SERIES

Work Out

English Language

'O' Level and GCSE

The titles in this series

For examinations at 16+

Biology	Physics
Chemistry	Principles of Accounts
Computer Studies	Spanish
English Language	Statistics
French	
German	
Mathematics	

For examinations at 'A' level

Applied Mathematics
Biology
Chemistry
English Literature
Physics
Pure Mathematics
Statistics

MACMILLAN
MASTER
SERIES

Work Out

English Language

'O' Level & GCSE

S. H. Burton

MACMILLAN

First published 1986

Published by
MACMILLAN EDUCATION LTD
Houndmills, Basingstoke, Hampshire RG21 2XS
and London
Companies and representatives
throughout the world

Typeset by TecSet Ltd, Sutton, Surrey
Printed at The Bath Press, Avon

British Library Cataloguing in Publication Data
Burton, S. H.
Work out English language.——(Macmillan
work out series).——(Macmillan master series)
1. English language——Grammar——1950–
I. Title
428   PE1112
ISBN 0-333-36700-6

Contents

Acknowledgements

The author and publishers wish to thank the following who have kindly given permission for the use of copyright material:

The Associated Examining Board for questions from the 1980 and 1982 'O' Level English Language Papers.

Jack Cross for an extract from his article 'Money matters', published in *The Guardian* (April 3, 1984).

A. M. Heath and Company Ltd on behalf of the Estate of the late **Sonia Brownell Orwell** and **Martin Secker and Warburg Ltd** for an extract from the *Collected Essays, Journalism and Speeches of George Orwell*, Vol. 4.

University of London University Entrance and School Examinations Council for questions from the 1982 and 1983 'O' Level English Language Papers.

University of Oxford Delegacy of Local Examinations for the June 1982 'O' Level English Language Paper.

A. P. Watt Ltd on behalf of **Frank Muir** and **Robert Langley** for extracts from their published work.

Every effort has been made to trace all the copyright holders, but if any have been inadvertently overlooked, the publishers will be pleased to make the necessary arrangements at the first opportunity.

The University of London Entrance and School Examinations Council accepts no responsibility whatsoever for the accuracy or method in the anwers given in this book to actual questions set by the London Board.

Acknowledgement is made to the Southern Universities' Joint Board for School Examinations for permission to use questions taken from their past papers but the Board is in no way responsible for answers that may be provided and they are solely the responsibility of the author.

The Associated Examining Board, the University of Oxford Delegacy of Local Examinations, the Northern Ireland Schools Examination Council and the Scottish Examination Board wish to point out that worked examples included in the text are entirely the responsibility of the author and have neither been provided nor approved by the Board.

Groups Responsible for Examinations at 16+

In the United Kingdom, examinations are administered by four examining groups and three examination boards. Syllabuses and examination papers for each group can be ordered from the addresses given here.

Northern Examining Association

Joint Matriculation Board
    Publications available from:
John Sherratt and Son Ltd
78 Park Road, Altrincham
Cheshire WA14 5QQ   (JMB)
Yorkshire and Humberside
    Regional Exam Board
Scarsdale House
136 Derbyside Lane
Sheffield S8 8SE
North West Regional Exam Board
Orbit House, Albert Street
Eccles, Manchester M30 0WL

Northern Regional Exam Board
Wheatfield Road, Westerhope
Newcastle upon Tyne NE5 5JZ

Associated Lancashire Schools Exam
    Board 12 Harter Street
Manchester M1 6HL

Midland Examining Group

University of Cambridge Local
    Examinations Syndicate
Syndicate Buildings, Hills Road
Cambridge CB1 2EU   (UCLES)
Southern Universities Joint Board
Cotham Road
Bristol BS6 6DD   (SUJB)
West Midlands Regional Exam Board
Norfolk House, Smallbrook
Queensway, Birmingham B5 4NJ

Oxford and Cambridge Schools
    Examination Board
10 Trumpington Street
Cambridge CB2 1QB
East Midlands Regional Exam Board
Robins Wood House, Robins Wood Road
Aspley, Nottingham NG8 3NR

London and East Anglian Group

University of London School
    Examinations Board University
of London Publications Office
52 Gordon Square
London WC1E 6EE   (L)
East Anglian Regional Exam Board
The Lindens, Lexden Road
Colchester, Essex CO3 3RL

London Regional Exam Board
Lyon House
104 Wandsworth High Street
London SW18 4LF

Southern Examining Group

The Associated Examining Board
Stag Hill House
Guildford, Surrey GU2 5XJ   (AEB)
Southern Regional Examining Board
Avondale House, 33 Carlton Crescent
Southampton, Hants SO9 4YL

University of Oxford Delegacy of
    Local Examinations Ewert Place
Summertown, Oxford OX2 7BZ   (OLE)
South-Western Regional Examining
    Board 23–29 Marsh Street
Bristol BS1 4BP

Scottish Examination Board

Publications available from:
Robert Gibson & Sons (Glasgow) Ltd
17 Fitzroy Place, Glasgow G3 7SF   (SEB)

Welsh Joint Education Committee
245 Western Avenue
Cardiff CF5 2YX   (WJEC)

**Northern Ireland Schools Examination
  Council** Examinations Office
Beechill House, Beechill Road
Belfast BT8 4RS   (NISEC)

Introduction

How to Use this Book

By using this book in the ways suggested here and amplified in the text, you can be confident that you will not be faced by unexpected or unpractised kinds of questions in your English Language examination. The knowledge and skills covered are those tested by the examiners, and all the practice questions have been either directly taken from or exactly modelled on the papers set by the various examining boards.

The instruction, revision and practice required in your last year of preparation for the examination are provided; and by combining four special features the book gives you all the help you need to get a good result. (1) It identifies and supplies examples of every kind of question that the examiners set. (2) It describes the qualities that the examiners will be looking for in your answers. (3) It shows you how to tackle each kind of question methodically, even when under examination pressures. (4) It provides you with a lot of practice questions *and* with worked-out answers to those questions so that you can judge your own performance and then see clearly how to bring your work up to the required standard.

Follow exactly the instructions provided in each chapter. They take you step by step through the correct method of dealing with each kind of question. Study the notes, commentaries and suggested answers accompanying the instructions to ensure that you master the recommended method.

Fully worked-out answers to many of the test papers and examination questions are provided at the end of the book. Do *not* look at the answer to any question until you have written down your own answer. Then, make a careful comparison between your answer and mine. Do not accept my answer uncritically. I have not made any deliberate mistakes, but there will be times when you believe that your answer is better than mine. Think hard. Then, if you still believe that your answer is better and you can put your finger on those qualities that make it better, you have taken a big step forward.

Revision

The revision material you need and the correct methods of using it are supplied in this book, but you should reinforce your preparation by reading as much as you can find time for. Read different kinds of writing — for example, novels, short stories, biographies, articles and news items in newspapers and magazines. Read in the careful *comprehending* way described in Chapters 3 and 4. Use your dictionary as you read so that you build up a large working vocabulary.

You should also obtain a syllabus and copies of recent papers from your own examining board — you will find the address on page ix. The syllabus gives details of your own examination and describes which kinds of questions are set in each paper. For example, it will tell you whether the composition question and the practical writing exercises are in separate papers (see Chapter 1), whether the comprehension question is a written test or a multiple-choice objective test (see

Chapter 3), whether the summary question is separate from or combined with the comprehension question (see Chapters 3 and 4).

Copies of recent papers will provide you with extra practice material to use when you have completed all the test questions and papers supplied in this book. You cannot have too much practice during your revision period.

The Examination

The essential techniques are explained in this book, but I want to draw particular attention to three points here: bad timing; careless reading; scrappy planning.

Bad timing is a frequent cause of failure in the examination. You cannot score marks for unanswered questions, and your maximum mark for a half-answered question is fifty per cent — even if your half-answer is perfect! It is essential to pace yourself carefully so that you give the correct amount of time to each answer. The practice questions in this book allow for and encourage a progressive speeding up, so that, when you are working under examination stress, you have trained yourself to answer each question within the time allocated to it.

Candidates in English Language often lose marks by careless reading of questions and by scrappy planning of their answers. You must give adequate time and thought to reading the questions and to planning your answers. Too many candidates imagine that they are wasting time unless they are scribbling furiously throughout the examination. That is why I have provided so many opportunities for you to practise accurate reading and thorough planning. You must be in full command of these vital techniques by the time you take your examination.

One last point: some examining boards set additional language questions to test your knowledge of vocabulary, usage and spelling. Your syllabus and past papers will provide the information. Whether your board sets such additional questions or not, do not fail to make full use of Chapters 5–9. Every English Language examination is a test of good English, and in all answers marks are deducted for faulty vocabulary, usage and spelling. Chapters 5–9 have a direct bearing on the writing of good English for whatever purpose. Do not be tempted to ignore them. Work through all the exercises and apply the lessons that they teach you when you are answering composition, comprehension and summary questions.

Good luck!

S. H. Burton

1 Composition

1.1 Definition and Description

(a) What is 'a Composition'?

All the examining boards require their English Language candidates to write 'a composition', although the syllabuses and question papers of some boards refer to it as 'an essay' or 'a piece of continuous writing'. The particular name employed makes no difference to the kind of answer expected from candidates. In the sense in which the terms are used in English Language examinations, 'a composition', 'an essay' and 'a piece of continuous writing' are one and the same.

- A composition is a sustained and continuous piece of writing on a subject chosen by the candidate from a list supplied in the examination paper.

(b) The Composition Question and the Writing Exercise

Most examining boards set two separate kinds of writing tests and require their candidates to answer both. Some boards set both tests in the same paper; others set them in different papers. Some boards refer to both tests as composition questions; others highlight the differences between them by referring to one question as 'a composition' and to the other as 'a writing exercise'. Candidates are allowed more time for the composition (usually one hour) than for the writing exercise (usually half an hour). More marks are allocated to the composition than to the writing exercise. The range may be from a maximum of 50 for the composition to a maximum of 30 for the writing exercise.

(c) The Differences between the Composition Question and the Writing Exercise

The subjects set in the composition question are of a different kind from those set for the writing exercise. Here are some typical syllabus descriptions of the two kinds of subjects and of the different responses expected from candidates.

1. In Paper I the composition question will test the ability of candidates to express themselves in continuous prose. A choice of subjects will be given but all the subjects will require personal involvement and individual response. In Paper II the composition question [the writing exercise] will test the ability of candidates to communicate what is required in a practical situation indicated in given material. A choice of questions will be provided.
2. Candidates will be asked to choose two subjects for composition, one from Section A and one from Section B. In Section A [the composition question] the subjects will be imaginative, allowing a free and individual response. Those in Section B [the writing exercise] will be factual, with clearly indicated material calling for a controlled response.

Comparison of some typical subjects recently set for the two kinds of writing tests brings out the distinction that the examiners make between them.

(i) *Examples of Subjects Set for the Composition Question*

1. A family feud.
2. Windows.
3. Describe the scene at a busy market in the week before Christmas.
4. Many people believe that corporal punishment and/or imprisonment should be used to deter young football hooligans and vandals. What do you think?

(ii) *Examples of Subjects Set for the Writing Exercise*

1. Write a letter to the mother of a friend of yours explaining why you are unable to accept her invitation to spend a few days at your friend's home during the summer holidays. Give your reasons clearly, but in such a way as to avoid hurting her feelings.
2. A group of foreign students is coming on an exchange visit to your home town. Write an introductory talk that you would give to them on one of the following topics:
    (a) Places of interest to visit in and around the town.
    (b) How to get the best out of local transport facilities.
    (c) Tips on suitable (and unsuitable) places to eat.
3. Write clear instructions on how to carry out one of the following:
    (a) Repair a puncture in a bicycle tyre.
    (b) Prepare suitable living quarters for a small animal to be kept as a pet.
    (c) Change films in a camera.

(d) Imaginative Writing and Practical Writing

The terms 'imaginative' (or 'creative') writing and 'practical' (or 'factual') writing are often used to describe the differences between the kind of answer required in the composition question and the kind of answer required in the writing exercise. The specimen questions printed in Section 1.1(c) showed that there is a clear distinction between the two kinds of writing. Further study of past papers will confirm that the subjects set in the two different questions are designed to test candidates in sharply contrasting ways.

Imaginative or creative writing

(i) Much of the material used in the composition must be imagined (created) by the writer, although its source is often (and best) found in personal experience.

(ii) The wording of the question invites a free and personal response from the writer.

(iii) The question is intended to be a 'trigger' for the writer's imagination. The emphasis is on self-

Practical or factual writing

(i) Much of the material to be used in the writing exercise is supplied in the wording of the question.

(ii) The wording of the question controls the writer's response. The instructions demand an answer that takes a given form and develops along preset lines.

(iii) The question limits the writer's answer to a given area of communication. Clear treatment of

expression and creativity: a subjective approach is required.

factual material is looked for. The candidate writes to the examiners' 'brief': an objective approach is required.

Because the composition and the writing exercise make such different demands, they are treated separately in this book. The writing of compositions of various kinds is demonstrated in this chapter, and ways of tackling practical writing exercises are demonstrated in Chapter 2.

(e) What the Examiners are Looking for

Both the composition question and the writing exercise are primarily tests of a candidate's ability to write well-organised, clear and accurate English. In each case the examiners are looking for a piece of writing that is:

- Carefully planned as an answer to the chosen question.
- Soundly constructed and clearly paragraphed.
- Written in well-made and varied sentences.
- Correct in its grammar, punctuation and spelling.

1.2 Compositions of Different Kinds

(a) Classifications

The examiners make it clear that compositions of several different kinds are set. Here is just one typical statement to that effect: 'Dramatic, impressionistic, narrative and discursive subjects will be included.' Study of all the syllabuses and of representative question papers provides the following classifications of composition subjects: (1) narrative; (2) descriptive; (3) discursive; (4) dramatic; (5) impressionistic.

Candidates must learn to identify the category to which their chosen subject belongs, for each kind of subject has its own special features and must be treated accordingly. For example, an impressionistic subject requires a more subjective approach than a discursive subject.

Both the *form* of a composition and the *style* in which it is written must be suited to the kind of subject that has been selected.

The notes that now follow list the distinguishing features of each kind of subject. The work-out sections of this chapter demonstrate how those features affect the planning and writing of compositions of each kind.

(b) Narrative Compositions

Narrative compositions tell (narrate) a story or give an account of a sequence of events. Their subjects are about *action*. For example: 'Write a story entitled *In the Nick of Time*'; 'Give an account of an exciting journey that you once made by land or sea or air'.

A story composition must have plot, characters and atmosphere. A plot is not needed for an account of events, but the narrator must introduce 'human interest' and set it against a realistic background. In both a story and an account of events the narration must move forward. Narrative compositions must not be static.

(c) Descriptive Compositions

Obviously, descriptive compositions describe! They describe a scene or a place or an object or a person. For example: 'Describe either the sights or the sounds at a busy bus station on a winter's day'; 'Describe the appearance, personality and home surroundings of someone well known to you, either of your own age or much older'.

The key to success is the writer's ability to find an imaginative approach to the subject and to shape the composition so that every detail contributes to the over-all effect that has been planned. Lacking that creative angle of attack, a descriptive composition is a mere list of details haphazardly strung together. Very boring.

(d) Discursive (Argumentative or Controversial) Compositions

A discursive composition is one in which the writer presents facts, ideas and opinions about a given topic and *arrives at a conclusion by reasoning*. Typical discursive subjects are: 'What gives "pop" music its following?'; 'Do you think that smoking should be banned by law?'; 'What are the good and bad points about television?'; 'Consider the arguments for and against fox hunting'.

The alternative names for discursive compositions – 'argumentative compositions' and 'controversial compositions' – indicate the kind of subjects set and the kind of treatment required.

A genuine interest in and some information about the chosen topic are essential. So, too, are a respect for facts, a balanced attitude to the opinions of others and a clear presentation of the writer's point of view.

Discursive (argumentative or controversial) subjects are: *discursive*, because they require writers to reason their way to a conclusion; *argumentative*, because they require writers to set out the arguments on both sides and to weigh them fairly; *controversial*, because they require writers to keep cool and think clearly about topics that stir up strong feelings.

(e) Dramatic (Conversational) Compositions

Dramatic compositions must be written in *direct speech*. Hence the alternative name 'conversational compositions'. Typical dramatic (conversational) subjects are: 'A lecturer and a student have had a disagreement. Write a dialogue between them in which the circumstances of their quarrel are made plain and in the course of which they come to a friendly resolution of their problem'; 'Write a short play by continuing the dialogue set out below in a manner which develops the dramatic situation'. (The first few lines of the dialogue are provided to introduce the characters and to establish the initial dramatic situation.)

Success in such compositions depends on the ability to write direct speech for two or more characters (dialogue) that sounds convincing and that develops the initial situation in an interesting way.

(f) Impressionistic Compositions

Impressionistic compositions are highly subjective and imaginative compositions. Several pictures are provided as part of the examination paper. The instructions then read like this: 'Write a composition suggested by one of the pictures on page 10 of this paper. Your composition may be directly about the subject of the picture, or may be based on some suggestion that you take from the picture; but there must be some clear connection between the picture and your composition. Your composition may take the form of a story or of a description.'

Another kind of impressionistic composition is based on a short poem (or an extract from a poem) printed on the examination paper. Candidates are instructed to describe the ideas or thoughts or feelings that the poem suggests to them (in other words, the *impressions* it makes on their minds). Or they may be told to write (in prose, of course) a description of a place or a person well known to them in circumstances similar to those described in the poem. Or they may be asked to write a story based on the poem.

Whatever the particular form asked for, a successful impressionistic composition requires close observation of the details of the picture (or careful reading of the poem), an imaginative response and a clear link between the given stimulus (picture or poem) and the candidate's writing.

1.3 Examination Techniques

(a) Planning Your Time

Most boards allow about 1 hour for the composition question. Divide it up as follows:

1. Read through the instructions carefully, making sure that you understand exactly what you have to do. (about 1 minute)
2. Study all the subjects 'on offer'. Consider each carefully and make your choice. (2 or 3 minutes)
3. Gather your material, select your material, decide on your 'angle of attack', plan your composition. (not less than 10 minutes)
4. Write your composition. (about 40 minutes)
5. Read it through, correcting any careless slips of phrasing, grammar, punctuation or spelling. (not more than 5 minutes)

Students are sometimes advised to write a draft of the composition on rough paper, to revise it and then write out a fair copy. I cannot agree with that advice. It takes 15 or 16 minutes to write out 500 words *legibly*, and there is simply not enough time in the examination to write a rough draft of the composition followed by a fair copy. In any case, if the planning has been thorough, the composition can be confidently composed straight onto the answer sheets. Any mistakes will be minor slips which can be corrected in the final read-through.

(b) Choosing Your Subject

It is most important to make the right choice first time. You cannot afford to work by trial and error. To start one composition, scrap it and start another would leave you hopelessly short of time. While preparing for the examination, you will have discovered where your strengths lie and which kinds of compositions you write best. That experience will help you to weed out the subjects that are not for you. Even so, think hard about your choice. Go for a subject that *interests* you. Assess your potential performance coolly. For example, you may have written good discursive compositions in your practice work, but do not assume that you are, therefore, limited to the discursive subjects offered in your examination paper. They may be on topics that do not really interest you and about which you have few ideas. In that case, careful consideration of the other subjects will probably result in a better choice.

(c) Planning Your Composition

Skimped and careless planning is the commonest cause of poor compositions. Three different (but linked) operations are involved: gathering material; selecting material; shaping the composition. Each of those operations is given detailed examination in the work-out sections of this chapter, where successful methods of planning compositions of all kinds are demonstrated.

(d) Length

The length required varies: 'not less than 450 words'; 'from 350 to 500 words'; 'about 500 to 600 words'. Often, length is stipulated in pages. For example: 'Your work should cover about three sides of the pages in your answer book. If your handwriting is unusually large or unusually small, you should make the necessary adjustment to the number of pages you fill. Average handwriting produces about eight words to the line.'

You should, of course, find out what length is required by your own examinations board, and your practice compositions should conform to that. Quality is always more important than quantity, although a composition of the minimum length must be written.

(e) Reading through and Correcting

Do not attempt major revisions of content or structure at this stage. It is too late to start rewriting your composition. An imaginative response to your chosen subject and careful planning should have resulted in a fluent and interesting piece of writing. In this final reading you can correct any grammatical, punctuation and spelling errors and reword any clumsy expressions. Be sure that your corrections are neat and clear.

1.4 Summing Up

The composition instructions printed below illustrate the points made in this chapter. Although they are addressed specifically to English Language candidates for the University of London General Certificate in Education, they provide essential guidelines for candidates in all similar examinations. (Key words in the instructions have been italicised for the purposes of this book.)

> Choose a subject from the list below about which you can write *interestingly; plan* your composition according to *the nature of the material* and the *form* (narrative, descriptive, discursive, dramatic, etc.); write in an *appropriate style* and take care with *grammar, spelling, and punctuation.* Your composition should be *450 words or more* in length, but, apart from that, will be assessed on the *quality*, not the quantity of what you have written.

No matter which particular board you are sitting for, you should tackle the composition question along those lines. Details of time allowed, of marks allocated and of length stipulated may vary slightly from board to board, but the examiners of all the boards are looking for similar qualities in candidates' compositions.

1.5 Work out Narrative Compositions

(a) Getting to Grips with Narrative Subjects

The subjects set for narrative compositions are of two distinct kinds:

1. Subjects that require you to write a *story*.
2. Subjects that require you to write an *account of events*.

In each kind of narrative composition the *action* provides the chief interest, but a story composition has some special features that are not required in a straight-forward narration of events. The following table sets out the characteristic qualities of each.

A story

(i) Must have a plot. It need not be complicated, but there must be a 'story line'. In a story things change. Perhaps a discovery is made or a problem is solved. Perhaps people's attitudes alter or their relationships with one another develop. In some important way a new situation is brought about and the story-teller must plan the events so that they lead to this development.

(ii) Needs characters to provide an interesting interplay of personalities and to create tension. There is no need to 'crowd the canvas' with people. Two characters will often be enough. The important thing is to involve people with events. A story is about people doing things.

(iii) Description of people and places is essential. The characters are placed against an interesting and convincing background. Much of the interest in a story is generated by the interplay of people, events and setting. A close connection between people and places creates an 'atmosphere'.

(iv) Dialogue (conversation between characters) is essential. People in stories talk to one another (as

An account of events

(i) Does not need a plot, but must progressively relate a sequence of events. The reader's attention is held by a series of incidents. The writer must provide links to connect successive events and to keep the narrative flowing in an interesting way. The action must move steadily forward from the beginning to the end. A successful narrative depends on a clear plan.

(ii) 'Characterisation' (in the story sense) is not required, but some 'human interest' makes for a lively narration. Perhaps the personality of the narrator 'comes through' or there are some interesting glimpses of the people taking part in the happenings. The emphasis, however, is on action rather than on character.

(iii) Description plays an important part in the narration. The emphasis is on action, but action does not take place in a vacuum. Details are needed to help the reader to follow the events. Interest is aroused by lively description of a realistic setting.

(iv) Dialogue is not essential, but it can sometimes be introduced to good effect. Speech in a straight-

9

they do in real life). As they talk, they come alive for the reader and the plot is carried forward. The changing situations of a story — see (i) — are often brought about by or revealed through dialogue.

(v) A story is a piece of fiction. Plot, characters and setting are invented by the writer. Personal experience must be drawn on to create convincing people and places — 'write about what you know' — but a story is essentially made up: imagined.

forward narrative composition is always directly related to the action. Its purpose is to advance the narrative flow.

(v) An account of events must be rooted in the writer's own experience. Firsthand knowledge of the happenings related — or of very similar happenings — is needed. Details may be invented to add life and colour, but this kind of narrative composition is essentially an imaginative treatment of actual events. It is not a piece of fiction, as a story is.

In some examinations the term 'anecdote' is used to distinguish between a story composition and a straightforward narrative composition. For example:

Write *either* a story *or* an anecdote based on one of the following: (i) a telephone ringing in an empty house; (ii) the non-arrival of an important letter; (iii) an ambulance speeding through a city on an icy morning.

An anecdote is the narration of an interesting or striking incident or a series of such incidents.

To sum up. If you decide to write a narrative composition, you must choose between:

A plotted composition
A story. All the events lead up to and help to bring about the situation with which the story ends. This final situation develops out of circumstances and events earlier in the story.

An unplotted composition
An account of events: a description of incidents: a relation of an experience: an anecdote. All these are examples of 'reportage'. They are narrations of interesting events happening in succession, one after another.

As this work-out section will show, 'unplotted' does *not* mean 'unplanned'. A clear plan is the basis of a successful composition of whatever kind.

(b) Thinking about the Subjects on Offer

Here are some typical examples of subjects set for narrative compositions.

(i) *Story Compositions*

1. 'The Humber, the Menai Straits, the Tay, Sydney Harbour, the Golden Gate — what tales bridges could tell!' Write a story in which a bridge plays an important part.
2. 'It was the weirdest-looking object I'd ever seen.' Write a story in which those words are used at an important moment.

3. 'Even the smartest crook can make a silly mistake.' Write a story, using those words as its opening.
4. 'I never did discover its hiding place.' Write a story that ends with those words.
5. Write a story entitled 'A Broken Promise'.
6. Write a story suggested by the following quotation:

Hark, they are going: the footsteps shrink,
And the sea renews her cry.
The big stars stare and the small stars wink;
The Plough goes glittering by.
It was a trick of the turning tide
That brought those voices near.
Dead men pummelled the panes outside:
We caught the breath of the year.

Vernon Watkins

Note that each of those subjects contains a requirement that the writer must observe. Number 1 imposes some control over the contents of the story. Numbers 2, 3 and 4 influence the plot by insisting on the inclusion of given words at a particular point in the story. Number 5 influences both contents and plot by specifying the title of the story. Number 6 is less direct in its controls, but it lays down the condition that the source of the story must be the impressions the writer receives from the poetry. (This kind of question, combining narrative and impressionistic subjects, is often set.)

Candidates who can write a good story sometimes miss their opportunity by failing to recognise possible story subjects. When the particular form that a composition must take is not specified, candidates are free to choose whatever form suits them best. For example:

Write a composition based on one of the following topics:
(a) A family gathering.
(b) Lost property.
(c) Nightfall.
(d) A journalistic scoop.
(e) An unwanted present.

Instructions worded like those permit any of the given topics to be treated as story material. They are, of course, equally available for and suited to straightforward narrative or descriptive treatment.

(ii) Straightforward Narrative Compositions

The instructions for the writing of an account of events, a description of incidents, a relation of an experience and an anecdote are worded in various ways. Here are some typical examples.

1. You were one of a crowd waiting for a celebrity to appear. Describe what happened.
2. Describe an experience in the course of which events occurred in a way that contrasted sharply with what you expected.
3. You saw a person knocked off a bicycle by a passing car that did not stop. Tell the story of what happened next.

4. 'I shan't do that again', you said. Give an account of the events that led up to that remark.

Only in the fourth example are candidates specifically instructed to give an account of events, but the wording of the others is a clear indication that straight-forward narrative writing (*not* story telling) is wanted. 'Describe what happened' (1) and 'Describe an experience' (2) instruct the writer to narrate a sequence of happenings. The composition is to take the form of a piece of 'reportage': an account of events that occurred one after another.

Do not be misled by the wording of the third example: 'Tell the story of what happened next'. That is not an invitation to write a story with a plot. It is an instruction to write an anecdote. The key words are: *what happened next*. An anecdote is not a story. It simply unfolds events in a straightforward chronological sequence. It does not bring about those plotted changes of circumstance and situation that are the essence of a story.

All these unplotted forms of narrative compositions — accounts of events, descriptions of incidents, relations of experiences, anecdotes — share the same essential characteristic: they run in a straight line from beginning to end. The writer must keep the narrative flowing. Any break in the continuity is a tiresome interruption at which the reader loses interest.

(c) Making a Choice

There are more narrative subjects in Section 1.5(b) than you will find on your question paper, since the examiners will offer you other kinds of composition subjects as well. However, for the purposes of this work out, we will suppose that they are all available. They represent most of the varieties of narrative subjects that you are likely to encounter, so it will be useful to consider them all while demonstrating how a good choice of subject can be made.

The work out is written in the first person singular because choosing a subject is essentially a personal decision. By showing you how *I* go about it, I can illustrate all the points that you will have to consider when you are looking for a subject that suits *you*. Then, in later sections, I shall gather and select material and plan and write the composition to provide a practical demonstration of methods that you can confidently use, whatever your choice of subject.

While steering you through the choice-making process, I do not assume that my choice of subject would be right for you. You may be able to write interestingly on a subject that is not for me. You may have ample material for a composition on that subject and the ability to make a good plan for it, whereas I am stuck for ideas and cannot see how to arrange what little material I have. The work out cannot tell you *what* to choose, but it can show you *how* to choose.

If I choose a story composition, I shall have to invent a plot. That is not easy, so I look first at the straightforward narrative subjects on offer, but none of them interests me so much that I feel confident of interesting my reader. I cannot see how I can tap my own experience to find the firsthand material that I need to write a lively composition on any of them.

Turning to the story subjects, I remember to look at those that *may* be written as stories ('A family gathering', 'Lost property', 'Nightfall', 'A journalistic scoop' and 'An unwanted present') as well as those that *must* be (numbers 1–6).

At first, I am tempted to have a go at 'A family gathering'. I think that my experiences at my Uncle Henry's house one Christmas provide me with useful material for characters and setting, although I cannot see plot possibilities. Of course, I might treat that topic by straightforward narration, using my imagination to provide some lively and colourful details.

'A family gathering' is a possible subject, but I do not warm to any of the others in that particular list. I cannot at once see plot material in them for stories and I am not very interested in the few ideas that they suggest to me for purely narrative treatment.

Turning to the subjects that are specified for story treatment, I reject the one in which a bridge is to play an important part. I think I *could* write such a story, but it would not come out of my personal experience. My story would be second-hand 'formula' writing; a stale imitation of stories that I have read. So, because I cannot see a way of putting something of myself into this particular story, I decide not to attempt it. Stories ought to be their writers' own creations. Only then can they be fresh and original and, therefore, interesting.

Subjects 2, 3 and 4 put me off by requiring me to include given words at particular points in the story. Many writers have the ability to carry out such instructions without losing their spontaneity. Indeed, the necessity of constructing a story line that brings the given words into the story at the right place seems to stimulate their imagination. But not mine. I know that my story would seem contrived and artificial. The plot would creak.

Again, I am not happy with number 5. I *can* sometimes write a story with a given title, even though that restricts my freedom to invent the contents and the plot; but I cannot recall interesting personal experience on which to base 'A Broken Promise'. (Now, if the given title were 'A Promise Fulfilled', I should have lively material ready for use and a good, simple plot needing just a little working up — but that isn't the title!)

I turn to number 6 and, as I read the lines of poetry, I find that I am getting strong impressions. The words are ringing bells in my memory, suggesting exciting possibilities for characters and setting; and I *think* I can see — rather dimly as yet — a possible plot.

At this point I make a time check and I realise that I have spent as long as I dare in considering possible subjects. My choice must be made. Which shall it be: 'A family gathering' or number 6? I can see good material for characters and setting in the former if I treat it as a story, but I have not had any ideas for a plot. If I treat it as a straightforward narrative, it may lack action. It begins to seem rather a static subject. Nothing much happened. On the whole, I think I see more scope in Number 6.

(d) Gathering Material

Write a story suggested by the following quotation:

> Hark, they are going: the footsteps shrink,
> And the sea renews her cry.
> The big stars stare and the small stars wink;
> The Plough goes glittering by.
> It was a trick of the turning tide
> That brought those voices near.
> Dead men pummelled the panes outside:
> We caught the breath of the year.

I open my mind to the words. They stir up recollections and imaginings which I jot down as they occur. All that matters at this stage is to capture ideas: selecting and planning come later.

night — hushed — glittering stars — the sound of the sea — that lonely cottage in Cornwall where we spent a family holiday — a nightmare

The quotation has triggered off a personal recollection and I can link the poet's words with my own experience. This is promising. I explore the possibilities further, reading the words again.

Within the general impressions, certain words seem to be making a particular impact:

Hark, they are going/footsteps shrink/sea renews her cry/a trick of the turning tide/voices near/Dead men pummelled the panes

I add to the raw material already jotted down, letting memory and imagination work together. Some of my notes are based on fact, some are inventions suggested by the words of the quotation. The distinction between fact and fiction is of no importance when material for a story is being gathered.

an autumn holiday — starry nights — the sound of the sea — a lamp-lit living-room — my parents downstairs reading — my bedroom very quiet — the sound of footsteps dwindling — along a path? — the 'cry' of the sea again — a rapping at the window — something outside trying to get in — returning to claim something? — what? — 'It's only the sound of the sea' — 'the tide has turned' — the owner of the cottage kept the village shop — talking to him — his stories of days gone by

I can now see exciting possibilities in the material I have gathered. It should give me scope for lively writing and an original treatment, for it springs partly from the quotation and partly from an experience of my own which the poet's words have brought back to me. I must work on the raw material and shape it.

(e) Selecting Material and Arriving at a Plan

There is still a lot to do before I can start writing my composition. The material I have gathered so far could be used in a straightforward narration of events, but I must now think out a plot so that I can turn an anecdote into a story. The connections between the words of the quotation and my raw material are well established, so I am at liberty to invent any details I need to construct a plot; and I am free to adjust the circumstances depicted in the poem to suit my story. I jot down some more notes, building up the material I have already gathered.

I had a nightmare — it frightened me very much — my parents weren't very pleased when I rushed downstairs into the living-room — 'Go back to bed. You've been dreaming.' — that big oak chest in the living-room — black with age — the initials 'I.R.T.' carved on the front — the man we rented the cottage from was called Tressilian — Reuben Tressilian — he kept the village shop and post office — his name over shop door — his family had lived in the cottage for many years — his great-grandfather was lost at sea in a great storm — we went to the shop for groceries the morning after I had my nightmare — he told us about his family that morning

I am beginning to see the bare bones of my story line and I feel confident enough to work on a more detailed plan. I set it out in two columns. The steps in which I shall tell the story are very carefully noted in the left column. In the right,

I make notes to help me to work out the details of character, setting and events as I go along. As I work on my plan, I reject some of the material I have already gathered and I alter and add to the rest.

(*Note:* As you study the plan that now follows, bear in mind that I have written it out at greater length than you — or I — would have time for in the examination. My purpose is to demonstrate the importance of thinking a subject through and becoming clear about how you are going to treat it *before* you begin to write. If you practise along the lines set out here, you will master the technique of sound planning. Then you can speed up and, in the examination, you will know how to construct a short outline plan on which a good composition can be based.)

(i) *The Plan*

1. Introduce characters and setting — brief description of family, cottage and surroundings.

father, mother, son — about ten — is story to be told in first or third person? — easier to bring about change in situation if son tells story as it happened — lonely cottage about 2 miles from nearest village — cottage near sea — sound of sea, especially at night

2. Sketch in holiday occupations and pleasures. Build up atmosphere before storm and nightmare.

warm autumn days — walks and picnics — cosy living-room — books and TV — son usually to bed at ten — parents stay up reading for a time — cottage interior described — important to bring old chest to reader's attention because it plays important part in story — initials 'I.R.T.' carved on chest — N.B.: chest not in living-room — place it on landing outside son's bedroom door

3. The night of the storm. Son's fear. Parents explain it away. They're right, of course — he's been dreaming.

son wakes up — roaring of wind and waves (perhaps earlier?) — sudden hush — tapping at window — footsteps on path — fear — son rushes downstairs — 'someone at my window, trying to get in'/'you've been dreaming: it's only the wind rattling the panes — grating of pebbles on seashore'

4. Next morning — to village to shop.

this is a quiet stage of story — storm has died down — his nightmare is over and explained away — bright, calm morning — night fears seem unreal

5. Introduce Reuben Tressilian. He keeps the village shop. Conversation. He tells them about his family.

R.T. owns cottage — rents it to holidaymakers — Tressilians have lived in cottage for years — all fisherfolk — (some of these details to come in earlier? — when cottage is first described?)

6. Climax of story begins here. First mention of Tressilian's great-grandfather.

initials on chest, 'I.R.T.', were great-grandfather's — he kept his valuables in it — story told about him — he was lost at sea in great storm — comes

15

7. Turning point of story here. Discovery made and situation changes. Son knows date of storm in which 'I.R.T.' was drowned.

back to find chest on anniversary of his death
care with details here — must be convincing — closely linked together to keep story moving — enough detail to keep reader in picture but don't clutter up the action — best if all told through dialogue? — son and Mr T. talking, but parents silent

8. End of story. Parents were wrong about 'nightmare' and son was right. Final situation follows from and is caused by 7.

don't over-explain — story ends crisply — parents realise what has happened, so does son — suggest this, rather than explaining — they look away — busy themselves in shop — mystery, but no loose ends

Now I can start writing. If I find, as I write the story, that I need to change any details or make minor adjustments to the sequence of events, I am free to do so. The plan is my guide and I shall stick to its main features, but I am not bound to follow it to the letter. I shall almost certainly think of improvements as the act of writing the composition stimulates my imagination; but I shall not make fundamental changes in the structure of my story while I am writing it. I cannot afford to make false starts or leave loose ends in the plot, so it would be dangerous to depart far from this carefully constructed plan.

(f) Writing the Composition

When I was ten, my father and mother and I went ~~for our holidays~~ to a lonely cottage on the Cornish coast for a week's holiday.

It was a lonely place, perched above the sea and not another house near it. There was a village about two miles away where the owner of the cottage lived. His name was Reuben Tressilian. He kept the village post office and
and
shop. ~~He~~ rented the cottage to holidaymakers.

We had a lovely holiday. The days were warm, and although it went cold at night, we were cosy in the cottage. It was comfortably furnished with
There was an open hearth in the living-room
interesting old pieces and pictures. ~~The living-room had a big fireplace~~ which made it very cheerful. We had brought books with us and there was a TV set. We spent our days walking, exploring the cliffs and picnicking. In the evenings we sat reading or watching television until they pushed me off to bed at about ten o'clock. I didn't mind. There was a big black oak chest on the landing outside my bedroom door and I often made up stories about it. Some initials were carved on the front and as I lay in bed I used to wonder who 'I.R.T.' was. I guessed that he was the big, bearded man wearing a fisherman's jersey in the old, faded photograph that hung on the wall above the chest.

furious
One night — I shall never forget it — there was a ~~big~~ storm. As we sat in the living-room, the wind roared in the chimney and we could hear the

16

waves crashing against the cliffs. I thought it was exciting, but I don't think my parents liked it much.

At ten o'clock my mother looked at the clock on the ~~mantlepeace.~~ mantelpiece. 'Off to bed now, Billy', she said. 'We're going to the village early tomorrow. I need some ~~food~~ supplies for the rest of the week.'

'I shan't be able to sleep', I said. 'Not with all this noise going on.'

'Nonsense! You'll sleep like a log. You've been out in the fresh air all day and you're yawning now.'

'Good night, Billy', my father said, rather firmly. 'Sleep well.'

As I went past the chest on the landing, I stopped to look at the old photograph. It was ~~moving~~ swaying slightly on its cord in the draught.

'Good night, I.R.T.', I said. 'Sleep well.'

In spite of the howling wind, I went to sleep at once. I didn't give old 'I.R.T.' another thought before I was off.

And then — I don't know how much later — I woke. I was cold and ~~I was frightened.~~ scared stiff. The noise ~~had stopped.~~ of the storm had stopped. There was a sort of hush, as if the night was holding its breath, and the moon was bright on the window.

Then I heard a crunching sound, like heavy footsteps on the gravel path at the back of the cottage; and — seconds later — 'tap, tap, tap' on the glass. It was as loud as the beating of my heart and there was a shadow on the pane.

Downstairs I ran and into the living-room.

'Quick!' I said. 'Come up to my room. There's something tapping at the window — trying to get in.'

'You've had a nightmare, Billy', my mother said. 'I'll get you some hot milk and you can drink it by the fire. Then back to bed you go.'

'It's the wind', my father said. 'And waves beating on the shore. Listen!'

He was right. The storm ~~had started~~ was raging again. The wind was shaking the tiles and the sea roared below the cliffs.

He came up with me and tucked the clothes round me. 'No more dreams, Billy. Sleep well.'

And, strangely enough, I did. No more dreams and no more shadows at the window.

After breakfast we set off for Mr Tressilian's shop. The day was calm and bright and we enjoyed our walk.

'You're having a good time?' Mr Tressilian asked as he reached things off the shelves and loaded up ~~the basket.~~ our baskets.

'Oh, yes', my mother answered. 'And it's such a lovely cottage. You've got some beautiful furniture there, Mr Tressilian.'

'All family stuff', he said. 'Tressilians have lived in the cottage for years. They were all fisherfolk, till I gave it up and settled down to shopkeeping.'

'Who was "I.R.T."?' I asked.

He looked a bit surprised, but he answered me.

'He was my great-grandfather — Isaac Reuben Tressilian. That's his photograph that hangs on the wall above the big chest on the landing. He was lost at sea in a great storm, many a year ago.'

'It was his chest, was it?'

'Oh, yes. He had it made the year he was married — the year he built the cottage. He kept his valuables in it. It was always kept locked when I was a boy, though his valuables — such as they were — had long vanished. My father used to tell us a story about that chest. He said that Isaac Reuben always returned on the anniversary of the storm. Looking for his chest, he was. So my father said. He didn't believe it, of course. Nor do I. It was just a story he liked telling us and we liked hearing.'

'He was drowned on the fifteenth of September, wasn't he?' I asked.

'Yes', Mr Tressilian said. 'He was — on the fifteenth of September 1865. How did you know?'

'It was the fifteenth of September yesterday', I said. 'And I think your great-grandfather came looking for his chest last night.'

I turned to my parents as I said it, but they pretended not to hear. My father was reading a newspaper that he'd taken off the counter and my mother was unusually interested in the label on a bag of sugar.

(g) Reading through and Correcting

As you can see, I made some improvements in the couple of minutes that I allowed myself for reading through and correcting. I put right some careless slips of the pen and I was able to tighten up the writing here and there. One or two clumsy expressions jumped out at me as I read through what I had written, and it was easy to find better ways of wording them.

On the whole, however, the writing went smoothly because I had put a lot of thought into gathering and selecting my material and constructing my plan. The *form* of my composition was clear to me before I began to write it, so it was not difficult to find a *style* of expression that was suitable.

(h) A Different Choice of Subject

You may be reluctant to choose a story subject and you are right to be cautious. Never attempt a story unless you can see, quite early on, how you can construct a plot for it. The plot may be very simple, but it must be convincing (no loose ends) and it must bring about an interesting development in the story. In the work out you have just studied I was able to see plot possibilities when the words of the poetry connected with an event that I recalled from my own experience. I had to work on the details, of course, but the outline of my plot began to come through at an early stage.

Like many writers, however, I do not often find it easy to construct a plot, so I usually look for a straightforward narrative subject rather than a story. I hope to find one that interests me and to which I can bring some firsthand experience.

You cannot expect always to find an ideal subject on the question paper, but things are never as bad as they seem in those first minutes as you read through the set topics and think despairingly, 'I can't write about *any* of these!' You can always find a subject on which you can write competently if you go about choosing and planning in the ways that I am demonstrating in this chapter.

Suppose the subject I chose in Section 1.5(c) had not been on offer. My second-string subject, you remember, was 'A family gathering', which the instructions permitted me to treat either as a story or as a straightforward (unplotted) narra-tive. Story treatment was ruled out for me because I could not see plot possibilities in the subject. As I considered it for straightforward narrative, I became less hopeful of success. I knew I could draw on personal experience and write interestingly about people and setting, but I knew also that my potential material lacked the essential ingredient of good narrative — *action*.

When a subject dries up on you like that, you have to look again at subjects that were not immediately attractive as you read through the questions for the first time. By thinking hard along methodical lines, you will find a topic that you can tackle successfully.

Ask yourself these two questions:

- What are the chief features of a good composition of this kind on this subject?
- What opportunities does this subject offer me to write a composition that contains those features?

The whole purpose of these work-out sections is to help you to find the answers to those questions.

In my own case, looking again at all the composition subjects offered in Section 1.5(b), I should have to choose this: 'You were one of a crowd waiting for a celebrity to appear. Describe what happened'.

For various reasons, that is not my ideal subject for a straightforward narrative composition, but it does bring an item of personal experience to mind and I think I can work that up into a competent piece of writing, fragment though it is.

Faced with subjects that do not look very attractive at first sight, comfort yourself with the old proverb: 'Necessity is the mother of invention'. Necessity is there, without doubt: the necessity to write a composition! Don't panic. Think coolly. Your powers of invention and recall are greater than you realise. Necessity will bring them to your aid and a sound technique will enable you to make use of them.

In the next sections of this chapter I shall describe the qualities of a good narrative and then go on to demonstrate how, bearing them in mind, I feel reasonably confident of writing a successful composition on a subject that I chose because I had to.

(i) Action: the Essence of Narrative

Any composition that the examiners' instructions identify as an account of events, a description of incidents or the relation of an anecdote must be centred on action. Nothing must distract the reader's attention from the action, for it is in the action that the interest lies.

Any other features of such a composition — descriptions of people and places, passages of dialogue, for example — are secondary to the action. Their sole purpose is to make the narrative more vivid and to hold the reader's attention as the action unfolds. Anything that impedes the narrative flow is a tiresome interruption.

(j) Pacing the Narrative

Varying the pace of the narrative is a sure way of gaining and holding your reader's interest. Action described at a uniform pace is not very exciting. Your reader will be as bored by a narrative that races breathlessly from start to finish as by one that proceeds throughout at a steady jogtrot.

Try to begin with a striking incident to capture attention. You can then afford a *brief* description of the circumstances in which the action is taking place and of the people involved. Then be sure to get the action moving again at once. It is often effective to let it run slowly at first, then — at a clearly indicated turning point — to quicken the pace so that the narration carries your reader forward to its climax. Pay special attention to the end. Are you going to finish with the action at its highest point? Or does your treatment of your subject demand a brief rounding-off? Either of these endings can be effective but, if you prolong your composition beyond the highest point of the action, do be *brief*. An anticlimax at the end is a painful let-down.

(k) Narrative Links and the Narrative Thread

To write a successful narrative, you must:

- keep your reader's attention on the action;
- make your reader want to know what happens next.

You cannot achieve those two aims unless your narrative is easy to read.

The provision of narrative links makes for easy reading. These links connect the successive stages of the action and carry the reader along. Without such links, the narrative thread is snapped. Do try to vary their wording. A monotonous succession of 'then . . . and then . . . next' is boringly obvious. The links should be unobtrusive.

The more carefully you plan your composition before you begin to write, the easier you will find it to provide the essential connections. Once the successive stages of the narrative are clearly set out in your plan, the sequence of events is established and you will be able to carry your reader through the action with only a sparing use of the more explicit verbal links. Incident will follow incident in a natural progression, and you will then not often need to provide obvious 'signals' that the action is moving on.

(l) Narrative Details and Descriptive Details

Some details play an essential part in carrying the action along. These are the narrative details that enable the reader to follow the course of events. For example, if your chosen subject hinges on a street accident and what followed, your reader *may* need to know the colour or make or size of a vehicle involved, or the age and appearance of the driver, or exactly where the accident happened.

You have to judge the relevance of each detail when you are considering whether to include it. Ask yourself: 'Does this detail help my reader to understand what is happening?' Obviously, you must provide the details that play an important part in the action, but be strict in your selection. A narrative cluttered with details is hard to follow. The reader's attention is distracted from the action.

The same considerations apply to descriptive details. Some are needed to make the narrative convincing and lively, but they must be sparingly used or the action will be held up. What matters most in a narrative is what happens. A few carefully chosen details will capture attention and hold interest, but your reader's main concern is with the events themselves.

(m) Human Interest

You are not creating 'characters' when you are writing a straightforward narrative, but people usually play the leading parts in the action. Just sketch them in with a few identifying details. It is especially important to do this when the events involve antagonism. Conflict may be present at the outset or it may be generated as the action unfolds. Skilfully revealed by a narrative in which the pace changes, conflict is a source of tension and rising excitement.

(n) Dialogue in Narrative

Though always less important than in a story, dialogue can be an effective means of identifying people and indicating that a new stage of the action is beginning. Keep it short. Too much talk interrupts the action. In a straightforward narrative, speech is useful to push the action along while, at the same time, informing the reader about who is doing what.

(o) Narrative Style

As we saw in Section 1.4, the style of any composition must be appropriate to that kind of composition. A quick-moving style is appropriate to a straightforward narrative. Short sentences, active verbs and a sparing use of adjectives are generally effective when striking and interesting events are being described.

Variations of style, however, are as desirable as variations of pace. A deliberate slowing of the action (to increase tension and lead into a climax) will be marked by a more leisurely style. Descriptive touches are more telling when the language used contrasts with that employed in the purely narrative passages. Quick-fire sentences are an indispensable medium for rapid action, but a narrative that rattles along in staccato bursts from start to finish is no pleasure to read. The writer needs to get his breath from time to time — and so does the reader.

(p) Work out Another Plan

With all those considerations in mind, I tackle the subject that I have been forced to select. I have no more time left for making a choice and none of the other subjects seems more promising. At least, I can see a way into this one and I must work methodically to make the best use I can of the possibilities that it seems to offer me.

> You were one of a crowd waiting for a celebrity to appear. Describe what happened.

(i) *Gathering Material*

I jot down the material that comes to mind, just as it occurs.

> crowd in square in front of town hall — curiosity led me to join it — gradually discovered what it was all about — local hero expected to appear on balcony — had been given civic dinner and freedom of borough — long wait — crowd patient and good-humoured — gradually turned bad-tempered   I wasn't

very keen anyway, so I left — read about events in local paper afterwards — eventual appearance — enthusiastic reception

That is not a lot to write about and it is sadly lacking in action. I shall have to build it up.

Fortunately, the instructions give me some useful pointers: '*You* were one of a crowd . . . Describe what happened.' I must narrate in the first person singular and I must stay with the crowd longer than I actually did! I can draw on my memories of the night and the crowd up to my departure, and I can reconstruct the later events by using the newspaper report as the basis of my invented material. Although my starting point is an actual event, I can make up any extra material that I need.

Also, I begin to see possibilities for changes of pace to create tension and rising excitement.

crowd is good-humoured — crowd gets bored — crowd gets angry — celebrity appears — crowd won over at once

And I can see how the action can be presented from various angles.

observer/narrator (me) — the crowd — the celebrity — the civic dignitaries (especially the mayor) — the police

From some or all of those angles, contrasts and conflicts can be introduced into the narrative to keep it moving and make it lively.

(ii)   *Selecting Material and Arriving at a Plan*

First, I shape my composition by mapping out the successive stages through which the narrative will be unfolded. As I work on the outline, I can reject material that does not fit in, adding whatever new material I need.

(1) I see a crowd. (2) I join in. (3) Eager anticipation — 'X' is to appear. (4) Long wait. (5) Crowd gets bored. (6) Crowd gets restless. (7) Rumours circulate. (8) Crowd gets angry. (9) Ugly mood develops. (10) Police inspector enters town hall. (11) 'X' appears on balcony accompanied by mayor? NO: mayor appears alone. (12) Crowd furious. (13) Mayor brings 'X' onto balcony. (14) 'X' talks to crowd, makes flattering speech. (15) Crowd's anger evaporates: happiness all round.

That gives me a satisfactory start. Now I can work out a detailed plan. As I fill in the gaps, I shall get a much firmer grasp of my subject. Some of the proposed incidents will be compressed or omitted; others will be expanded. New ideas will occur. I shall be establishing firmer links, varying the pace, introducing stronger human interest, looking for conflicts and contrasts, placing snatches of speech at strategic points in the narrative. Overall, what I aim to do is to increase the excitement of the narrative without destroying its credibility.

A good plan will firm up the possibilities that I have begun to see: possibilities that were not apparent when I first began to gather my material. I am now confident that, if I can get my plan right, I can write a fluent composition on this subject.

(iii) *The Plan*

1. Jump straight into the action. I am part of the crowd when the narrative begins: part of it but detached from it — there's a narrative angle here.

   perhaps like this? — 'We want Mel! We want Mel!' There must have been ten thousand people packed into Bursley Town Square that night . . .

2. *Brief* description of situation. Action has been launched and reader now needs to know what it's all about.

   names essential — reader must be helped to believe in narrative — Mel Jones, captain of Bursley football team — Bursley Town Square packed with people waiting for him to appear on balcony after civic dinner and award of freedom of borough — cold dark night — square and town hall floodlit

3. Pick up action again. Crowd has been waiting a long time. Mood is changing.

   introduce little old man standing next to me in crowd — he's a useful way of carrying action forward and he's another 'angle' — he provides me with useful details about events — he's not a fan

4. Action quickens. Crowd getting very restless. Jokes rather savagely about mayor and councillors.

   'things'll get rough soon' (l.o.m. is talking to me) — 'it's gone ten now and he was due on balcony at nine'

5. Rumours begin to fly through crowd. Action hotter.

   'He's not coming out'/'mayor's driven away'/'it's all over'/'dinner's going on till midnight'/'toasts and speeches'

6. Crowd angry now. People surge forward. Police on two hall steps look apprehensive.

   'We'd best be going, lad.' — but impossible to shove through pushing mob

7. Police inspector enters town hall in a hurry.

8. Mayor appears on balcony. Tries to make himself heard.

   groans — jeers — crowd in ugly mood

9. Mayor turns away. Goes back in. Climax of narrative begins here.

   fury of crowd — l.o.m. and I in danger of being crushed — trying to get away — perhaps better to go with crowd? confusion reigns — cheers and jeers — scuffles break out

10. Mayor returns. Mel Jones is with him. Some people can see him but most cannot.

11. Mel Jones begins to speak. Crowd gradually calms down. Listens. Cheers. Loves it. Purrs with self-congratulation. Good humour all round.

    just hint at his soothing words: a phrase or two will be enough — 'fellow townsfolk . . . great honour . . . yours as much as mine' — acid comment from l.o.m.: 'half of them can't hear a word he's saying'

12. We make our escape. Action dies down. Keep this very short. I look back. Balcony is empty but they are still there — happy and singing in the cold dark night.

    'Good night, lad. Those idiots'll wait all night for another dose of syrup.'

Obviously, your plan for a composition on that subject would be different from the one that I have just worked out; and I do not claim more for mine than that it provides ample material arranged in an effective order. You might give your narrative a different 'slant', emphasise other aspects of the action, or — of course — write about a completely different series of events occurring in wholly different circumstances. It is in the composition question above all the others that the examiners invite and reward an entirely personal response from candidates.

Even so, we all need the help that comes from a methodical approach to writing. By applying the techniques demonstrated in these work-out sections, you can make a good choice of subject, explore thoroughly the possibilities that it offers you, and then write a composition that does justice to the imaginative thinking that you have put into it.

1.6 Work out Descriptive Compositions

(a) Facing the Problem

A descriptive composition seems easy compared with the other kinds. A story demands a plot; an account of events must be securely strung on a narrative thread; a dramatic composition tests the technical skill of writing realistic dialogue; an impressionistic composition exacts an imaginative response to a visual or verbal stimulus. In comparison, a descriptive composition appears to offer the writer much more freedom.

In fact, this apparent freedom can be a trap, for a descriptive composition makes its own special demands. You will probably not have difficulty in finding plenty of material for the descriptive subjects offered to you, but it is not easy to sort that material out and arrange it in an effective order of presentation.

(b) What You Must Do

A good composition, of whatever kind, has a beginning, a middle and an end. That sounds obvious, but it is a fact that is often overlooked when a descriptive subject has been chosen. Unless the material is presented in a clear progression *from* the beginning, *through* the middle, *to* the end, a descriptive composition is just a ragbag of details. Descriptive items haphazardly thrown together cannot hold the reader's interest, however vivid and telling they are in themselves.

A descriptive composition must have *unity*. In other words, it must be a complete and self-contained piece of writing, all the *parts* of which contribute to the *whole*. To impose unity on your material, you have to do a lot of imaginative thinking and careful planning before you begin to write.

(c) Some Typical Descriptive Subjects

1. Write a description of a scene that you know well, bringing out its special character.
2. Write a descriptive composition entitled *either* (a) 'A lonely place' *or* (b) 'A night scene'.
3. My best friend.
4. Overheard remarks.
5. Breakfast.
6. A room of my own.
7. Describe the scene *either* at a railway station *or* at a public swimming-pool.

8. The river.
9. The street market.
10. Closing time at the supermarket.

(d) Making a Choice

A good choice depends on two factors: your interest in and personal experience of the subject; your ability to 'see into' the material that you gather and to find an 'angle of attack'.

Your material will not ring true unless you have some personal experience of what you are describing. For example, do not choose subject 10 in the above list if you have never been in a supermarket at closing time. Again, you will certainly have abundant personal experience from which to draw your material for subject 5, but what a very dull catalogue of details your composition will be unless you can find an 'angle' on it. A subject such as that demands a fresh and lively approach.

The wording of the first subject on that list sums up two very important points about descriptive writing. It instructs you to describe something that you know well (a scene in that case) and to bring out its special character.

- Whatever its particular subject, a descriptive composition must be about something (or somebody) you know well *and* bring out the special character or significance that it has for you.

(e) Working out a Descriptive Subject

I have chosen subject 5, 'Breakfast', for the purposes of this work out. As a candidate in the examination I should probably choose subject 2(a), 'A lonely place', because there is one particular moorland scene that I know especially well and I feel confident that I could describe it in a way that would bring out the very special character that it has for me. But the subject 'Breakfast' gives me a better chance of demonstrating two important techniques:

1. How to gather fresh and interesting material for a descriptive subject that could easily seem stale and secondhand.
2. How to find a personal angle of attack from which to plan a descriptive composition that is lively and original.

(i) *Gathering Material*

Think in particular terms, not in general terms. Not breakfasts in general, but breakfasts (or a breakfast) that *you* have taken part in. Open your mind to the subject and gather personal, not abstract, material.

> bacon and eggs – toast and marmalade – tea or coffee – a bowl of cornflakes and a rush – snatched piece of bread and butter – the bus leaves in 5 minutes – what a lovely day it's going to be! – what shall we do? – oh, lord, it's snowing! – where's Jean? – not out of bed yet – she'll be late again – breakfast/*break* fast – first meal of the day – new life – lovely – smells – toast's burning – no hurry – pass the butter – milk's boiled over – can't stop – what a start to the day! – why is everyone so grumpy? – yawn – switch that noise off – oh, this sun!

(ii) *Looking for an Angle of Attack*

Because I have been thinking about the subject in personal and particular terms — in other words, finding my material in my own experience — I am becoming aware of a pattern. My ideas have been jotted down just as they occurred, but I can see a way of shaping them:

rush/leisure
good humour/bad temper
enjoying food/bolting food
fine weather/bad weather
zest/apathy

A strong contrast underlies the apparently haphazard collection of ideas. That contrast provides me with an angle of attack.

(iii) *Finding a Theme*

Following up this way of looking at my subject matter, I see that a theme is emerging: 'Breakfast as it *can* be, contrasted with breakfast as it usually *is*'. This emerging theme will now direct all my thinking and planning because, with it in mind, I can see how to describe breakfast in a purposeful way. For me, the subject now has a particular character and significance that I am aiming to express through my description. With that theme I can give my composition unity. Every descriptive detail that I include will bear on the theme.

Again, I can now make a plan that has a clear-cut shape. I can find a good beginning, link each paragraph to the others, arrive at an effective ending, because I have found a central idea to shape my writing. I know what I want to say.

Finding 'the idea behind the description' is the hardest job when you are writing a descriptive composition: the hardest and most important, for a composition without a theme is a mere catalogue of descriptive details, lacking unity, plan and purpose.

(f) Some More Descriptive Subjects

Sometimes the examiners' instructions draw your attention to the importance of providing a theme and implicitly warn you against producing a mere catalogue of details. Note the wording of this question (University of London, G.C.E., January 1983):

Treasured possessions.
(You may wish to describe some of the things you value most and show why you would hate to lose them.)

By including the words *and show why you would hate to lose them*, the examiners are saying, in effect, 'A mere catalogue is *not* what we want. We want to read descriptions of the things you treasure that show us *why* you treasure them.'

If you were tackling that question, you would have to take that theme as your guide as you gathered and selected your material and arrived at your plan. Here are some of the considerations that I would bear in mind.

1. Personal and particular thinking — *my* treasured possessions. I'll make a list.
2. How many? I can't find time or space for more than three or four. In any

case, although I don't want to lose any, there aren't more than a few that I'd *hate* to lose. If I include too many, I can't bring out the significance of those that really matter.

3. Which shall I include? The *most* treasured, of course; but it's not easy to say which they are. Think hard about this, by going on to 4.

4. *Why* would I hate to lose each one? Let's have another look at the list I've made and start sorting them out by asking that question: my copper ring, because it was given to me by a very special person/my radio, because I get so much pleasure from it/my tool kit, because it's so useful/my post office savings book, because it's worth money. . .

5. I'll choose four possessions, each of which I'd hate to lose for a different reason. That will give my composition variety and, therefore, added interest.

6. Order of presentation? I must think ahead. How to arrive at an interesting *sequence* is a problem. I musn't make it a simple list of one thing following another. I know: start with the most *valuable* one (in money terms, that is); go on to the most *useful* one; go on to the one that gives me most *pleasure*; end with the one that isn't worth very much in money terms but *means most to me* because of the person who gave it to me.

7. That's the outline settled. Now I can work out a detailed plan. I've got to know *before* I begin to write exactly how I'm going to tackle the descriptions. Take the radio, for example. What sort of description can I give of that? What details are relevant? The theme gives me my way in. I'd hate to lose it because of the pleasure it gives me. How does it do that? Because of its splendid tone? Because of its world-wide wavelength coverage? Because it's small and portable? Whichever of its features are the ones that make it most treasured are the ones to describe in detail.

Directed thinking of that kind is the basis of a successful plan.

Getting the order right was a problem when dealing with that subject, but many descriptive subjects are so worded that the order of writing is plain. For example:

Describe the changing activities of your street from dawn to dusk of a summer's day.

If I choose that subject, I know where to begin (at dawn) and I know where to end (at dusk); but I must put more thought into it than that. The structure will be loose unless I can link the beginning and the end to round it off. If I can find a way of doing that, I shall be able to impose a unity on my composition, making each detail and each part contribute something important to the whole. Descriptive writing that is full of unrelated bits and pieces is very boring.

I try out several ideas and, in the end, decide on this as a unifying link.

dawn — day beginning — light   both are quiet times — the day begins
dusk — day ending — dark   and ends in silence

I think again. It's not as good as I thought it was! My street isn't very quiet at dusk! So I try for a unifying idea by working along different lines: the street is long; shops and houses on both sides; trees, street lamps, pavements, doorsteps; people walking, talking, laughing, shouting; cars moving, cars parked. I must take up a viewpoint — present the scene from an angle. Where? From a particular window? — whose? Downstairs window or upstairs? Or see the scene from a flight of steps? — church steps? — a memorial? — a monument? — a statue? (possibilities here: bustle of street contrasting with quietness).

Whichever point of view I select, I can unify my composition by seeing and hearing everything from it. It is *my* street, after all, so I should be able to communicate its changing activities and personality as time passes over it on a summer's day.

Again, inside the imposed time limits, I must select particular descriptive moments. I can't describe everything that happens at every successive minute of the day. Even if I could, it would be a rather boring and long-winded progression of 'then . . . and then . . . and then'!

Something like this might work: (1) dawn; (2) nine o'clock; (3) lunch time; (4) mid-afternoon; (5) dusk. I see the possibility of a three-part structure there. Beginning: (1). Middle: (2), (3) and (4). End: (5).

I suggest that you now work on some of the descriptive subjects in Section 1.6(c), gathering, selecting and arranging your material in the ways I have demonstrated. Find your angle of attack and establish your theme for each subject. Then make a detailed plan for one of them and write the composition.

1.7 Work out Discursive Compositions

(a) What the Examiners are Looking for

The special features of discursive (argumentative or controversial) compositions were described in Section 1.2(d). The subjects set are concerned with facts, ideas, opinions, and the examiners are looking for:

- a genuine interest in the subject and an adequate fund of information about it;
- the ability to give due weight to a contrary opinion, while coolly and reasonclearly and fairly;
- the ability to give due weight to a contrary opinion, while cooly and reasonably rejecting it;
- the ability to set out an argument step by step and to arrive at a sensible conclusion.

To satisfy those requirements, a composition must be carefully planned and clearly expressed.

(b) Some Typical Discursive Subjects

1. Do you agree with the view that at a time of high unemployment women should give up their jobs so that unemployed men can get work?
2. 'We are squandering the natural resources of the planet and future generations will have to pay for our selfishness.' Put the case for three or four practical measures that you think we could and should take to safeguard the future of our children.
3. Do you agree that watching television is a waste of time?
4. Argue the case *for* or *against* the reintroduction in Britain of *either* capital punishment *or* corporal punishment.
5. 'Since alcohol causes as much suffering as any of the illegal drugs, the sale and consumption of alcoholic drinks should be banned.' What are your views on that statement?
6. 'No subject should be compulsory at school or college, for we never learn well what we learn unwillingly.' Suppose that you sympathise with that

point of view but, even so, believe that *one* particular subject should be compulsory. Make out your case.

7. Present your case for *either* believing *or* not believing in *one* of the following: (i) extraterrestrial life; (ii) the Loch Ness monster, or any other monster; (iii) ghosts; (iv) fortune-telling.

8. Do you agree with those who argue that everyone at the age of 18 should be conscripted into the armed forces for a period of military service?

9. 'We live in a world of which one half is affluent and the other half is poverty-stricken.' What are your views and what remedies would you advocate?

10. 'To derive pleasure from the death of living creatures is an abominable thing. I'd abolish hunting and all other kinds of blood sports.' What are your opinions on this contentious subject?

(c) Making a Choice

First, ask yourself whether you have enough knowledge of a particular subject to be able to write a composition of the required length. You do not have to be an expert to write well on any of the subjects offered, but you are expected to have the general information that a thoughtful person interested in the subject would have picked up from reading and talking about it and/or from discussions on television or radio. As you have seen, ideas for story, narrative and descriptive compositions are often generated as you gather and plan your material, but you will not obtain the material you need for a discursive composition by that method. Again, if you are short of information, this probably means that you are not very interested in the subject; and interest in your chosen subject is a prerequisite for successful writing.

This is not to say that a discursive composition must be crammed with facts. The examiners are less concerned with the quantity of your information than with the use you make of it in setting out your argument. Even so, to be able to deploy an argument and arrive at a sensible conclusion, you must have some knowledge of the subject.

(d) Read the Question Carefully

Consider very carefully the particular 'line' that the examiners are asking you to pursue. Are you being asked to put a case *for*? Are you being asked to consider both sides? Are you being asked to propose improvements? Marks are often thrown away because the candidate does not obey the instructions. For example, subject 7 on the list in Section 1.7(b) instructs you to present your case for *either* believing in *or* not believing in . . .'. There, you are not invited to consider both sides but to argue for or against belief. Because balanced views are wanted, it is always sensible to show an awareness of the opposing case, but a full exposition of it in this composition would be a waste of time. You would be marked on the part of the composition that obeyed the instructions. The other part would not be read.

Look at subject 6: 'Suppose that you sympathise with that point of view . . .'. In other words, do not debate that point of view in your composition. Take it for granted and deal with the meat of the question, which comes later.

(e) Planning and Style

A well-developed argument is required. It must be reasoned, balanced, thoughtful and interesting. It must, therefore, be based on a careful plan in which your ideas are arranged in a logical sequence. When you are planning, think in terms of a three-part structure: (1) introduction; (2) body of argument; (3) conclusion.

The introduction is best confined to one paragraph. Four or five paragraphs will suffice for the body of the argument. The conclusion is the destination towards which you have led your reader throughout the composition. It knits up the strands of your case and expresses your final opinion. Make it pithy. One paragraph should be enough if your argument in the body of the composition has been thoughtfully directed.

A clear, easily read style is essential. Your reader's attention should be concentrated on *what* you are writing, not distracted by *how* you are writing it. Firm, varied sentences and a crisp, accurate choice of words will sustain interest in and win agreement with the argument you are putting forward.

Never get carried away by the strength of your feelings. You are expected to have opinions and to express them, but in a reasoned manner. The point is well illustrated by subject 10 on the list in Section 1.7(b): ' "To derive pleasure from the death of living creatures is an abominable thing. I'd abolish hunting and all other forms of blood sports." What are your opinions on this contentious subject?' The quotation used as a 'subject trigger' expresses strong feelings, but the examiners are asking you to give your *opinions* on the controversial topic fired off by the quotation. What they want is a reasoned discussion of the question raised by the vehement words of the quotation. They expect you to have a decided point of view, but your conclusion must be reached by thoughtful argument. Your use of language should reflect your cool and reasoning approach to the subject. A discussion conducted in emotional terms — 'abominable', for example — would not be appropriate.

(f) Work out a Plan

As a rule, you know what your conclusion is before you begin to plan. The subject interests you. You have some information about it and you know what you think about it. Your problem is how to use your information in a developing and reasoned argument that justifies your opinions on the subject. In a sense, you are planning backwards from your conclusion and it is often helpful to do your preliminary thinking in this order:

1. This is what I think about this subject.
2. What are the facts and what are the arguments that lead me to this conclusion?
3. How can I best set out those facts and those arguments to show that I have good reasons for coming to my conclusion?

I shall now work out a plan for a composition on subject 5 on the list.

> 'Since alcohol causes as much suffering as the illegal drugs, the sale and consumption of alcoholic drinks should be banned.' What are your views on that statement?

I know that I do not agree that the sale and consumption of alcoholic drinks should be banned. What are my reasons? What facts am I relying on? (1) Alcoholic drinks need not be harmful. (2) There is some medical evidence to suggest that *moderate* drinking is beneficial. (3) Moderate social drinking is a source of pleasure. (4) Banning harmless pleasure can never be right. (5) In any case, a legal ban leads to law-breaking (e.g. the crime that accompanied prohibition in America; the evasions and severe punishments in some countries today).

Having jotted down my own positive reasons for the opinion I hold, I look at the arguments that underlie the proposition with which I am disagreeing. I must take opposing views into consideration if my argument is to stand up. (1) Yes, alcohol *can* cause suffering. (2) Whether it causes *as much* suffering as the illegal drugs, I do not know; and nor does the author of the statement. The proposition is very sweeping. (3) I suppose that cocaine and heroin — the so-called 'hard drugs' — are meant by 'the illegal drugs'. Their sale to and use by the general public should certainly be banned (even though they have their proper and beneficial *medical* uses). (4) The proposition makes no distinction between 'the illegal drugs', the general use of which *must* be harmful, and alcohol, the use of which *may* be harmful — but only when it is *misused*.

I have now sorted out my ideas. I know *where* my argument is going. I know, roughly, *how* it will get there. As I work out my plan, I have two remaining problems to sort out: (1) Where do I begin? (2) In what order shall I develop my argument?

(i) *Plan (with Notes)*

1 Introduction

Must be 'punchy' to gain reader's attention. Must make it plain that I am beginning a thoughtful discussion of the subject. *One* paragraph along these lines: the statement quoted is an assertion, not a reasoned opinion — it ignores the distinction between alcoholic drinks, which may be harmful, and hard drugs, which must be — on this dubious basis, it calls for an indiscriminate ban.

2 Body of Argument

Here I must do three things: (1) demonstrate weakness of proposition; (2) deploy my positive arguments for permitting sale and consumption of alcoholic drinks; (3) lead reader step by step towards agreement with my conclusion. Thinking about those three tasks suggests the following sequence of paragraphs.

PARAGRAPH 1

Cannot be denied that immoderate drinking causes mental and physical suffering — many alcoholics — families distressed — hospitals burdened — but this is misuse, abuse, of alcohol.

PARAGRAPH 2

Benefits of alcohol that statement ignores — social pleasure — medical evidence in favour of moderate use.

PARAGRAPH 3

Dangers of prohibition — the American experience — modern examples — law evasion and law enforcement — crime inevitably accompanies prohibition.

Some habits are so vicious, some substances so dangerous as to warrant banning —
for reasons given, not alcoholic drinks — most people use them as source of harmless pleasure — cannot justifiably take away the pleasure of a majority because a
minority misuses it.

CONCLUSION

One pithy paragraph, knitting together strands of argument. Banning pleasure
always dangerous and rarely justified. Considering the inevitable harmful consequences of a legal ban, the case against alcoholic drinks is too weak to support
their prohibition.

(ii) *A Note on Appropriate Language*

As you already know, emotional terms and excited writing must be avoided. You
will not convince your reader by shouting. The cool, thoughtful tone of a good
discursive composition calls for a degree of formality in its style, but do not confuse formality with pomposity. Long-winded sentences and 'big', would-be
important words will not impress your reader. An easy, plain style is the best, but
do not use slang or colloquialisms (see Chapter 6).

1.8 Work out Dramatic Compositions

Remember that a dramatic (or conversational) composition must be written in
direct speech, but — as you will see from the work out — you can use 'stage directions' to help to develop the action and to suggest the emotions and attitudes of
the characters. A dramatic situation is tense and exciting because the characters
are in some sort of confusion or conflict. The action rises to a climax and then
ends with a quick clearing up of the confusion or resolution of the conflict.

(a) A Typical Question

>   *David McKenzie, a young man of eighteen, is sitting at the table of a
>   living-room making a model from a kit; his sister, Jacky, a bright-eyed
>   nervous teenager, is curled up in an armchair watching television. Their
>   father, who has just returned from work, is recovering his spirits by trying
>   to read the evening newspaper.*
>   *There is an insistent ringing of the doorbell. Mrs McKenzie is heard going
>   to answer it, and there are muffled sounds of a serious conversation out-
>   side. The door of the living-room opens violently. She appears, disturbed
>   and shaking.*
>   Mr McKenzie [*casually looking up*] : What is it, dear?
>   Mrs McKenzie [*breathlessly*] : There's a policeman at the door.
>   David: Oh, no!
>   *Jacky quickly unrolls herself from the chair and switches off the television;
>   she looks anxiously at her father and bursts into tears.*

Write a short play by continuing the dialogue in a manner which develops
the dramatic situation. (You are advised to continue the method of setting

out the dialogue, but *do not copy out the extract*. If you wish, you may introduce one or two more characters or add a further scene.)
(L., January 1982)

(b) Work out: Stage 1

Analyse the given dramatic situation out of which you must develop a short play.

  (i) Peaceful domestic scene suddenly interrupted by arrival of policeman.
 (ii) Four characters briefly introduced:
      David McKenzie (brother) — sitting working at model — quiet — eighteen
      Jacky McKenzie (sister) — bright-eyed, nervous — watching TV — curled up — teenager
      Mr McKenzie (father) — tired after work — trying to read newspaper
      Mrs McKenzie (mother) — disturbed — shaking — opens door violently
(iii) Another character — policeman — as yet an unknown quantity

(c) Work out: Stage 2

Identify possible dramatic 'growth points'.

  (i) Jacky's reaction — looks anxiously at father — bursts into tears — frightened of father's reaction — thinks she knows why policeman has called — nervous person, so assumes that policeman's visit means trouble for her
 (ii) David McKenzie's exclamation ('Oh, no!') — is that caused by annoyance at interruption or does he think something is catching up with him? — quiet character, so has possibilities for surprising dramatic development
(iii) Father — no reaction given, so can be used in any way that develops drama — father-figure, so give him authority and some control over events — remember, he's tired and wants to read his paper in peace
 (iv) Mother — upset — bewildered — worried — not so much an actor in the drama as a reactor to events?
  (v) Policeman — why has he called? — obviously the mainspring of the action — provide a harmless reason for his visit but do not reveal it at once — in meantime, let other characters react in confused, nervous or angry way

(d) Work out: Stage 3

Outline development of dramatic situation.
   Suppose the policeman has called to interest the McKenzies in a police/public co-operation in a 'neighbourhood watch' scheme.
   Suppose David thinks he wants information about his motor bike. The licence is due for renewal.
   Suppose Jacky thinks he saw her and her friends leaving a disco late the previous evening. They were happy and excited and making a lot of noise. Perhaps there has been a complaint? What will her father say?
   Leave Mr and Mrs McKenzie in bewilderment. He's fed up because he's tired and wants to relax. She's anxious about her children. Give Mr McKenzie an active role. Give Mrs McKenzie a passive role.

Thinking it out has provided: (1) a development of the given dramatic situation; (2) action that rises to a climax; (3) an ending that untwists the strands of the action and resolves the tension.

(e) Work out: Stage 4

Write the dramatic composition in accordance with the instructions supplied.

Mr McKenzie [*wearily*]: What on earth does he want? You'd better bring him in. Oh, do be quiet, Jacky! What's the matter?

Jacky [*between sobs*]: We didn't mean . . . it was only fun . . .

David [*searching through his wallet*]: I filled it in the other day. Don't say I didn't post the blessed thing.

> *By this time, Mrs McKenzie has brought the policeman into the living-room. He is a young man, with a pleasant smile.*

Policeman: I'm sorry to disturb you, but I'd like to have a talk.

> *Jacky and her mother speak at the same time and nobody hears what they are saying. The policeman looks enquiringly at Mr McKenzie, whose patience is wearing thin.*

Mr McKenzie: I wish somebody would tell me what this is all about. Jacky, keep quiet until you have something sensible to say. Don't upset yourself, Alice. There's nothing wrong — as far as I know.

David McKenzie [*waving an envelope*]: It's here! All filled in and signed — *and* the money's inside. If I catch the last post, they'll get it tomorrow.

> *David makes for the door, smiling happily, but the policeman speaks to him before he can reach it.*

Policeman [*firmly*]: If you could just give me a moment . . . I'm particularly anxious to talk to young people, like you and your sister.

Jacky [*tearfully*]: I'm sorry, but — honestly — I don't know how to . . .

Mr McKenzie: Where d'you think you're going, David? Sit down. [*He turns to the policeman.*] Perhaps if you sat down too, we'd get somewhere. I think my two children have gone off their chumps.

Mrs McKenzie: Oh, yes, do sit down. I'll go and get us all a cup of tea. I'm sure you'd like one?

> *She turns towards the kitchen door, pleased to have something practical to do.*

Policeman: Well, that's very kind of you, but perhaps you'd just listen to me first. You are all concerned in this.

Jacky: No! You've got it wrong. It wasn't *their* fault. They weren't there. They were here, at home, when . . .

Mr McKenzie: Jacky, if I have to tell you to shut up once more, I'll go as barmy as you. [*He turns to the policeman.*] Now, young man, I think I can guarantee you a few minutes of silence. What's it all about?

Policeman: We're trying to start a neighbourhood watch scheme. Each station in our division is contacting the households in its area. There's to be a public meeting in the Town Hall at 7.30 next Tuesday and I'm here to invite you all to it.

David McKenzie [*putting the envelope back in his wallet*]: So that's it! Oh, what a pity! I can't go on Tuesday — it's my training night.

Jacky [*very enthusiastically*]: Oh, what a good idea! I'll be there and I'll bring some of my friends.

Mrs McKenzie: Tuesday, you say? I'm afraid I can't. I always spend the evening with Gran on a Tuesday. She's getting on, you know, and she looks forward to Tuesdays.

Mr McKenzie [*very firmly*]: I think we shall be well represented at the meeting, officer. Jacky's very keen — you can see that. And I'm sure David will put off his training for once. He takes a lot of interest in legal matters, don't you, David?

> *David is about to answer, but he looks again at his father's expression and changes his mind.*

Policeman: I'll leave these leaflets for you to read before the meeting. [*He hands one to David and one to Jacky.*] Thank you for your interest and I'll look forward to seeing you next Tuesday evening. I don't think I'd better have that cup of tea, thank you, Mrs McKenzie. I've got several more houses to visit.

> *Mrs McKenzie shows the policeman out. David returns to his modelling. Jacky reaches for the television switch.*

Mr McKenzie [*picking up his newspaper*]: Now, David, you'd better go and post that letter. And don't tell me it doesn't matter. If a policeman's visit reminded you of it, it matters all right. And, Jacky, you can forget about television for half an hour. Celebrate your lucky escape — whatever it was — by helping your mother in the kitchen. *I'm* going to read my paper.

1.9 Work out Impressionistic Compositions

(a) The Examiners' Instructions

As you saw in Section 1.5, a composition on an impressionistic subject may be written in the form of a story. It may also be written as an unplotted narrative or a description, or in *any form that the particular instructions permit*.

Whether the provided stimulus is verbal (a few lines of poetry) or visual (a picture or a series of pictures), the examiners usually invite candidates to respond by writing *one* of several different forms of composition which they stipulate. Which form of composition you choose is entirely up to you, provided that it is one of the forms permitted by the question.

The instructions sometimes refer to an 'essay'. For example: 'Write a story, a description, or an essay suggested by *one* of the pictures on pages 4 and 5.' The term *essay* is often used as a synonym for 'a composition', but, as it is used in the instructions just quoted, it means a composition of a particular kind: *not* a story, *not* an unplotted narrative, *not* a description, but an exposition (and an exploration) of the *ideas, thoughts* and/or *feelings* that are suggested to you by the poetry or the picture.

To familiarise yourself with the range of instructions, study the list of typical questions given in the next section. Before doing so, however, remind yourself of the stipulation that applies to *all* impressionistic compositions of whatever form: the composition must be directly and clearly connected with the given poetry or picture. That is its starting point.

(b) Some Typical Impressionistic Questions

1. Using the picture on page 5 as a starting point, write a story or a descriptive essay.
2. Write a story, a description or an essay suggested by *one* of the pictures on the accompanying sheet. Your composition should be directly about the

subject of the picture or take some central suggestion(s) from it: *there must be some clear connection between the picture and your composition.*

3. Using the following lines of poetry as a starting point, write a story or an essay.
4. Write a composition based on the accompanying picture postcard.
5. Write a composition suggested by the following quotation.
6. Write on an idea suggested by the picture below.
7. Write on an idea, *or* on places, *or* on persons, suggested by the following lines.
8. Look at the photograph printed below and then answer *one* of the following:
    (i) Write a story in which the driver of the car in the picture plays an important part.
    (ii) Write a story entitled 'The car that broke down'.
    (iii) What ideas about transport does the picture suggest to you?
    (iv) Write an essay based on the thoughts and feelings that the picture suggests to you.

(c) Work out Your Methods

Revise Section 1.5, where a sound method of writing an impressionistic composition is demonstrated in full detail.

In that work out the stimulus was poetry and the form chosen for the composition was a story. Here are some notes on how to use a pictorial stimulus to write compositions of various kinds.

(i) *Picture Subjects*

The picture material is included in the examination 'pack' of questions, answer books, writing paper, etc., that you will find on your desk. It may be a photograph of a dramatic scene, or a 'still' from a television play or a film. It may be a news picture from a paper or a magazine, or it may be a landscape or a townscape. It may be a photographic reproduction of a work of art. It may be a strip cartoon. It may be comic or serious; strictly realistic or imaginatively suggestive. The range of possibilities is large, but whatever the subject or the nature of the picture, your composition must spring out of a close and imaginative response to it.

(ii) *A Story Composition Based on a Picture*

Imagine that you are one of the people in the picture, or imagine that you took the photograph or that you painted the picture. This way, you involve yourself in the possibilities of action, get to know the people, find an angle from which to tell your story.

Having identified with one of the people in the picture or with the photographer or artist, let your thoughts play on possible relationships (enmity, love, rivalry, support, and so on) between your 'angle character' and other people in the picture. The seeds of your plot lie here.

Study facial expressions, gestures, clothes, ages, postures, and so on, as shown in the picture. Sharp observation of such details will provide descriptive material and plot development for your story.

Only when you have 'interpreted' the picture in this way, by an imaginative exploration of *what* is happening and *why* it is happening, can you use it as the springboard for a story.

(iii) *A Descriptive Composition Based on a Picture*

Study the picture closely, with a sharp eye for its details. You will find yourself responding imaginatively to some particular item. A frowning face, an open window, a shadow on a doorstep, a child's smile, a car without a number plate, a smart hat worn at a rakish angle . . . such are the pictorial hints that will start you off.

Look for your 'angle of attack' (see Section 1.6(d)) in the interaction of a detail with the overall impression that the picture makes. That crucial angle of attack may be discovered either by narrowing down your focus from the picture as a whole to a particular detail, or by focusing first on a detail and then widening your view to take in the whole picture. Try both ways of searching for your viewpoint.

Once you have established your angle of attack, move in an ordered sequence from your starting point to your planned ending. Unless you consistently maintain your chosen angle, you will let in irrelevant details and weaken the structure of your composition. Unity (each detail and each part contributes to the impact of the *whole*) is vital. Remember: 'No false starts and no loose ends.'

(iv) *An Essay Based on a Picture*

See Section 1.8(a) for the meaning of the term *essay*, as used here.

Instructions such as 'Write an essay based on the impressions you receive from this picture' or 'What thoughts (and/or feelings) does this picture suggest to you?' require a different kind of answer from those we have been considering earlier. They limit you by excluding narrative or descriptive forms of composition, but they offer you great freedom of imaginative response to the picture. Provided that your subject matter is triggered off by something in the picture (and is clearly seen by the reader to be so evoked) you can allow your imagination to journey beyond the picture's bounds.

(v) *Model Structure*

Many candidates find that the following model structure provides a sound basis for a picture composition of the kind we are discussing here.

1 INTRODUCTION

Brief but vivid description of the 'trigger detail' in the picture and of your immediate response to it. One paragraph.

2 BODY OF COMPOSITION

Three or four paragraphs describing the associated ideas, thoughts and/or feelings that the 'trigger' has set off in your mind. It is essential to link these paragraphs so that each leads your reader on to the next. You must establish a clear forward flow of ideas, thoughts, feelings.

3 CONCLUSION

A final paragraph, rounding off the imaginative journey on which you have taken your reader. It is structurally effective and imaginatively satisfying to return to the trigger detail from which the essay began.

2 Practical Writing

2.1 General Characteristics

In the practical (or factual) writing exercise you are given certain material which must be used in a practical, everyday situation indicated by the examiners' instructions. The exercise tests your ability to write briefly, clearly and accurately. Because the instructions strictly control both the contents and the purpose of your writing, the exercise is sometimes called 'directed writing'.

Now revise Sections 1.1(c) and 1.1(d).

(a) Time, Length and Marks

The time allowed for the writing exercise ranges from 15 minutes to half an hour. Most boards expect an answer of not more than one side in length. Maximum marks allotted range from 10 to 30.

(b) Purpose and Form

The writing exercise provides you with the opportunity to show that you can:

- write correct English;
- make accurate use of given information;
- carry out instructions.

The answer required may be in the form of:

- a letter;
- a report;
- a short article;
- a set of instructions;
- an ordered explanation;
- an outline of a point of view;
- an outline of advice on some problem.

(c) Style

A plain, 'no frills' style is appropriate to the practical purpose and factual content of the writing exercise. The letters, reports, instructions, etc., that are called for are best expressed in simple terms, with no wasted words or purple patches. 'Transactional' writing (writing that gets things done) is successful when it is crisp, clear and very much to the point, so your use of language must be objective, unemotional and controlled.

2.2 Work out Letters

The examiners' instructions may or may not draw your attention to the importance of correct layout and the need to observe the conventions of letter writing. Whether they do so or not, your letter must always be set out properly and you must always conform to the conventions. Failure to do so is penalised.

(a) Work out 1

factual material provided and practical situation indicated

writing task set — the writer is given two objectives

There is a proposal to resite the market in your town by moving it from its present open-air site in the town centre to a covered hall being built by property developers. This proposal has caused bad feeling between its supporters and its opponents. Write a letter to the Editor of your local newspaper, stating your own views and attempting to reconcile the two sides.

---

writer's address — see notes

12, Grove Road,
St Mary's Way,
Boroughtown.
BT7 12GR
31 March 1985

recipient's name and address — formal letter

The Editor,
Boroughtown News,
6, West Walk,
Boroughtown.
BT4 6WW

correct salutation for Editor

Sir,

It is not surprising that the proposal to resite our market has caused so much bad feeling. Its supporters see only the advantages offered by a modern, spacious, weatherproof market. Its opponents regret the ending of a long tradition. Our market has been held in the Square for over three hundred years. Its stall-holders give us excellent service throughout the year. The objectors also argue that the move will cause market prices to rise to pay for increased rents in the new hall.

My own view is that the advantages of the move outweigh the disadvantages, but I sympathise with the objectors and I believe that their case merits a reasoned answer. If the market committee of the borough council would publish details of the new stall rents, the objectors would know whether their fears are justified. They also deserve an assurance that the layout of the new hall will be as convenient and efficient as the arrangements that we are used to.

I believe that the present bad feeling would be greatly reduced if those two suggestions were followed up.

Yours faithfully,

formal close *Yours faithfully* matches salutation *Sir* — no full stop after signature

Brian Jones

1 The Layout of Addresses

Choose either of the following styles. Whichever you choose, be consistent. Do not start with one style and change to the other.

Style 1	*Style 2*
12, Grove Road,	12 Grove Road
St Mary's Way,	St Mary's Way
Boroughtown.	Boroughtown
BT7 12GR	BT7 12GR
Closed punctuation.	Open punctuation.
Indented lines (except postcode).	Blocked lines.
The comma after the house number is optional.	If well-written, this is a neat and uncluttered address layout.
No full stop after St — it is a contraction (= *Saint*), not an abbreviation.	

2 The Date

All letters must be dated. The date form shown is clear and neat:

day (numerical)	month (in full)	year (in full)
31	March	1985

There are many other date forms. The following are often used:

31st March 1985; March 31st, 1985; 31.iii.85

Economy and clarity argue for the form used in the work out.

3 The Recipient's Name and Address

Must be included in formal letters. Out of place in informal letters. May be written above body of letter, as in work out, or below.

4 Salutation

The recipient of the letter must be 'greeted'. This greeting is called the 'salutation': *Dear So-and-so*. Formal ('business') letters require formal salutations. These are: *Dear Sir/Dear Madam*; *Dear Sirs* (to a Company); *Sir* (to the Editor of a newspaper). The correct salutations for 'non-business' letters are: *Dear Mr Jones*; *Dear Mrs Jones*; *Dear Miss Jones*; *Dear Ms Jones*; *Dear Tom*; *Dear Jane*; *Dear Uncle Fred*; etc.

5 Punctuation of Salutation

When indented paragraphs are used in the letter, it is customary to end the salutation with a comma.

Dear Mr Jones,
           Thank you for your letter . . .

Note the capital for the first word of the letter. When the paragraphs are not indented, omit the comma at the end of the salutation.

Dear Mr Jones
Thank you for your letter . . .

6 Formal Close

Before 'signing off', the letter writer uses a *formal close*. The formal close must 'match' the salutation. Like this:

Dear Sir		*Dear Mr Jones*	
Dear Madam	} *Yours faithfully*	*Dear Mrs Jones*	} *Yours sincerely*
Sir		*Dear Sally*	

If the salutation does not name the recipient, the formal close is *Yours faithfully*. If the salutation does name the recipient, the formal close is *Yours sincerely*. Note that *Yours* begins with a capital Y, but *faithfully* and *sincerely* begin with small letters. There is no punctuation after the signature.

(b) Work out 2

address to be used

recipient of letter

date clue for letter

diary language not always suitable for letter to aunt

You are on holiday with some family friends, the Robinsons, at 6, Quayside Cottages, Hartsea, Devon. On a morning walk along the cliffs, you witness the rescue of a person cut off by the tide. Write a letter to your Aunt Amy, describing the adventure. Make use of these notes from your diary.

Friday 13 August. Early walk along cliffs. Robinsons' dog Toby wittering away on cliff top. Barking like fury. Looked down. Figure on beach waving frantically. Faint calls. What to do? Return for help? Sound of helicopter. Hovered overhead. Then down cliff face. Winchman brought stranded walker up. Elderly woman. Bit shaken; not hurt. Took her to Robinsons. Surprise, surprise! Miss Agnes Smith — old family friend of theirs. Mrs R and Miss S quite overcome — shock/relief. Mr R's joke. Plans for party at Miss S's hotel tomorrow.

---

6 Quayside Cottages
Hartsea
Devon
14 August 1986

Dear Aunt Amy,

I promised you a letter, but I didn't think I'd have quite such exciting news to send.

Yesterday, I took the Robinsons' dog, Toby, for an early morning walk along the cliffs. Suddenly, he got very excited and started barking furiously. I looked over the cliff and saw a figure on the beach below, waving frantically at me. I could hear faint calls for help and I decided I must return to the cottage. I couldn't do anything on my own.

Then I heard a helicopter in the distance. Quite soon, it was hovering overhead and then it descended the cliff face very slowly and care fully. The winchman was lowered and he lifted the stranded walker off the beach.

When they got her to the cliff top, I saw that she was an elderly woman. She was a bit shaken, but she assured them that she was not hurt, so they asked me to guide her back to the village.

Mrs Robinson came out to greet us and you can imagine how surprised she was to recognise the rescued woman as Miss Agnes Smith, an old family friend of theirs. It was quite a shock for them both and they were rather upset by it all, until Mr Robinson made them laugh by saying that this was an unusual way of paying calls!

We're having a celebration party at Miss Smith's hotel tonight and I must start getting ready now.

With lots of love,
Your affectionate niece,

Jane

(i) *Notes on Work out*

1 *Layout and Conventions*

The information required for the address was included in the instructions. (Style 2 was chosen for the layout, but style 1 would have been equally correct.) The date clue was also important. Notice the use made of it by Jane. The salutation *Dear Aunt Amy* was matched by the signing off, which accurately reflected the kinship and good feeling between writer and recipient.

2 *Style*

This is an informal letter (contrast it with Work out 1) in which colloquialisms (*didn't, I'd*, etc.) are appropriate. However, the slang expressions used in the diary notes were rightly rejected as being unsuitable in tone. Though not formal, this letter is from niece to aunt and slang would be ill-mannered. Jane very nicely achieved the easy, conversational style that the occasion required.

3 *Contents*

The letter writer was instructed to describe the adventure, but neither time nor length allowed space for descriptive detail, so a bare outline of events was required. A brief introductory sentence supplied a realistic beginning for the letter. Similarly, the last clause of the final sentence provided a neat and convincing ending.

(c) Work out 3

You notice this advertisement in your local paper:

Junior assistant required to work initially in Accounts Department of small but growing local firm, specialising in the preparation of research reports for electronics industry. Must be mathematically competent and willing to undertake part-time study for further qualifications in areas to be agreed. Apply in writing to Box 27, Bramshall Clarion, Mill Lane, Bramshall, BH12 6ML, giving details of qualifications and experience. Two referees required.

You left school 2 years ago with five O levels and since then have had work experience relevant to the post advertised. You have applied for admission to an electronics course at your local F.E. college and are waiting for the result of your application. Write a letter to the address given, applying for the advertised job.

---

16 Smith Street
Bramshall
BH8 16ST

30 June 1986

formal letter: recipient's name and address required →

Box 27
The Bramshall Clarion
Mill Lane
Bramshall
BH12 6ML

formal salutation →

Dear Sirs,

letter 'headline' provided: reader can 'tune in' to contents at once →

Junior Assistant in Accounts Department

start with personal details: list all qualifications and other achievements in non-academic fields →

      I believe that my qualifications and experience make me a suitable candidate for the above post.

      I am 18 years old and I left Bramshall Central Comprehensive School in July 1984 with five O levels: English Language (Grade 2); English Literature (Grade 2); Mathematics (Grade 1); General Science (Grade 2); French (Grade 3). I also gained life-saving and woodcraft badges in the Guides and I was secretary of the school discussion club.

highlight aspects of experience that suit you for job →

      I then worked with Comma Electric for a year, gaining varied experience in components assembly and in the customer relations department.

      In the past year, I have had experience of part-time voluntary work in the Bramshall Youth Centre. I have now applied for admission to the first year electronics course at Bramshall F.E. college and, if you appoint me to the vacancy in your firm, I shall ask to be transferred to the evening course in order to pursue the further qualifications to which your advertisement refers.

formal close *Yours faithfully* →

Yours faithfully,

Mary Young

clear and convenient way of listing referees →

Reference may be made to the following:
1. Mr J. K. Tompkins, M. A., Headmaster, Bramshall Central Comprehensive School, BH4 5CC.
2. Miss A. C. Bednall, Personnel Officer, Comma Electric, BH16 1TE.

2.3 Work out Reports

(a) What the Examiners are Looking for

When the writing exercise takes the form of a report, the examiners expect you to be:

- accurate in carrying out the instructions;
- logical in the arrangement of the contents;
- clear and brief in expression.

A report must be written in continuous prose (*not* in note form), but headings and/or numbered sections may be used as an aid to clear presentation. The test of a well-written report is the ease and clarity with which it can be read and understood.

Questions of this type are often set:

> Your student council committee has asked you to report on the cafeteria service provided in your school or college. Write your report, suggesting practical ways in which the service could be improved.

(b) Layout: Headings

By its very nature, a report is an essentially practical piece of writing, intended to be *used*. It has been asked for by some person or some organisation. It is on a precise subject. It is needed for a particular purpose at a particular time. Therefore, it must be accurately and clearly identified. Always supply headings that provide the necessary details. The report called for in the question just quoted requires these headings:

> *To:* Student Council Committee, Fairplace F.E. College
> *From:* X. Y. Bloggs
> *Subject:* College cafeteria service
> *Date:* 15/9/86

(Note that all-numeral date forms are acceptable on reports, memoranda and brief notes. On letters, the date form recommended in Section 2.2(a) should be used.)

(c) Layout: Internal

Headings and/or numbered sections are usually required in the body of a report. They are essential when it contains numerous and varied items, and even the comparatively straightforward reports asked for in your examination are made much clearer by such divisions. Internal headings and/or numbered sections act as 'signposts' to the logical order in which a report is set out. Thus, they assist the reader to comprehend the contents quickly and clearly.

(d) Logical Order: Findings and Recommendations

When you have assembled the material for your report, sort it out into a logical order of presentation. In the question quoted in Section 2.3(a), you are instructed to do two things: (1) investigate the cafeteria service; (2) make practical suggestions for improvements. Logically, then, your report should consist of two main sections: (1) Findings; (2) Recommendations.

Since you will probably need to include more than one item under each of those internal headings, some such plan as this will be suitable:

1. *Findings*
   (i) or (a)   ⎫   arranged in a logical order when the
   (ii) or (b)   ⎬   material for the report has been
   etc.   ⎭   assembled — see below
2. *Recommendations*
   (i) or (a)   ⎫   arranged in a logical order after
   (ii) or (b)   ⎬   the findings have been sorted out
   etc.   ⎭   — see below

The precise nature and number of the sub-divisions under each main heading cannot be decided in advance. After you have jotted down the material for your report, you can then work out the classifications into which it can sensibly be divided. For example: favourable items; unfavourable items. Then you can decide upon the *order* of presentation: favourable items before unfavourable items — or vice versa?; proceed from most important item to least important item (*descending* order)?; proceed from least important item to most important item (*ascending* order)?

Provided that you are aware of the necessity of establishing a logical order, a scheme to suit the nature of the report will emerge as you sort out your material.

(e) Work out

practical situation indicated: instructions given

Your student council committee has asked you to report on the cafeteria service provided in your school or college. Write your report, suggesting practical ways in which the service could be improved.

(i) *Stage 1 of Work out*

Jot down the material as it occurs to you. In an everyday situation you would gather this material by observing, asking questions and making notes. In examination conditions you must draw on your experience of the system to provide the material for the report.

> poor quality of snacks, sandwiches especially — lack of variety and imagination — hot and cold drinks expensive and not good — food, except for standard hot meal at lunch, poor value for money — hot lunch very good, varied, plenty of it, but too expensive for most students to eat every day — long queues — takes far too long to get to food bar — seats uncomfortable, and not enough — too much noise — lack of social atmosphere — cafeteria closes at five, no chance of hot drink or snack after lectures, evening students not catered for at all

(ii) *Stage 2 of Work out*

Suggestions for improvements have been asked for, so the logical order of presentation seems to be : (1) favourable items; (2) unfavourable items. Recommendations will then follow logically from the latter. Again, looking for ways of sorting the material out into sensible groups, you can see that the unfavourable items fall into three classes: (1) food; (2) surroundings and conditions; (3) opening hours. Of these, food is undoubtedly the most important, so take that first.

1. Findings

plan for report is emerging from close, analytical study of findings	

(a)   Favourable items
(b)   Unfavourable items
   (i)   food
   (ii) surroundings and conditions
   (iii) opening hours

The details of this 'display code' — '(a), (b), (b)(i)', etc. — will not necessarily be followed in the report itself. Here they are useful in setting out the emerging plan for the report.

(iii)   *Stage 3 of Work out*

The instructions asked for practical suggestions about ways of improving the cafeteria service. Now that the findings have been assembled and arranged in a logical order of presentation, the recommendations follow on logically. It is important to distinguish between what can and should be done immediately and what might be done in time and with extra funds. Those considerations suggest the logical order in which to present the recommendations.

2. Recommendations

recommendations follow logically from ordered presentation of findings and are themselves presented in a logical order

(a)   Food   Detailed recommendations for immediate action can be made.
(b)   Surroundings and Conditions   Detailed recommendations for immediate and medium-term action can be made.
(c)   Opening Hours   Long-term problem because of serious financial implications. General recommendations can be made.

(iv)   *Stage 4 of Work out: Writing the Report*

REPORT

To: Student Council Committee, Fairplace F.E. College
From: X.Y. Bloggs
Subject: College cafeteria service
Date: 15/9/86

1. Findings

(a) Students consider that the hot lunch is a good meal, providing a variety of well-cooked dishes.
(b) Most students, however, rely on the snacks because they cannot afford the hot lunch. The snacks — especially the sandwiches — are of poor quality. They lack variety and they are over-priced. The same criticisms apply to the hot and cold drinks.
(c) Lunchtime queues are long and tiresome. The seating is uncomfortable and inadequate. There is too much noise in the cafeteria and a lack of social atmosphere.
(d) Cafeteria service closes at 5.00 p.m. Consequently, students cannot obtain refreshments after lectures, and evening students are not catered for at all.

2. Recommendations

    (a) Food   Immediate action can and should be taken to improve the quality and variety of the snacks and drinks. No additional funds are required to effect this improvement, just more care and imagination. A student/cafeteria staff liaison committee should be set up at once.

    (b) Surroundings and Conditions   As a first step, more chairs should be provided. Then, queues, overcrowding and noise could all be reduced by more thoughtful timetabling. If half the morning lectures ended at 12 noon and the other half at 1.00 p.m. (with a consequent adjustment to afternoon lectures), the pressure on the cafeteria would be halved. Lunch service would have to be extended to 2 hours, but this should not cost more than present resources would allow.

    (c) Opening Hours   I recognise that an extension beyond 5.00 p.m. would be costly, but I recommend that this problem be taken to the college authorities for urgent action as soon as financial conditions permit.

2.4 Work out Articles and (Newspaper) Reports

(a) Qualities to be Aimed at

Note, first, that the examiners' instructions often refer to a piece of writing intended for a newspaper or magazine as 'a report'. Such a report is very different from the kind of report worked out in Section 2.3. Its heading (or 'headline') is brief and eye-catching. It is not divided into sections and sub-sections (though it is clearly paragraphed). It does not make recommendations.

An article is less concerned with events than is a newspaper or magazine report. For example, you would probably be asked to write a *report* of a village meeting called to discuss a local issue and to write an *article* about one of the speakers at that meeting. A report is more 'newsy' than an article. However, the distinction is not always sharply drawn. Instructions phrased like this are common: 'Write an article, suitable for your school or college magazine, reporting the major events (sporting *or* academic *or* artistic) of one term in the past year'.

As set for the practical writing exercise, an article and a (newspaper or magazine) report are very similar. The theoretical distinction between them does not affect the qualities looked for in your answer.

- An article or report written for a newspaper or magazine must be accurate, lively and readable.

(b) Two Kinds of Questions

In one kind of question the examiners supply you with the information that you must use in the article. In such cases pay very careful attention to the instructions. Careless reading costs marks: a point illustrated by the following questions.

1. Write an article for your school or college magazine, selecting your information from the notes below.
2. Write a report for your local paper, using all the information given below.
3. Write a report for publication in your college magazine, based on the notes supplied and any other information that you may wish to add.

The other kind of question stipulates the subject on which your article must be written, but leaves you to provide all the information. For example: 'Write an article for your local paper, reporting a measure proposed by the council and the strong feelings (for and against) that this has provoked'. Note that you are *not* asked for *your* opinions. Objective reporting is required. (Compare that question closely with the one set in Section 2.2(a).)

(c) Work out

Write an article for your local paper about Councillor Brown, your newly elected mayor, selecting your information from the facts supplied below.

Brown, Arthur Henry. b. Fairplace, 30 November 19–. Third son of William Henry Brown, foreman fitter Fairplace Engineering and a member of Fairplace Borough Council until his death in 19–. Educated at Fairplace Central School. Left at 16. Apprenticed to Fairplace Engineering. Later joined export sales division. Widely travelled. Numerous international conferences. Eventually managing director, his present post at Fairplace Engineering. Keen sportsman: Fairplace R.U.F.C. 1st XV; F. cricket club, captain 1st XI. Also F. dramatic soc. and civic soc. Member of Borough Council for past 10 years, Independent (Castle Ward), chairman library committee, member watch committee. In acceptance speech stressed desire to attract more industry to F. Hoped his year in office would be remembered for industrial expansion: 'more jobs and better jobs'. Married Mary Jones (Fairplace born) in 19–. Three children (two daughters, one son) now attending F. Sixth Form College

(i) *Stage 1*

The problem of order must be solved first. Think about the nature and purpose of the set task. You have to present facts about the new mayor in a way that will interest readers of your paper. A straightforward chronological arrangement of facts ((1) birth; (2) education; (3) early career; and so on) would work, but it might be rather dull reading. Can you think of a more interesting order? Here is one possibility.

NEW MAYOR'S AMBITIONS FOR FAIRPLACE

PARAGRAPH 1

A local family man

PARAGRAPH 2

Successful career — wide experience of industry and foreign travel lead to top job

PARAGRAPH 3

Yet, a Fairplace-centred life — local activities and local politics

PARAGRAPH 4

His ambitions for his term of office

PARAGRAPH 5

Conclusion: Councillor Brown, a mayor for our town and our times

The paragraph headings used in that outline will not appear in the article. They are useful signposts at this stage, when the objective is to group together and then to set out in a logical and interesting order the items of information supplied. You can probably improve on the suggested outline, but it does point out the possibilities for a livelier article than strict chronological order seemed to offer.

(ii) *Stage 2*

The reader's attention must be gripped by the beginning of the article and, an outline plan having been settled on, it is a good idea to try out one or two opening sentences. You do not have to distort the facts or to copy the broken English of the tabloids to be interesting. 'Fairplace's new mayor is a Fairplace man.'/'A truly local man is now Fairplace's first citizen,'/'Rooted in local life, our new mayor brings wide experience to his high office.' You may not use any of the trial openings exactly as worded (I am certainly not satisfied with any of those), but jotting them down tunes you in to the spirit of the article and helps you to get off on the right foot.

(iii) *Stage 3*

Think hard about your ending. Have it clearly in mind before you begin to write. Aim for a pithy and memorable summing up of the body of the article. No repetition, of course; but something that will stay in the reader's mind as epitomising the content and tone of the article. Look back at the outline. Paragraph 5 may suggest a good way of ending.

(iv) *Stage 4: Write the Article*

NEW MAYOR'S AMBITIONS FOR FAIRPLACE

Arthur Henry Brown was born on November 19— in the heart of the community whose first citizen he now is. The third son of William Henry Brown, foreman fitter at Fairplace Engineering and borough councillor until his death in 19—, he was educated at the Central School, leaving at the age of 16 for an apprenticeship with his father's employers. His marriage in 19— to a Fairplace girl, Mary Jones, strengthened these local ties, and their three children (two daughters and a son), students at Fairplace Sixth Form College, now follow in the family's footsteps.

Councillor Brown's apprenticeship was succeeded by an outstanding career in the export sales division, involving world-wide travel and attendance at many international conferences before he was appointed to his present post of managing director of Fairplace Engineering, the firm that he joined as a school-leaver.

Despite his many business commitments, he has always been involved in Fairplace activities. He played for the rugby club's 1st XV and was captain of the cricket club's 1st XI. His membership of the dramatic and civic societies was a reflection of his interest in the arts and in local history. Ten years ago, his election as a councillor (Independent, Castle Ward) led to service on the watch and library committees and the chairmanship of the latter.

His much-applauded acceptance speech, as mayor, epitomised his long and many-sided involvement with the life of our town. Above all, he said, he wanted his term of office to be remembered for the prosperity that would follow industrial expansion. 'More jobs and better jobs for Fairplace', in his own words.

Regardless of party ties, the people of Fairplace have welcomed their new mayor. An energetic and forward-looking man, deeply rooted in the community and devoted to its welfare, Councillor Brown is a mayor for our town and our time.

2.5 Work out Instructions, Descriptions, Explanations, etc.

(a) Typical Questions

1. Give instructions (not in note form) on how to do *one* of the following: (i) recharge a flat car battery; (ii) build a kite; (iii) replace a faulty plug on an electrical appliance; (iv) prepare a nourishing soup.
2. Describe the layout of and the services offered at *one* of the following: (i) a public library; (ii) a filling station; (iii) a D.I.Y. store.
3. What advice would you give to a first-year student at your school or college to help him or her to settle in as quickly and happily as possible?
4. Write a leaflet for distribution to your fellow-students urging them to support a campaign for better library facilities.
5. You have been asked to speak briefly for or against *one* of the following: (i) that the voting age should be reduced to 16; (ii) that bicycles should be licensed in the way that motor vehicles are; (iii) that professionalism in sport should be abolished. Write your speech.
6. A visitor from overseas has asked you to suggest a place of interest in your locality suitable for an excursion. Write a brief description of an outstanding building or beauty spot that would be worth a visit.
7. A relative or friend about to travel abroad for the first time has asked for your advice. Write helpful tips on *one* of the following: (i) passing through customs; (ii) travelling light; (iii) language problems.
8. You want to encourage a friend to take up your own favourite hobby or pastime. Describe its attractions and rewards.
9. Advise a friend who is thinking of buying a camera on how to make a good choice.

(b) What You Must Do

Although the instructions may be worded in very different ways, the practical writing exercise is always a test of your ability to organise your material and to write clearly and to the point.

You must work out your plan before you begin to write. To work out a satisfactory plan, you must:

- arrange the individual items into sensible groups;
- decide on a logical order of presentation.

(c) Parts, Stages, Steps

When a straightforward subject has been set, thinking along these lines will help you to organise your material. Suppose you have chosen to describe the layout and equipment that you would expect to find in a well-planned kitchen. A number of unorganised items will spring to mind at once. They can be arranged into workman-like groups by thinking of the *parts* in relation to the whole. The essential parts of a kitchen are: cooker; sink(s); worktops; seating; lighting; utensils; etc. An organising idea has been found. If you are giving advice on how to perform some transaction, such as applying for a passport or a driving licence, divide the transaction into its *stages*. If you are giving instructions on how to build a kite or make a dress, divide the process into *steps*.

By following that method, you will train yourself to think analytically about your subject and — before plunging into the writing — you will be able to solve the two main problems posed by the writing exercise: 'Where do I begin?' and 'Where do I end?'

(d) More Complicated Subjects

The parts/stages/steps approach will not always work. For example, numbers 3, 4, 5, 6 and 9 in the list in Section 2.5(a) are so worded as to require a different solution of the organisational problem. Giving instructions on how to build a kite (question 1(ii)) is best done in a series of steps, whereas 'advice to help him or her to settle in as quickly and happily as possible' (question 3) must be organised differently. The plan has to take strict account of the task set, a point illustrated in the following work out.

(e) Work out

Advise a friend who is thinking of buying a camera on how to make a good choice.

(i) *Stage 1*

Jot down thoughts just as they come.

lens qualities, resolution, maximum aperture, etc. — exposure control, none/ automatic/manual — film format, disc, 110, 35 mm — shutter speeds — size and weight — etc.

(ii) *Stage 2*

Look for a way of organising the items.

The essential parts of a camera can be grouped by function: (1) shutter; (2) lens; (3) exposure system; etc.

After a few moments, it is clear that the system of grouping tried out above is of no help in organising the material for this particular question. Organisation into parts grouped by their function would be a sound enough base for a plan if the task set were to describe a camera, but that is not what the instructions require. I have to advise on a good *choice* of camera. I must try to find another way of organising the material.

A good *choice* can't be made until you know what you want to do with the camera: what kind of photographs you want to take — sports (action) — portraits — landscapes — family snapshots — one kind of camera is a good choice for one kind of job, another kind is needed for a different job . . .

I think I have now found a way of organising my material into a suitable answer.

(iii) *Stage 3*

Keeping in mind the task set, group the items accordingly and decide on the order of presentation.

1. Good choice depends on what kind of work the camera will be used for.
2. Simple family snapshots need only a simple camera.
3. More ambitious photography needs a more sophisticated instrument. For example: action/shutter speeds; portraits and close-ups/viewfinder; etc.
4. Conclusion: decide what you want to do with your camera, then you can decide what features are essential.

(iv) *Stage 4*

An outline plan has been worked out, grouping the items and getting them into a logical order of presentation. The exercise can now be written.

ADVICE ON CHOOSING A CAMERA

points 1 and 2 of plan taken together in opening paragraph →
Your choice of camera depends on the kind of photographs you want to take. There are many very good, simple cameras that will take excellent family snapshots. They have fixed focusing and automatic exposure control. Consequently, they are practically foolproof to operate. They are light and portable and some of them are very cheap.

sufficient detail to support the point being made →
However, those simple cameras are no good for more ambitious photography, such as sports shots, portraiture, close-up studies, landscapes, and so on. For such work, you will need a more complicated and more expensive instrument. Undoubtedly, a single lens reflex camera (an 'SLR') is the most versatile and accurate instrument yet designed. It offers you a range of shutter speeds and apertures that will cope with any problem. Its viewfinder is incomparable for brightness and precision, and its focusing system is unbeatable. A range of interchangeable lenses will equip you for any photographic task. The more expensive models give you a choice between automatic and manual exposure control.

personal, informal phrasing is in keeping with the task set: 'Advise a friend . . .' →
In a nutshell, your choice lies between the cheap, light, easy-to-operate snapshot camera and the dearer, heavier, more complicated, but much more versatile SLR. When you have decided what kind of a photographer you want to be, I shall be able to give you more detailed advice.

(*Note:* More detail is included in the plans in Sections 2.2 to 2.5 than you (or I) would find time to include in the examination, but I want you to practise along the lines suggested in those sections until you have mastered the techniques of planning. Then you can speed up, and jot down a skeleton outline in the examination that will provide you with a sound plan for a clear and cogent exercise in practical writing, of whatever form you choose from the questions on offer.)

3 Comprehension

Comprehension tests and summary writing are compulsory questions in the English Language papers of all the examining boards. In some papers the same passage is used for both; in others two passages are provided, one for comprehension and the other for summarising. The mental activities involved in the two processes are closely linked: accurate summarising depends on thorough comprehension.

3.1 Tackling the Questions

(a) The Meaning of 'Comprehension'

The verb *to comprehend* means 'to grasp with the mind; to take in'. Keep that definition in mind as you answer comprehension questions. Comprehension is understanding *in depth*: grasping with the mind, taking in, the material with which you are dealing.

(b) How Marks are Lost

Generally speaking, candidates do not score high marks in the comprehension tests. This poor performance is caused by two chief errors: (1) failure to comprehend, in the sense just defined; (2) failure to read the questions carefully.

(c) Recommended Method of Tackling the Questions

Concentrated and imaginative reading of the set passage is the essential basis of success in comprehension. You must read with close attention and with a determination to discover and respond to the author's intentions, grasping the meaning of the passage as a whole and in detail. The following method is recommended.

1. Read the passage right through once, then jot down on rough paper a brief note that sums up its contents. For example: 'Writer argues that we must conserve the earth's natural resources'/'Description of the drought in 1974 and of its effects on an isolated moorland community'. Do *not* read the questions before you have completed this first reading and gained a good general understanding of the passage.
2. Bearing in mind your summary of the contents, read the passage through a second time, tracing the development of the contents and noting key words and phrases that throw light on the writer's intentions and on the spirit of the passage. You are 'reading between the lines' now, noticing *what* is said and *how* it is being said, and really getting under the skin of the contents.
3. Those two readings have enabled you to *comprehend*, in the true meaning of the term. Now read through *all* the questions. Do *not* start to answer them

until you have read them all. Most marks are lost through misunderstanding the meaning of the questions. As you read the questions, each throws light on the others. When you have read all the questions, make a third quick reading of the passage.

4. Now start to answer the questions. Work through them methodically, in order. If you are stuck for an answer, do not spend too long agonising over it. Leave a space and go on to the next question. You will often find that a question that seems baffling when you first try to answer it, seems easy after you have answered later questions. It falls into perspective and the answer 'emerges' as you work through the others.

5. Copy out your answers neatly and clearly on the answer sheet provided, leaving time for a quick check at the end to look for and correct any careless slips.

3.2   Written-answer Tests and Multiple-choice Objective Tests

(a) The Difference between the Two Types

Comprehension tests are of two types. In one type the questions call for written answers. In the other type several answers to each question are printed on the paper and candidates are instructed to indicate the correct answer, using an answering code provided in the instructions (see Section 3.7). Because the multiple-choice objective tests do not require written answers, candidates have to answer more questions than in written-answer tests.

(b) The Similarities between the Two Types

Though very different in layout and procedures, the two kinds of tests require the same kind of mental activity. Correct answers to both types of questions depend on three factors: (1) thorough comprehension of the passage; (2) complete understanding of each particular question; (3) total accuracy in carrying out the instructions.

(c) Carrying out the Instructions

(i)   *Written-answer Tests*

Because comprehension questions requiring written answers necessarily appear in a great variety of wording, they are dangerously easy to misunderstand and to answer in the wrong way. The closest attention must be given to the wording of each particular question. For example, if you are asked for an answer in the form of a sentence, a one-word answer or a phrase answer will not do. If you are asked for a sentence answer and you do not provide one, you cannot get the marks, even if the contents of your answer are accurate. On the other hand, if you are asked for a one-word answer, nothing else will be acceptable. If you are asked to give three reasons to account for something stated in the passage, give three reasons. If you write down two, you will get marks for two. If you write down more than three, you will be marked on the first three: the remainder will be ignored. You get no marks for doing what you were not told to do. Note the marks allotted to each question and be careful to allow yourself more time for a 5 mark question than a 1 mark question.

(ii) *Multiple-choice Objective Tests*

An answering code is laid down in the instructions and must be followed strictly. (Examples of various codes often used are given in the work-out sections.) The code may seem complicated. If you are not sure that you understand it, check with the invigilator before you begin to answer. Failure to use the answering code correctly would cost you all your marks, even though you knew the right answers.

3.3 What is Tested

(a) Kinds of Passages Set

You may be questioned on a passage (or passages) of prose or of poetry. Narrative, descriptive, discursive, dramatic or impressionistic writing may be used for the test, and the contents may be humorous, serious, satirical, factual, subjective, objective . . ., and so on. The range is limited only by the examiners' estimate of the degree of difficulty that you can be fairly expected to tackle.

As you sit in the examination room and read the passage(s) for the first time:

- do not panic if you know nothing of the subject about which it is written — previous knowledge is not required;
- remember that all the questions can be answered by a candidate of average ability who reads the passage and the questions carefully;
- remember that all the facts needed to answer factual questions are contained in the passage;
- remember that non-factual questions can be answered by an intelligent and imaginative study of the passage.

(b) Grasp the Meaning, Think Things out, Use Your Imagination

The questions test your powers of understanding and they also test your ability:

- to respond to hints and suggestions made by the writer — *implicit* meanings not actually spelt out;
- to draw sensible conclusions from stated facts;
- to develop a line of argument.

Broadly, then, the questions are designed to test your ability to understand, to think and to use your imagination.

(c) Classifications of Question Types

1. Questions about the *subject matter*, the *contents*, the *meaning* of the passage. These questions ask you *what* the writer said.

   EXAMPLES

   (i) Using the information supplied in paragraph 2, state how old X was when this event took place.
   (ii) List three ways in which Y made himself popular.
   (iii) State in one sentence Z's reasons for refusing the offer.

2. Questions about the *style* in which the passage is written. These questions ask you *how* the writer uses language. You may be asked about the use of imagery and figures of speech, about sentence and paragraph structures.

EXAMPLES

(i) Bring out in your own words the force of the metaphors in the following, paying particular attention to the italicised words: '... the marsh *yawned* in the summer heat' (1.–); 'Graham threw the *babbling* telephone down in disgust' (1.–).

(ii) What is the effect of the short sentence at the end of the fourth paragraph?

(iii) Why, do you think, did the author leave unfinished the sentence at the beginning of the last paragraph?

3. Questions about *vocabulary*. These questions ask you about the writer's use of particular words, especially (a) the use of unusual or difficult words: (b) the use of ordinary words in a fresh and surprising way; (c) the choice of precisely the right word to convey the exact meaning. Questions about vocabulary may be directed to matters of content or to matters of style (*what* is written or *how* it is written).

EXAMPLES

(i) Explain the meaning of the following words as they are used in the passage: vertiginous (1.–); calumny (1.–); misappropriated (1.–).

(ii) Express in your own words the meaning of: '... yet deferential when self-interest prompted' (1.–).

(iii) Give one word meaning the same as each of the following as it is used by the author: temperate (1.–); wan (1.–); smear (1.–).
(*Note:* Be careful to supply a word having *the same grammatical function* as the word in the passage. For example, 'smear' could be used as a noun or as a verb. If the author uses it as a noun, you must supply a noun as a synonym. If you answer with a word that is not the same part of speech, you are not supplying a word that 'means the same.')

4. Questions that test your ability to make an *imaginative response* to the passage.

EXAMPLES

(i) In what tone of voice do you think X replied to Y? Give one reason for your answer.

(ii) In one sentence, describe how A felt about B's decision.

(iii) 'This, C felt, was the moment for the flamboyant gesture that her fans had been encouraged to expect of her.' What do those words tell you about C's character and motives?

5. Questions that test your ability to *think* about the contents of the passage, especially the writer's use of reasoned argument.

EXAMPLES

(i) Select two statements that justify A's refusal to accept the truth of the report.

(ii) Name three facts that prove how ill-prepared B was for his new post.

    (iii) Comment briefly (not more than 50 words) on the argument used in the last paragraph, stating your reasons for agreeing or disagreeing with the author's conclusion.

Those are examples of typical questions set in written-answer comprehension tests. The questions (and the answers) in multiple-choice objective tests are presented differently, but — as you will see in the work outs — they test the same qualities: grasp of facts; imaginative response; thinking capacity.

3.4 Work out 1 (with Notes): Written-answer Test

Read the following passage carefully and then answer the questions on it.

(20 marks)

a descriptive passage

    I stood at the window and smoked a small cheroot. Across the rooftops I could see the darkened hump that was Carlisle Castle. I peered at it through the gloom with a strange fascination. The sky behind the turrets looked mottled and angry, touched with red from the city street-lamps like the ham-
5 mered bottom of a copper pot. It was a sky to steer away from, to button up against—a cloud-hung, wind-blown, rain-spattered sky. I shuddered. For the next few days, rain or wind, sleet or shine, my only shelter would be the tiny tent in the haversack on my back as I followed the trail of the Border Line across 110 miles of some of the wildest and most spectacular scenery in
10 Britain. It would not be an easy walk.

    Unlike Offa's Dyke or the Pennine Way, the Scottish Border was not a national footpath and because of the scarcity of highways had managed to remain largely intact, unspoiled by the incursion of the main summer tourist routes. It was a unique region, once the most disputed territory in the
15 country, with wild hills, ancient castles and famous abbeys which had seen more turbulence and bloodshed than the rest of these islands put together. I would be following in the footsteps of those outlaws of ancient times who spread terror and devastation along the Border counties and I would be treading where the Border Line itself was conceived in more than a thousand
20 years of the bloodiest battles in our history.

    I peered silently at the huddled outline of the castle. Beneath the neon-splashed sky it looked oddly out of place, and yet it caught the very essence of the Border. It was some fortress: a symbol of austerity, no doubt, for the prisoners of the Wars of the Roses who were confined there. It had with-
25 stood siege for nine months against Parliamentary forces during the Civil War and had entertained Bonnie Prince Charlie. It was also the scene of one of the earliest commando raids when, in 1596, the bold Buccleuch crossed the Esk with eighty men and pounded on the castle gates, demanding the release of Kinmont Willie.

summary of contents: the author recalls his thoughts and feelings at Carlisle on the night before he set out to walk the Scottish Border

30 Stirring stuff: but that is what the Border was all about. For the next few days I would be recapturing some of the colour and tradition that made it such a romantic and fascinating locality.

    I turned and peered at my hotel bed. It looked snugly inviting. Might as well make the most of it, I thought. I stubbed out my cheroot, took off my
35 clothes and switched off the light.

Robert Langley

(a) Choose *four* of the following words. For each one give a word or short phrase which could be used to replace it in the passage without changing the meaning.

mottled (line 4)   conceived (line 19)
spectacular (line 9) tradition (line 31)
disputed (line 14)   snugly (line 33)

(4 marks)

(b) Explain *in your own words* the meaning of *two* of the following expressions:

  (i) spread terror and devastation (line 18)

  (ii) caught the very essence (line 22);

  (iii) a symbol of austerity (line 23).

(4 marks)

(c) What does the author tell us of the castle's history? *Answer in your own words.*

(3 marks)

(A.E.B., June 1982)

(d) Using information from the first paragraph only, describe the author's reactions to the view from his hotel window.

(3 marks)

(e) What was the author intending to do when he left the hotel?

(2 marks)

(f) Re-state, *in your own words*, how the Scottish Border differed from Offa's Dyke and the Pennine Way.

(2 marks)

(g) Which phrase suggests that the author's feelings were roused by the history of the Border?

(2 marks)

ANSWERS

(Like the marginal comments printed alongside the passage, the notes accompanying these answers are to help you in your preparation for the examination. They do not *form part of the answers and they would* not *be included with them in the examination.)*

(a)   mottled (line 4) = blotched
spectacular (line 9) = striking
disputed (line 14) = fought over
conceived (line 19) = brought into being

(*Note:* I have given the four answers asked for and that is where I would *stop* in the examination; but, for the purposes of this work out, I shall demonstrate how to answer the other questions.)

tradition (line 31) = lore
snugly (line 33) = cosily

NOTES

1. The answers are clearly set out so that the examiners have no difficulty in recognising which word is being explained. Always space out your answers clearly and indicate which question you are answering.
2. In each case I chose the synonym that seemed to fit most closely the meaning demanded by the context of the original word. For example, I chose *blotched* rather than *spotted* as a synonym for *mottled*, and if you read lines 4 and 5 again, I think you will see why. However, *spotted* would certainly be accepted as a correct answer.
3. The instructions permitted me to use a short phrase instead of one word

where I felt it necessary. In the case of *disputed*, I felt that I needed the phrase *fought over*. There are other possibilities (*argued about* is one), but nearby words such as *castles, turbulence* and *bloodshed* (lines 15 and 16) suggested that a strong expression was needed to fit the sense of *disputed*.

4. In each case, I used a word or phrase having the same grammatical function as the word I was replacing. For example, *snugly* is an adverb and so is my chosen synonym *cosily*.

(b)
    (i) The outlaws filled all the Border with fear and laid waste to it.
    (ii) The castle symbolised the true nature and character of the Border.
(*Note:* Two answers were asked for and two have been given, so stop! *For work-out purposes only*, the third question is answered here.)
    (iii) To its prisoners, the castle represented stern and comfortless living.

NOTES

1. Each answer is given the 'numeration' of the question to which it refers (**(b)** (i), (ii), etc.). Therefore, there is no need to waste time by writing out each of the expressions that is being explained. (Contrast with question **(a)**, in which the separate words to be explained were not numbered and were, therefore, written out in the answers.) Even though the answers are numbered, each is given plenty of space, to help the examiners to read it quickly and to prevent confusion.

2. I had to explain the meaning of each expression *in my own words* and I found it a help to link each clearly to the context in which it was used in the passage. It was the outlaws who spread terror and devastation; the castle that caught the very essence; the castle that was a symbol of austerity for its prisoners. Once I had reminded myself who or what each expression referred to in its context, it was not so difficult to think out synonymous phrasing for each.

(c) The castle housed prisoners in the Wars of the Roses. It held out for nine months against the Parliamentarians in the Civil War. Bonnie Prince Charlie stayed there. In 1596, when Kinmont Willie was a prisoner in the Castle, the bold Buccleuch attacked it in an attempt to free him.
(*Note:* As the instructions stipulated, I confined myself to the castle's *history* and I used *my own words*.)

(d) The castle had an inexplicable attraction for him and the stormy sky made him shiver as he thought of what lay ahead.
(*Note:* Only information given in the first paragraph may be used in this answer. Two aspects of the view are mentioned there: the castle and the sky. His reactions to both are described in the answer.)

(e) He was going to start a long walk, 110 miles along the line of the Scottish Border.

(f) The Scottish Border was not an officially designated walkers' route like Offa's Dyke and the Pennine Way.
(*Note:* I did not find it at all easy to restate the difference *in my own words*. The author's words are: '. . . was not a national footpath'. Judge for yourself how well or badly I have explained that as 'an officially designated walkers' route'.)

(g) 'Stirring stuff' (line 30)

(*Note:* A short answer, but a difficult question! I was tempted to choose *colour and tradition* or *romantic and fascinating locality*. The wording of the question, however, made me decide that *Stirring stuff* was the right answer: '. . . feelings were *roused*' surely corresponds to being 'stirred up'? But you must judge for yourself.)

Having read my answers and notes, go through the passage and the questions again. Examine the wording of each question closely and use your dictionary when you are considering my answers. A critical consideration of my work out will teach you a lot about answering comprehension questions. In fact, I think I have made a pretty good job of the answers, but I am sure you can make improvements here and there.

3.5 Work out 2 (without Notes): Written answer Test

(a) How to Use this Work out to Best Advantage

1. Study the passage, using the method set out in Section 3.1(c), *before* you read the questions.
2. Read through *all* the questions *before* you read the answers.
3. Study each question and the particular lines of the passage to which it refers *before* you read the answer.
4. Consider carefully the merits of each answer *before* going on to the next, studying both its contents and the way in which it is expressed. Use your dictionary and refer to the notes in Section 3.4 while you are assessing the accuracy of the answer and the appropriateness of its wording.

(b) Work out

Read the following passage carefully and then answer the questions on it.

(20 marks)

Having to write a preface after labouring for five years to produce a book is an unnerving experience and something of an anti-climax; rather like an elephant who has succeeded at long last in giving birth to her calf being then required to balance a bun on her head.

5   But a preface has its uses. It can give readers a whiff of the author's style and an indication of his potential as an inducer of tedium, thus enabling them to moderate their enthusiasm, lower their sights, and so prepare themselves for the main body of the work. A preface can also give the author a few precious moments alone with a person who has bought the book, or is
10   having a free read of it in a bookshop, or has borrowed it from a library by mistake, in which the author can explain what the book is about.

There have been many descriptions of what history is, but there are probably as many ways of looking at the past as there are writers and historians prepared to look. This book is an attempt to look at social history from
15   the viewpoint of people who were alive at the time and were not at all happy about what was going on.

As in most histories, my book is concerned with great personages and great deeds but the concern is with their imperfections, not their glories;

with the aspects of them which caused contemporaries to treat them with
20 scorn, fury or ridicule. The approach is that of the judge who before considering sentence asks, 'Is anything known against?' Thus the Wordsworth
in this book is not the great nature poet but the Wordsworth with clammy
hands and no sense of smell; Rousseau is not the philosopher who tried to
reform education but Rousseau the despiser of intelligent women. Embed-
25 ded in the text are more than a thousand expressions of human displeasure,
culled from poems, prose writings, letters, critical commentaries and reported speech. These range in power from mild disapproval to blind hate.

In no sense is this book offered as a work of scholarship—the author
would not make so bold—but as a highly personal account of social history
30 seen from a rather unusual point of view. It is hoped that when this account
is added to the more orthodox view of history, the reader will end up with a
slightly more stereoscopic picture of the past. Each chapter cannot possibly
tell the whole story of course, so the aim has been to be representative rather
than exhaustive.

Frank Muir

(a) Explain **in your own words** the author's feelings about having to write a preface to his book.   (3 marks)
(b) According to the author, what does the reader gain from the preface? **Use
your own words.**   (4 marks)
(c) What purpose does a preface serve as far as the author is concerned? (2 marks)
(d) In what respect does Muir's book differ from most histories?   (3 marks)
(e) Explain in your own words the meaning of the following:
    (i) 'from mild disapproval to blind hate' (line 27)
    (ii) 'to be representative rather than exhaustive' (lines 33–34).   (4 marks)
(f) Choose **four** of the following words. For each one give a word or short phrase
    that could replace it in the passage without changing the meaning.
        required (line 4)   culled (line 26)
        approach (line 20)   scholarship (line 28)
        embedded (lines 24–25)   orthodox (line 31)   (4 marks)
(A.E.B., June 1980)

ANSWERS

(a) The author feels daunted by a task that seems rather deflating after the
    prolonged labour of writing the book.
(b) The preface gives the reader a preliminary taste of the way in which the
    author writes and, by preventing him from having too high an expecta-
    tion of the book, puts him in the right frame of mind for reading it.
(c) The preface enables the author to talk quietly to the reader on his own
    and to explain the contents and purposes of the book.
(d) Unlike most histories, Muir's book does not deal with the triumphant
    deeds of great people, but with their human frailties. It is about the weak-
    nesses that their contemporaries saw in them, not the successes for which
    they are now remembered.
(e)
    (i) from gentle dislike to extreme and unreasoning detestation
    (ii) to present typical examples rather than to include everything

(f)

required (line 4) = obliged
culled (line 26) = gathered
scholarship (line 28) = erudition
orthodox (line 31) = usually accepted

3.6 Written-answer Comprehension Paper

(a) How to Use This Test Paper to Best Advantage

1. Do *not* look at the answers until you have answered all the questions on both passages to the best of your ability.
2. Write out your answers just as you would in the examination, so that you can make a thorough comparison between your answers and mine.
3. Note the examiners' instructions very carefully: *all* the questions set on *both* passages must be answered; and marks will be deducted for incorrect and clumsy English.
4. Candidates are allowed 1¾ hours for this paper. Time yourself accurately to see how long you take, but do not worry if at this stage of your preparation you take longer than the permitted time. You will speed up with continued practice.
5. Use your dictionary when you need to, and look back at the advice given earlier in this chapter when you want help. It is much more important to work through these tests steadily and thoroughly than to race along in an attempt to finish on time. You will learn a lot by answering these questions thoughtfully. In later tests you can practise working against the clock. As you gain experience, you will find that the examiners' time limit gives you comfortable room for the thorough reading and careful thought required for success.
6. Make detailed comparisons between your answers and mine. Refer closely to the passages and to the questions, and try to understand the reasons for any major differences between us. Do not be afraid to stand up for your own answers whenever you think that you are right and I am wrong, but do not jump to the conclusion that I am wrong! Work it out.

(b) Test Paper (Answers on pages 165–166)

Time allowed: 1¾ hours
Maximum mark: 100
Answer both questions
This paper tests your ability to read with understanding and to think about what you have read. Do not hurry. You have two fairly long passages in front of you, but time enough for reading them. You will be wise to get to know each passage well before attempting to answer any of the questions set on it.

Remember that this is an examination in English Language. It is important not only to answer the questions correctly but also to write your answers in clear, careful English, with proper attention to spelling and punctuation.

1. Read carefully the following passage, and answer the questions set on it.

Every year many millions enjoy the National Trust's open spaces. This freedom of access is one of the chief purposes of the Trust. None the less, its very volume creates serious problems. A careful tally on a bank holiday weekend at Clumber Park in 1964 recorded 106 000 visitors. In the following year
5 at Hatfield Forest there were 28 300 cars, and at Runnymede 80 000. Two hundred sacks of litter have been collected on Box Hill after a Whitsun weekend. With the dumping of refuse and derelict cars on Trust property, litter begins to assume a quality of nightmare. No less worrying is the persistent hooliganism at many properties, particularly those near industrial centres
10 such as Allen Banks in Northumberland. Even well intentioned visitors tend to damage trees, break fences and start fires. Uncontrolled dogs worry sheep, and on certain open spaces there is interference with the commoners' grazing rights.

A grave problem is the long-term effect of an excessive number of visitors
15 on plant and animal ecology. If more than a given number of people pass over a dale or mountain path, regeneration becomes impossible and erosion follows. The bald and widening tracks scarring Dovedale and certain favourite cross-country routes in the Lakes are sad indications of this. At Kinver Edge in Staffordshire and Kynance Cove in Cornwall, which are much visited, the
20 sward over large areas has been completely destroyed and erosion has set in. Consequently it has proved necessary to close and fence parts of the land in order to restore the natural ground cover. Sand dunes pose a similar problem, for with constant access erosion is unavoidable.

The problems raised by the increase in the number of visitors can be tackl-
25 ed in two ways. The first is a proportionate increase in the number of wardens. The Trust accepts this as an expensive necessity. They now constitute a growing army, recruited to help, advise and control the public. Many wardens are countrymen, sometimes naturalists or retired foresters, and their knowledge contributes directly to the pleasure of visitors. Happily, people
30 are often ready to serve as part-time wardens in a voluntary capacity. On the Longshaw estate in Derbyshire there is a rota of forty voluntary wardens, and at Brownsea Island, where the fire danger is acute, no less than fifty people in the summer give unpaid service as watchers and wardens.

The second course open to the Trust, and one to which its publicity must
35 be progressively directed, is to achieve a wider dispersal. An airman or a buzzard surveying the wide range of Trust properties would see some that seem to stir like anthills and others that preserve an almost Saxon solitude. The Trust's aim must be to spread the load, alleviating the pressure where it grows intolerable and dispersing it to spaces that may still be called 'open'.
40 There is little danger in this. Solitude will always remain for those who wish to find it.

Apart from closure, which is contrary to Trust policy and which can only be justified for limited periods in desperate cases, there is a third course which the Trust may in extremity be forced to adopt at certain properties if
45 numbers continue to increase as they have done in the last decade. It is the control of access by rationing. The brake could be applied either by charging an admission fee, or by limiting the numbers admitted on a given day. The Trust hopes that such measures can be avoided. They would only be necessary at peak periods. It is well to recall that most wardens have a well earned

50   rest for six months, that dense visitor-traffic is usually as temporary as the
     holiday season, and that many of the airman's most restless anthills enjoy a
     long winter quiet.

                              Robin Fedden, *The National Trust, Past and Present*

(a) Explain *freedom of access* (line 2).   **(2 marks)**
(b) Say briefly what you understand by **any two** of the following words:
    (i)   *regeneration* (line 16);
    (ii) *erosion* (lines 16, 20 and 23);
    (iii) *decade* (line 45).   **(6 marks)**
(c) In lines 28–29 the author says that some National Trust wardens are naturalists
    or retired foresters, *and their knowledge contributes directly to the pleasure
    of visitors*. How do you suppose this happens?   **(3 marks)**
(d) What is meant by serving *in a voluntary capacity* (line 30)?   **(3 marks)**
(e) *many of the airman's most restless anthills enjoy a long winter quiet* (lines 51–
    52).
    (i) What does the author mean here by *anthills*?
    (ii) What *airman* is he referring to?   **(6 marks)**
(f) Write a paragraph of some 100–120 words summarising the ideas expressed in
    the passage to cover the following points:
        —the main problems caused by the popularity of National Trust properties;
        —the steps the Trust is taking, or would like to take, to deal with these
         problems;
        —the further steps that the Trust might unwillingly have to take.**(20 marks)**

2. Read carefully the following passage, and answer the questions set on it.

       Fiammetta had all the characteristics demanded of a prima donna: a mag-
    nificent voice well trained, an extremely beautiful person, a temperament
    passionate, fearless and headstrong. In body she was small, so that one mar-
    velled such a superb volume of voice could pour out of such a fragile vessel—
5   she was not in reality fragile, however, but brimming with a restless vitality,
    healthy, tough. Italian by birth, with an abundance of dark hair and huge
    dark eyes (grey or violet? Freeman never knew) which by some unusual
    coloration of iris and pupil had at times a silvery and starry appearance.
    Fiammetta dressed with the most exquisite taste; in ordinary life extremely
10 neat, elegant, sophisticated, on the stage she could wear the flaunting cos-
    tumes of operatic heroines with all the savage verve they required.
       She was to sing the title-role in a production of *Carmen* for which Freeman
    was designing fresh costumes and scenery. Freeman considered this opera
    'old hat', but had been assured by those in charge that he was employed
15 especially to give freshness and originality to a somewhat stale theme. He
    had accordingly let his imagination gallop: the glowing result pleased him,
    and when he heard Fiammetta sing at rehearsal, his pulses quickened with
    delight. It appeared, however, that Fiammetta wished to sing in yellow in-
    stead of the traditional scarlet. Freeman was summoned to a conference on
20 stage and informed of this desired change in an imperious tone. A new design
    for the dress would of course be needed.
       'It can of course be done if you postpone the opening night for a month
    or two', said Freeman with a smile.
       'You require two months to design one dress?' said Fiammetta haughtily.

64

25　(Her Italian-English, uttered in one of the finest contraltos of the century, was delicious.)

'By no means. But if the colour of Carmen's dress is changed, all the other costumes and the scenery must also be changed, or she will not appear the main character.'

30　'That is nonsense. Never have I heard such nonsense.'

'I think you're being a little unreasonable, Freeman', said the stage manager anxiously.

Freeman shrugged his shoulders.

'If the signorina wishes to be a mere blur against the background, let it be 35　so by all means, but take my name off the programme.'

'Now, Freeman!'

'What is that, a blur? I do not understand this word', said Fiammetta, looking round the group angrily.

Nobody ventured to enlighten her, and there was an uncomfortable pause.

40　'Something such a beautiful Carmen should never be', said Freeman eventually, laughing.

Fiammetta gave him a glance in which, as Freeman clearly saw, disdain was mingled with calculation. He was not surprised therefore when she suggested that they should lunch together and talk over the matter, not surprised 45　when he presently found himself alone with her in her suite at the hotel. He was not surprised, because her intention to use the power of her beauty to get her own way about the dress was throughout sufficiently obvious.

Sure enough, she began to flatter and soothe him, to gaze up into his eyes with that expression of admiring interest which is always so seductive, so apt 50　to lead a man into those intimate confidences which place him in the power of the recipient. Freeman had had sufficient experience, in various preceding *amourettes*, of this enticing look, to know exactly what it meant: he therefore watched Fiammetta with a smile—he had no objection in the world to being seduced, but nothing would induce him to yield about the yellow dress. 55　Fiammetta, it would seem, felt this, for she grew angry.

'You do not think me beautiful, Mr Freeman?' said she, her wonderful eyes sparkling with rage.

(They really sparkled, thought Freeman, surveying them admiringly; in her case the *cliché* was literally true.)

60　'On the contrary, signora', he replied pleasantly: 'I think you the most beautiful woman I have ever seen.'

'Then why do you remain so cold? Come, kiss me! Do not be afraid.'

'I am not afraid', said Freeman in an easy tone, laughing: 'but it is only fair to tell you that I am capable of taking many kisses and yet not making 65　you a yellow dress.'

He rose and gave her a little bow, to take his leave.

'And yet you call yourself an honourable man?'

'No', said Freeman, pausing. 'I have no such pretensions. I have come up out of the gutter and carry no sentimental luggage.'

70　'And I too, you fool!' cried Fiammetta, springing to her feet. 'I too am of the gutter. I am as relentless as you are yourself. I take what I want.'

'Ah! Now we understand each other.'

'Stay, then', said Fiammetta, stretching out to him her small hot hand, on which the diamonds glittered.

75　'No. It is the dress you want, not the man', said Freeman, turning away. He spoke soberly, but felt violence rising in him like fever.

She threw herself between him and the door.

'Are you so certain, Freeman?' she cried, panting.

'Don't try to lie to me!' shouted Freeman, plunging into rage.

80   For a moment they stood glaring at each other, furiously angry; then they both began to laugh.

'I shall not make you a yellow dress', said Freeman stubbornly.

'*Basta!* What do I care?'

'But I will design a beautiful new scarlet dress; the old one is too dull, too
85   spiritless for such a guttersnipe as you', concluded Freeman, laughing and taking her in his arms.

Phyllis Bentley, *Crescendo*

(a) (i) What is a *prima donna* (line 1)?
    (ii) *She was to sing the title-role in a production of 'Carmen'* (line 12). What do you understand by *title-role*? **(4 marks)**

(b) Turn to lines 13–17.
    (i) *Freeman considered this opera 'old hat'*. Explain *'old hat'*.
    (ii) *the glowing result*. What impression does *glowing* create for us?
    (iii) *his pulses quickened*. What does this mean? **(9 marks)**

(c) *It appeared, however, that Fiammetta wished to sing in yellow instead of the traditional scarlet* (lines 18–19).
    (i) What is the meaning here of *traditional*?
    (ii) Freeman argues that if Fiammetta is to sing in yellow the opening night of the opera will have to be postponed by a month or two. Why, in his view, would so long a postponement be necessary? **(6 marks)**

(d) *'What is that, a blur? I do not understand this word'*, said Fiammetta (line 37).
    (i) *Nobody*, we are told, *ventured to enlighten her*. Why was that, do you suppose?
    (ii) How would you have explained to her what Freeman meant? **(6 marks)**

(e) *Fiammetta gave him a glance in which, as Freeman clearly saw, disdain was mingled with calculation* (lines 42–43).
    Give briefly the meanings of (i) *disdain*, (ii) *calculation*, as they are used in this context. **(6 marks)**

(f) *And yet you call yourself an honourable man?* (line 67).
    In the lines that immediately follow this remark, explain the following phrases:
    (i) *I have no such pretensions;*
    (ii) *I have come up out of the gutter;*
    (iii) *carry no sentimental luggage*. **(9 marks)**

(g) In a paragraph of some 15–20 lines (120–150 words), state the cause of the quarrel between Fiammetta and Freeman, and trace the course of their dispute to a conclusion that proves satisfactory to both of them. **(20 marks)**

(O, June 1982)

3.7 Multiple-choice Objective Tests

(a) Number of Passages and Questions

Some examining boards using multiple-choice objective tests of reading comprehension set more than one passage; others set just one. The number of questions set also varies. For example, a recent University of London paper consisted of three passages, with 10 questions on the first passage, 26 questions on the second and 24 questions on the third: 60 questions in all, to be answered in 1¼ hours. A recent Associated Examining Board paper consisted of one passage with 25 questions, to be answered in 50 minutes. You will, of course, familiarise yourself with the particular requirements of your own board and practise accordingly.

(b) The Meaning of 'Objective'

Whatever differences there may be in the number of passages and questions set, the same principle underlies all multiple-choice tests of reading comprehension. It is this: since candidates do not write their answers in words of their own choosing, the marking of the answers is free from any personal ('subjective') judgement on the examiners' part. That is why these tests are called 'objective'. The answers are either right or wrong. In written-answer tests — as you saw in Sections 3.3–3.6 — not only the contents of an answer but also the way in which it is phrased affects its accuracy and suitability as a response to the question. Its merit is assessed partly on how it is worded. This problem does not arise in answering (or, therefore, in marking) multiple-choice objective tests of reading comprehension.

(c) But the Aims are the Same!

Even so, both written-answer and multiple-choice objective tests of reading comprehension have the same purposes: to examine the candidate's ability to understand what is read, to reason about it and to make an imaginative response to it (see Sections 3.2 and 3.3).

(d) Instructions and Answering Codes

The examiners' instructions and stipulated method of indicating your answers require very careful reading. Indeed, you could say that comprehending the instructions is a necessary part of the comprehension test! There is nothing unfair about this, but the fact remains that candidates sometimes throw marks away by neglecting to study the instructions with concentrated attention. The degree of concentration required is illustrated by the following extracts from papers recently set by two different boards.

ANSWERING THE QUESTIONS

1. Attempt all items. Each correct answer will score 1 mark. No deduction will be made for wrong answers.
2. Indicate your answers on the answer sheet by shading the upper part of the box on the appropriate letter; e.g. if the answer to item 8 is thought to be C, it should appear as:

Only one answer must be indicated. Any other form of answering is incorrect and will not score.
3. If you change your mind, shade in the lower part of the box you have marked and mark the letter you now think correct; e.g. to cancel C and enter A instead, it should appear as:

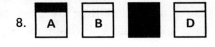

(A.E.B.)

For each question there are five suggested answers, A, B, C, D and E. When you have selected your answer to the question, find the row on the answer sheet with the number of that question and draw a *horizontal* line to join the dots under the letter for the answer you have chosen.

For example, the answer C would be marked as shown.

A	B	C	D	E
(· ·)	(· ·)	(——)	(· ·)	(· ·)

Mark only one answer for each question. If you change your mind about an answer, rub out the first mark carefully; then mark your new answer.

There are 60 questions in this test. You are advised to answer all the questions. You will score one mark for each correct answer; no marks will be deducted for incorrect answers or omissions.

(L.)

Instructions and answering codes such as these may look formidable at first sight, but if you study them closely, you will realise how clear and unambiguous they really are.

The work out that follows shows you how to carry out instructions for answering a short multiple-choice objective test. Further practice is provided in this book and you will, of course, go on to study and practise other past papers set by your board.

3.8 Work out 3 (with Notes): Multiple-choice Objective Test

This is the first of three tests of reading comprehension set in one paper by the University of London in January 1982.

COMPREHENSION PASSAGE 1

DIRECTIONS

1. Read the passage carefully and then answer the questions.
2. Each passage has five suggested answers. Select the best answer to each question and mark the answer to that question accordingly.
3. Record your answer to each question by drawing a line TO JOIN THE DOTS under the letter corresponding to the answer you have chosen, thus (●——●). Make sure that each of your answers is shown by a clear, black horizontal line.

Georgina had always claimed the status of a boy. She fought like a boy—it was understood that she must fight alone and unsupported. For this was the rule—if Richard or I had gone to help her even when she was over-mastered, then all the boys of the village would have descended upon us to vindicate
5   our laws of war, and Georgina herself would have been more infuriated by our intervention than by even the most humiliating defeat. But the same laws of war now entitled me to go to Georgina's help—so as soon as the second girl caught Georgina by the arms, I also flew to battle. But as I was

not only much lighter even than Georgina, but also, I suspect, so terrified
10   that I scarcely knew what I was doing, I was swept at once into the ditch
with one careless swing. Georgina was now thrust down on top of me and
held there by the big girl who now seemed both puzzled and remorseful; she
kept on asking her companions what she was to do with the little ———.

At last, to the great relief, I think, of the Battwell girls as well as ourselves,
15   a certain labourer, a neighbour of ours called Sam Weaver, a tall and power-
ful man, came by and asked with some indignation what they were doing
with us, and heard the story. It was corroborated sufficiently by the scratches
not only on the big girl's hands and cheek but on the hands of the girl who
had held her. Sam, a just man, then apologised for Georgina, tucked her
20   under his arm, picked up his sack in the other hand and conveyed them both
away to the Coytes' stables where he judged my father would be found, and
there planted my sister, a truly miserable object with her swollen blood-
stained face, her mud-covered clothes, before my father, and related the crime.

---

1. According to the first sentence (line 1) Georgina had always insisted that she
   A was as strong as a boy
   B should be treated as a boy
   C was as independent as a boy
   D should be known as a boy
   E was as brave as a boy

2. Which one of the following words is closest in meaning to 'vindicate' as used in line 4?
   A Determine
   B Satisfy
   C Explain
   D Obey
   E Uphold

3. 'Remorseful' (line 12) means that the big girl seemed
   A baffled by what she had done
   B offended by the little boy
   C tired of the whole affair
   D unable to make up her mind
   E sorry for what had occurred

4. After pushing Georgina and the narrator into the ditch, the 'big girl' (line 12) was all the following EXCEPT
   A unwilling to hurt them more
   B unsure of what to do next
   C anxious to be friends with them
   D sorry for what she had done
   E relieved when an adult intervened

5. Sam Weaver's first question implies that he thought that
   A his neighbour's children were being bullied
   B Georgina had started yet another fight
   C the fight had involved only girls
   D Georgina might have been severely injured
   E they were playing some silly game

6. Which one of the following is closest in meaning to 'indignation' as used in line 16?
   A Dignity   D Bitter scorn
   B Righteous anger   E Resentment
   C Animosity

7. The 'story' (line 17) told by the girls was probably that
   A Georgina had attacked them quite violently
   B the fight had been one against one
   C Georgina had broken the accepted laws of war
   D the two smaller children had fallen in the ditch
   E Georgina wanted to be treated as a boy
8. Which one of the following words is closest in meaning to 'corroborated' as used in line 17?
   A Confirmed
   B Justified
   C Emphasised
   D Revealed
   E Explained
9. Judging from the passage, the 'crime' (line 23) was most probably that Georgina had
   A covered her hands and face in blood
   B attacked the Battwell girls
   C involved her brother in a fight
   D made Sam indignant and apologetic
   E been pushed down into a muddy ditch
10. Sam Weaver finally decided that
   A Georgina needed his protection from the girls
   B he would like to see Georgina punished
   C Georgina was responsible for what had happened
   D he would carry the distressed child home
   E Georgina's wounds needed some attention at once

ANSWERS

	A	B	C	D	E
1	(· ·)	(—)	(· ·)	(· ·)	(· ·)
2	(· ·)	(· ·)	(· ·)	(· ·)	(—)
3	(· ·)	(· ·)	(· ·)	(· ·)	(—)
4	(· ·)	(· ·)	(—)	(· ·)	(· ·)
5	(—)	(· ·)	(· ·)	(· ·)	(· ·)
6	(· ·)	(—)	(· ·)	(· ·)	(· ·)
7	(—)	(· ·)	(· ·)	(· ·)	(· ·)
8	(—)	(· ·)	(· ·)	(· ·)	(· ·)
9	(· ·)	(—)	(· ·)	(· ·)	(· ·)
10	(· ·)	(—)	(· ·)	(· ·)	(· ·)

(Study these detailed comments on that test. They provide the advice you need when tackling multiple-choice objective tests of reading comprehension.)

1. Do not expect to find an even distribution of correct answers. In that test, **D** is not the correct answer to any of the questions and I did not allow that to worry me while I was choosing my answers. I marked **B** as correct four times; **A** three times; **E** twice; and **C** only once. Nor is there any pattern of correct answers: 2 is **E** and so is 3; 7 is **A** and so is 8; 9 is **B** and so is 10. You must not be concerned about the number of times you select each letter or the sequence in which the letters occur in your answers. Candidates sometimes allow themselves to be influenced by irrelevant thoughts such as, 'It must be **D**'s turn now' or 'Oh, it can't be **C** for the third time running'. Considerations of that kind should play no part whatever in your thinking. Answering a multiple-choice objective test is not a guessing game. Your job is to think out and then mark the correct answer to each question, regardless of how many times it is **A** or **B**, and so on.

2. You must consider *all* the suggested answers to each question *before* you make your selection. Do not jump to conclusions. Remember that the suggested answers have been very carefully framed to test the accuracy of your reading and your ability to think things out and to make an imaginative response to the passage. Consequently, you must put all the answers through a mental sieve. Some you will quickly reject as inaccurate. Others will merit further consideration. Perhaps they are *partly* true, but *not* the answer that the question requires. These are the hardest to eliminate. Perhaps they *would* be true *if* the question were framed differently. Perhaps they *are* true in relation to later or earlier statements in the passage, but *not true in relation to the sentence(s) to which the question is directed*. You must weed out all the possibilities patiently before you can decide on the one suggested answer that fits *all* the facts and meets *all* the circumstances. For example, in the test just answered:

   Question 1
   According to the first sentence (line 1), Georgina had always insisted that she

   A was as strong as a boy
   B should be treated as a boy
   C was as independent as a boy
   D should be known as a boy
   E was as brave as a boy

   Reread the sentence to which the question specifically directs your attention: 'Georgina had always claimed the status of a boy'. The key word is *status*. It means 'standing' or 'position'.
   Now put the suggested answers through your mental sieve:

   A The sentence does *not* say that.
   B The sentence says that she claimed the status ('position' or 'standing') of a boy. Therefore, she must have insisted on being treated as a boy, since only such treatment would accord with the status she claimed. (If she was not treated as a boy, she could not have the status of a boy.)
   C She certainly behaves as independently as any boy could do, but that in-

formation comes from the rest of the passage, *not* from the sentence on which the question is based.

D Nothing in the first sentence (or anywhere else in the passage) supports that interpretation of her claims.

E She certainly behaves as bravely as any boy could do but, again, that information comes from the rest of the passage, *not* from the sentence on which the question is based.

That thorough sieving of all the suggested answers shows that the only one that fits *all* the facts is **B**.

Now work through all the other questions and answers in that test as methodically as I have just taken you through Question 1. You will be amply rewarded for the time you spend and the trouble you take, for it is *essential* to understand the demands made by these multiple-choice objective tests and to train yourself to meet them.

3. Questions 4 and 10 merit special study. The particular problems they pose are typical of questions often set.

Question 4

This demands especially close and imaginative reading of both the question and the passage. The instructions tell you to pick out the suggested answer that is *not* an accurate description of the big girl's state of mind. All the suggested answers *except* **C** are true statements. **C** is *not* a true statement; therefore, it is the *correct* answer! Here is a full work out of the question, showing how to arrive at the required answer.

A is a correct statement of her feelings, because the passage states that she was 'remorseful'. (She must have been unwilling to hurt them more if she was remorseful for what she had already done to them.)

B is a correct description of her feelings, because the passage states that she was 'puzzled' and tells us that she 'kept on asking . . . what she was to do . . .'.

D is a correct description of her feelings, again because the passage states that she was 'remorseful'.

E is a correct description of her feelings, because we are told of 'the great relief . . . of the Battwell girls'.

C is an *incorrect* description of her feelings. As we have just seen, the passage provides evidence that she was unwilling to hurt them more, unsure of what to do next, sorry for what she had done, relieved when an adult intervened; but there is no evidence whatever to support the statement that she was 'anxious to be friends with them'. Therefore, **C** is the required answer.

Question 10

This is the most difficult question, I think, for the correctness of the answer is determined by *one* word in the question: *finally*. A full work out demonstrates this all-important point.

E can be eliminated at once. Sam Weaver does *not* give her wounds attention.

D can be eliminated next. He does *not* carry the distressed child home. He carries her to Coytes' stables 'where he judged my father would be found'.

A can be eliminated next. Nothing in the passage suggests that he thought she needed protection, once he had heard the story and seen the scratches on the other girls.

We are now left with **B** and **C** as possible answers. He certainly did decide that Georgina was responsible for what had happened (**C**), but was that what he *finally* decided? Surely what he *finally* decided was that he would like to see Georgina punished (**B**)? He could not decide on that *before* he had decided that she was responsible for what had happened. Again, having taken her to Coytes' stables and having 'planted' her in front of a responsible adult ('my father'), he *related the crime*. He would not have done that unless he had finally decided that he would like to see Georgina punished.

B is the correct answer.

3.9 Multiple-choice Objective Test (1 Passage)

(a) How to Use this Test Paper to Best Advantage

1. Work through all the questions and decide on your answers *before* you look at the answers provided on page 166.
2. Time yourself accurately. You will probably not have difficulty in answering the paper within the time allowed, but do not worry if you exceed it. Your pace will quicken as you accustom yourself to these tests and, at this stage, careful practice is more important than speed.
3. If any of your answers differ from those I suggest, work through the relevant questions again very methodically (see Section 3.8, NOTES) to find the causes of the discrepancies.

(b) Test Paper (Answers on Page 166)

Time allowed: 50 minutes

ANSWERING THE QUESTIONS

1. Attempt all items. Each correct answer will score 1 mark. No deduction will be made for wrong answers.
2. Indicate your answer on the answer sheet by shading the upper part of the box on the appropriate letter; e.g. if the answer to item 8 is thought to be C, it should appear as:

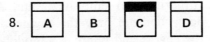

Only one answer must be indicated. Any other form of answering is incorrect and will not score.
3. If you change your mind, shade in the lower part of the box you have marked and mark the letter you now think is correct: e.g. to cancel C and enter A instead, it should appear as

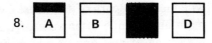

4. Do not linger over any item; if time permits, return later to reconsider omitted items.
5. Read the passage right through before filling in any answers.
6. In this test each item consists of a question or an incomplete statement followed by four suggested answers or completions. You are to select the most appropriate answer in each case.

At the Aller Moor pumping station, near Burrow Bridge, the story of the Somerset Levels is told by the shining, silent machinery that L. W. Musgrave, its custodian, has in his care. The Somerset River Authority, surely one of the most enlightened and skilful of public bodies, and certainly one faced

5 with tasks of unusual complexity, has established a museum here, containing specimens of the famous Appold patent centrifugal pump and of various types of Eastons, Amos and Anderson engines — the machinery that made efficient drainage of the Levels possible.

The Aller Moor engine was in use from 1869 to 1955, and Mr Musgrave

10 was 22 years old when he came to serve this fire-eating monster. He came on contract, having no fixed hours of work, in return for £12 a year, a free house and free fuel. His job was to see that there was always a head of steam to perform the vital work of pumping and to ensure that the complicated system of sluices was regulated efficiently. From four a.m. to seven every

15 day he tended the engine, its boilers and its fires; then rode his bicycle to whatever 'rhine' (the local name for a drainage channel) he was ditching or banking or cleaning, for it was understood that he would support himself and his family by day-labour, his work at the station being solely for the £12, the house and the fuel. His wife saw to the engine and the sluices in his

20 absence, for when pumping was necessary the fire-box had to be stoked every twenty minutes. His work in the pre-dawn period of the day was to rake out clinker, set the banked-down fire roaring and, above all, see that enough fuel was hauled into the shed to meet the stoking needs of the long day. Three tons of coal went into that hungry maw during a full day's pump-

25 ing, and his wife had all she could manage without the back-breaking labour of hauling the coal from the wharfside dump. The fuel came up from Bridgwater by barge in those days, costing 15s. a ton. When the old engine ceased its active life in 1955 its fuel was costing £7 a ton. Tredegar steam coal was the best of all in thermal efficiency, but it was dusty both in the

30 engine shed and in the house; Lydney coal was, therefore, the usual choice. 'Nobody', says Mr Musgrave, 'who hasn't fired for power knows the real difference between one kind of coal and another.'

He talks of those hard early days at the station with complete absence of self-pity, regarding his long working life as having been full of interest, and

35 taking a quiet, modest pride in his service to his fellow men and to the authority that employed him. As well he may. His work at Aller Moor demanded not only the engineering skill involved in operating and servicing the engine and pump — a model capable of lifting 13 000 gallons a minute — but detailed understanding of the intricate drainage system. The internal

40 drainage boards of the Levels were then independent and the Aller Moor Board was responsible for the safety of a huge area threatened by the Parrett and its tributaries. For many a year, the livelihood and, often, the lives of hundreds of people depended upon L. W. Musgrave and a handful of others employed to keep at bay the floods that for centuries past had annually over-

45 whelmed this part of the West Country. The rhines had to be inspected and maintained: mile after mile of carefully sited drainage ways, the blocking or breaching of any one of which could destroy the system. At the station, the work was not simply a matter of stoking a boiler and setting a pump to work at fixed times. The height of the main drainage channel — the River Parrett

50 itself — was but one of the factors involved. This fluctuated with the times of the tides in Bridgwater Bay and with the weather there and inland. As Mr Musgrave says, 'If't was rough, he [the tide] would be early.' Thus, the tidal charts hanging in the engine house, though conveying vital information

to the operator, had to be interpreted in the light of local knowledge and
55 their predictions had to be modified by the experience of years. The tide
that enters the river at its mouth rushes upstream, past Aller Moor, and on as
far as Langport, 19½ miles inland. Its height and rate of flow conditioned
what could and could not be done to get the water out of the main Aller
Moor rhine which, with hundreds of feeder dykes, kept the drainage area
60 free of floods *so long as* the main rhine could discharge into the Parrett and
the Parrett, in its turn, discharge into the sea. Sometimes it was possible to
let gravity do the work, when the Parrett was low; but gravity is a capricious
ally on the Somerset Levels! As a rule, the engine worked hard to drive the
pump, lifting water out of the rhine and forcing it into the Parrett's brim-
65 ming course. There were times, though, when this could not be done, for the
steam pump had to be stopped when the static head exceeded five feet. As
he bicycled back from a day's rhine-digging, the Aller Moor engineer watched
the smoke issuing from the station's 70-foot chimney. By its shape and
colour — plume or streamer, white, black or grey — he could make a shrewd
70 guess at how much stoking and coal-hauling he would have to do before he
could go to bed.

S. H. Burton, *The West Country*

---

1. Which one of the following is nearest in meaning to *custodian* as used in line 3?
   A treasurer
   B engineer
   C gaoler
   D guardian
2. In the first sentence it is implied that the machinery at Aller Moor is
   A new
   B no longer looked after
   C no longer in use
   D the property of its custodian
3. In lines 3–5 the writer claims for the Somerset River Authority all the follow-
   ing qualities EXCEPT
   A imagination
   B acquisitiveness
   C competence
   D resourcefulness
4. All the following makers' names designate machines that made efficient drain-
   age of the Levels possible. They all refer to the same kind of machine EXCEPT
   A Anderson
   B Appold
   C Eastons
   D Amos
5. Which one of the following is nearest in meaning to *rhine* as used in this
   passage?
   A a small or large ditch constructed to carry flood water away
   B a man-made lake for water storage
   C a large stream with steep banks
   D a rapidly running river
6. To serve the 'fire-eating monster' Mr Musgrave had to
   A extinguish the blaze
   B clear out the rhines
   C make new banks
   D maintain a head of steam and control the sluices

7. In which of these ways was Mr Musgrave remunerated when he started work?
    1 by receiving free domestic fuel
    2 by receiving a rent-free house
    3 by being paid £12 a year
  A 1 only
  B 1 and 2 only
  C 1 and 3 only
  D 1 + 2 + 3
8. The *day-labour* referred to in line 18 consisted of
  A maintenance work on the rhines
  B stoking the fire at the pumping station
  C hauling coal
  D regulating the sluices
9. According to the passage, Mrs Musgrave deputised for her husband in his absence because
  A she was glad to earn extra money
  B she wanted something to do
  C the fire had to be stoked frequently
  D the coal varied in quality
10. *Clinker* (line 22) is nearest in meaning to
  A a blocked flue
  B a clinched nail
  C hard lumps of incombustible matter
  D coal
11. The expression *that hungry maw* (line 24) refers to
  A the boiler furnace
  B the flood water
  C the River Parrett
  D the barge that transported the coal
12. Which one of the following is nearest in meaning to *thermal* as used in line 29?
  A hot
  B temperature
  C dust control
  D heat-producing
13. Mr Musgrave's retrospective view of his working life contains all these elements EXCEPT
  A quiet pride in having served the public
  B a sense of injustice
  C a justified recollection of having served his employer well
  D memories of the interest his work brought him
14. The work at the pumping station required all the following qualifications EXCEPT
  A full knowledge of the flood-prevention system
  B an understanding of the authority's legal powers
  C the mechanical skills needed to operate the engine and the pump
  D the ability to service the machines
15. Each of the following statements can be substantiated by evidence provided in the passage. Which *two* of them prove that the flooding of the Levels had been both a dangerous and a frequent occurrence?
    1 the internal drainage boards used to be independent bodies
    2 the Aller Moor Board was responsible for a huge area threatened by the River Parrett and its tributaries
    3 the livelihood and, often, the lives of hundreds of people depended on the pumping and draining

4 During many previous centuries this part of the West Country was annually overwhelmed by floods

A 1 and 2
B 2 and 3
C 2 and 4
D 3 and 4

16. Which one of the following is nearest in meaning to *breaching* as used in line 47?

A stopped up
B badly made
C pierced
D neglected

17. According to the writer, all the following are true EXCEPT

A the dykes had to be inspected and repaired
B the rhines were a mile long
C the water channels could become blocked
D damage to one rhine could destroy the whole drainage system

18. The writer indicates that the height of the River Parrett was

A not of major importance to the pumping
B at a constant level
C one of the considerations to be taken into account
D dependent upon the repair of the rhines

19. All these factors affected the height of the main drainage channel EXCEPT

A the head of steam available
B the times of the Bridgwater Bay tides
C the weather in the bay
D the weather inland

20. The writer makes all the following statements about the tidal charts EXCEPT that

A they were all the operator needed
B they were an essential basis for the operator's decisions
C local knowledge was needed to extract correct information from them
D their forecasts had to be adjusted in accordance with the experience of the operator

21. In the passage it is stated that Langport is

A nearer than Aller Moor to the sea
B further away than Aller Moor from the sea
C the same distance as Aller Moor from the sea
D 19½ miles away from Aller Moor

22. According to the passage, on which *two* of the following factors did the success of the whole drainage operation ultimately depend?

1 the efficient working of the feeder dykes
2 the efficient working of the Aller Moor drain
3 the transference of flood water into the River Parrett
4 the discharge of flood water by the Parrett into the sea

A 1 and 2
B 1 and 3
C 2 and 3
D 3 and 4

23. In the passage (line 62) it is implied that the force of gravity

A could be utilised to do most of the work
B did not always work in favour of the pumping
C raised the height of the Parrett
D caused the Parrett to run swiftly

24. Which *two* of the following does the writer suggest the homeward-bound engineer could deduce from the shape and colour of the smoke?

    1 the strength of the wind
    2 the quantity of coal being used
    3 the likelihood of rain before night
    4 the condition of the feeder rhines

A 1 and 2
B 1 and 4
C 2 and 3
D 3 and 4

25. From evidence stated or implied in the passage all the following facts can be deduced EXCEPT

A that the Somerset Levels are vulnerable to severe flooding
B that extensive drainage operations ceased in 1955
C that Langport is on the River Parrett
D that the River Parrett flows into Bridgwater Bay

ANSWER SHEET

1	A	B	C	D	14	A	B	C	D
2	A	B	C	D	15	A	B	C	D
3	A	B	C	D	16	A	B	C	D
4	A	B	C	D	17	A	B	C	D
5	A	B	C	D	18	A	B	C	D
6	A	B	C	D	19	A	B	C	D
7	A	B	C	D	20	A	B	C	D
8	A	B	C	D	21	A	B	C	D
9	A	B	C	D	22	A	B	C	D
10	A	B	C	D	23	A	B	C	D
11	A	B	C	D	24	A	B	C	D
12	A	B	C	D	25	A	B	C	D
13	A	B	C	D					

3.10 Multiple-choice Objective Test (2 Passages)

[Answers on page 167. Refer to Section 3.9(a) before you start to answer this paper.]

Time allowed: 50 minutes
Maximum mark: 39

How to answer the test
1. For each question there are five suggested answers, **A, B, C, D** and **E**. When you have selected your answer to each question, find the row on the answer sheet with the number of that question and draw a *horizontal* line to join the dots under the letter for the answer you have chosen.
   For example, the answer **C** would be marked as shown.

A	B	C	D	E
(· ·)	(· ·)	(——)	(· ·)	(· ·)

2. Mark only one answer for each question. If you change your mind about an answer, rub out the first mark carefully, then mark your new answer.
3. There are 39 questions in this test. You are advised to answer all the questions. You will score one mark for each correct answer; no marks will be deducted for incorrect answers or omissions.

COMPREHENSION PASSAGE 1
Questions 1 to 12 are based on this passage.

Horse-chestnuts would always be, to us, the appropriate ammunition to hurl at Luther Brimlow because, one tremulous October afternoon as we were gathering them, there suddenly was Luther's pimply face poked through the hedge and Luther's voice taunting us: 'Kids! Kids! Playing with conkers!'

5   Blanche and I were so absorbed in our task that, as often happened when we were together, each had completely forgotten the other and was wrapped in childish self-communion. She was gathering the horse-chestnuts into her apron, I into my pockets, and I am sure that to her, as certainly to me, this action was mechanical. Our minds were elsewhere, bemused by the tender

10   autumnal sky, and the sun's gentle warmth, and the crackle and rustle of the beautiful leaves beneath our feet, and the haze of a bonfire that was burning nearby. But though thus apart, we had the power of flying together in one defensive organism, as swiftly as two drops of mercury become one when they touch. So now we glared back at Luther Brimlow's face sneering at us

15   through the hedge.
'Who are kids?' Blanche demanded truculently.
'You are.'
'Why?'
'Playing with conkers.'

20   'Well, what do *you* do with yourself?'
'Sums.'
I could see Blanche's fingers curling crisply round a chestnut, prepared for the throw, and my ammunition was ready, too. But, somehow, that answer stilled us both. We continued to glare at Luther Brimlow's face, but now it

25   was not so much the face of the boy next door as of a monster outside the
range of our comprehension.

    Sums!

    If, while we were eating cake, someone had announced a preference for
coke we could not have been more astonished. And so, for that time, the
30   enemy was able to withdraw, with not a shot fired from our side. When his
face was beyond the hedge and he could be heard but not seen, he announc-
ed: 'I've saved up one pound two and a penny.'

    It seemed magnificent, but still we had nothing to say about it.

    'Bet you don't know what that would bring in at five per cent', the voice
35   taunted us, and we certainly didn't.

    'One and a pennyfarthing', Luther announced with triumph, and we heard
him scuttle across the road to his father's house.

Questions 1 to 12 are based on **Passage 1**. Read the passage carefully and then
answer the questions. Each question has five suggested answers. Select the best
answer to each question and mark the Answer Sheet accordingly.

    1. *Taunting* (line 4) is best explained as meaning that Luther's voice was
        A mocking ridiculously
        B jibing provokingly
        C sneering contemptuously
        D bawling teasingly
        E laughing sarcastically
    2. 'Wrapped in childish self-communion' (lines 6–7) is best explained as meaning
       that the two children were
        A pretending to talk to themselves as if alone
        B aware subconsciously of the presence of each other
        C taken up entirely with their own private thoughts
        D able to communicate without speaking to each other
        E willing to share their pleasure in their task
    3. All the following contribute to the representation of the October afternoon
       (lines 9–12) EXCEPT
        A reference to the experience of different senses
        B loose sentence-structure to express the dreamy mood
        C terms suggesting mildness and absence of extremes
        D frequent employment of rare and unusual vocabulary
        E words chosen which echo the sounds described
    4. The 'power' referred to in line 12 is best explained as the children's immediate
       readiness to
        A allow one to speak for both
        B retreat together in order to defend themselves
        C hasten to stand side-by-side to protect each other
        D choose attack as the best form of defence
        E adopt a common united attitude when attacked
    5. *Crisply*, as used in line 22, is best explained as meaning
        A stiffly and gradually
        B instinctively
        C quickly and firmly
        D secretively
        E easily and pliantly

6. Luther's answer stilled them both (line 24) probably because they
   A could not understand anyone liking sums
   B regarded all sums as very difficult
   C did not really know what he meant
   D were ashamed of their own ignorance
   E thought he was too clever for them

7. *Glare* (line 24) indicates that Blanche and the narrator were looking at Luther with
   A alarm
   B bewilderment
   C amazement
   D hostility
   E alertness

8. They looked at Luther as though he were a 'monster' (line 25) because
   A his face was very ugly and covered with pimples
   B he was taunting them and threatening to attack them
   C his rude interruption had utterly ruined their afternoon's pleasure
   D he preferred going to school to playing with conkers
   E his answer made them think he must be extremely abnormal

9. 'Outside the range of our comprehension' (lines 25–26) is best explained as indicating that Blanche and the narrator felt unable to
   A understand how Luther or anyone could like sums
   B remember meeting anyone quite like Luther before
   C think of an appropriate answer to Luther
   D perceive how they should deal with Luther
   E grasp what Luther had been talking about

10. If the comparison of eating cake to eating coke (lines 28–29) is applied to the events of the afternoon, 'eating cake' would represent
    A communing with oneself
    B eating chestnuts
    C gathering horse-chestnuts
    D playing conkers
    E preparing to attack

11. 'It seemed magnificent' (line 33) implies that Blanche and the narrator
    A recognised that Luther had scored over them
    B felt impressed by Luther's knowledge of the exact amount
    C admired Luther for having saved up his money
    D suspected that Luther was boasting about his savings
    E thought Luther's savings made up a huge sum

12. According to the passage as a whole, all the following are true of Blanche and the narrator EXCEPT that they
    A sensed each other's moods and feelings
    B were always aware of each other's presence
    C shared strong likes and dislikes
    D came to each other's aid if attacked
    E spent much time in each other's company

COMPREHENSION PASSAGE 2
Questions 13 to 39 are based on this passage.

It was our third job that night. Until this thing happened, work had been without incident. There had been shrapnel, a few bombs, and some huge

fires; but these were unremarkable and have since merged without identity
into the neutral maze of fire and noise and water and night, without date
5 and without hour, with neither time nor form, that lours mistily at the back
of my mind as a picture of the air-raid season.

And there we were—Len, Verno and myself—playing a fifty-foot jet up the
face of a tall city warehouse and thinking of nothing at all. You don't think
of anything after the first few hours. You just watch the white pole of water
10 lose itself in the fire and you think of nothing. Sometimes you move the jet
over to another window. Sometimes the orange dims to black—but you only
ease your grip on the ice-cold nozzle and continue pouring careless gallons
through the window. You know the fire will fester for hours yet. However,
that night the blank, indefinite hours of waiting were sharply interrupted—
15 by an unusual sound. Very suddenly, a long rattling crack of bursting brick
and mortar perforated the moment. And then the upper half of that five-
storey building heaved over towards us. It hung there, poised for a timeless
second, before rumbling down at us. I was thinking of nothing at all and
then I was thinking of everything in the world.

20 In that simple second my brain digested every detail of the scene. New
eyes opened at the sides of my head so that, from within, I photographed a
hemispherical panorama bounded by the huge length of the building in front
of me and the narrow lane on either side.

Blocking us on the left was the squat trailer pump, roaring and quivering
25 with effort. Water throbbed from its overflow valves and from leakages in
the hose and couplings. A ceaseless stream spewed down its grey sides into
the gutter. To the other side of me was a free run up the alley. A couple of
lengths of dead, deflated hose wound over the darkly glistening pavement.
Charred flotsam dammed up one of the gutters. A needle of water fountained
30 from a hole in a live hose-length.

Behind me, Len and Verno shared the weight of the hose. They heaved up
against the strong backward drag of waterpressure. All I had to do was yell
'Drop it'—and then run. We could risk the live hose snaking up at us. We
could run to the right down the free alley. But I never moved. That long
35 second held me hypnotised, rubber boots cemented to the pavement. Ton upon ton of red-hot brick hovering in the air above us numbed all initiative. I
could only think. I couldn't move.

Six yards in front stood the blazing building. A minute before I would
never have distinguished it from any other drab Victorian atrocity happily on
40 fire. Now I was immediately certain of every minute detail. The building was
five storeys high. The top four storeys were fiercely alight. The rooms inside
were alive with red fire. The black outside walls remained untouched. Like
the lighted carriages of a night express, there appeared alternating rectangles
of black and red that emphasised vividly the extreme symmetry of the win-
45 dow spacing: each oblong window shape posed as a vermilion panel set in
perfect order upon the dark face of the wall. There were ten windows to
each floor, making forty windows in all. In rigid rows of ten, one row placed
precisely above the other, with strong contrasts of black and red, the blazing
windows stood to attention in strict formation. Orange-red colour seemed to
50 bulge from the black framework like boiling jelly that expanded inside a
thick black squared grill.

Three of the storeys pivoted over towards us and hung flatly over the alley.
Through smoke-fogged fireglow the moonlight had hitherto penetrated to
the pit of our alley through declivities in the skyline. Now some of the moon-
55 light was being shut out as the wall hung ever further over us. The wall
shaded the moonlight like an inverted awning. Now the pathway of light

above had been squeezed to a thin line. That was the only silver lining I ever believed in. It shone out—a ray of hope. But it was declining hope, for al-although at this time the entire hemispherical scene appeared static, an
60 imminence of movement could be sensed throughout.

A wall will fall in many ways. It may sway over to the one side or the other. It may crumble at the very beginning of its fall. It may remain intact and fall flat. This wall fell as flat as a pancake. It clung to its shape through ninety degrees to the horizontal. Then it detached itself from the pivot and
65 slammed down on top of us.

The last resistance of bricks and mortar at the pivot point cracked off like automatic gun fire. The violent sound both deafened us and brought us to our senses. We dropped the hose and crouched. Afterwards Verno said that I knelt slowly on one knee with bowed head, like a man about to be knighted.
70 Well, I got my knighting. There was an incredible noise—a thunderclap con-densed into the space of an eardrum—and then the bricks and the mortar came tearing and burning into the flesh of my face.

Len, Verno and myself were all dug out. There was very little brick on top of us. We had been lucky. We had been framed by one of those symmetrical,
75 oblong window spaces.

Questions 13 to 39 are based on Passage 2. Read the passage carefully and then answer the questions. Each question has five suggested answers. Select the best answer to each question and mark the Answer Sheet accordingly.

13. 'Work had been without incident (lines 1–2) is best explained as meaning that their work had been without any
    A important air-raids
    B real dangers
    C exceptional occurrences
    D serious problems
    E major fires

14. 'These were unremarkable' (line 3) is best explained as meaning that for the writer the earlier happenings of the night were
    A everyday
    B trivial
    C unnoticed
    D commonplace
    E insignificant

15. Which two of the following best explain the meaning of 'these . . . have since merged without identity' as used in line 3? The events referred to
    1 occurred in close and rapid succession
    2 had contributed to an overall impression
    3 did not affect him personally
    4 were blotted out by later experiences
    5 could not be recalled separately
    A 1 and 4 only
    B 1 and 5 only
    C 2 and 3 only
    D 2 and 5 only
    E 3 and 4 only

16. The writer's picture of the air-raid season is described as a 'maze' (line 4) probably because he

A was firefighting in a network of very narrow streets
B had no real hope of ever getting out alive
C felt completely bewildered by all the noise and excitement
D remembered the period in a confused and disordered way
E kept rushing haphazardly from one fire to another

17. The main impression given by the first paragraph (lines 1–6) is that the writer
A had for the most part, a general recollection of his experiences during air-raids
B attended so many fires that he paid no attention to the danger
C saw fire-fighting as a job that had to be done in war-time
D became bewildered by the noise and confusion of the air-raids
E was trying to dispel the horrors of the fires from his mind

18. In the first paragraph (lines 1–6) all the following words and expressions contribute to the sense of experiences indistinctly remembered EXCEPT
A 'without incident' (line 2)
B 'without identity' (line 3)
C 'neutral' (line 4)
D 'with neither time nor form' (line 5)
E 'mistily' (line 5)

19. The men were 'thinking of nothing at all' (line 8) because their minds were
A dazed by the fear of death
B completely concentrated on their work
C fascinated by flowing water
D so accustomed to the job
E avoiding any thought of the danger

20. 'You don't think of anything after the first few hours' (lines 8–9) shows that, according to the writer, fire-fighting was often
A frightening
B monotonous
C exhausting
D dangerous
E frustrating

21. The water from the hose is described as a 'pole' (line 9) for all the following reasons EXCEPT that it was
A long and narrow
B vertical
C almost straight
D solid-looking
E round in cross-section

22. The firemen eased their grip on the nozzle (line 12) only when they
A were thinking of nothing at all
B began to grow tired of their work
C knew their dangerous task was finished
D saw the fire was temporarily under control
E shifted the jet to another window

23. *Careless*, as used in line 12, chiefly indicates that the firemen
A tended to forget the dangers of their situation
B did not worry about the cost of the fire-fighting
C gave little thought to what they were doing
D were not bothered about the damage caused by the fire
E relaxed once the fire had been finally subdued

24. Which *two* of the following are implied by the use of 'blank' in line 14?
1 Nothing much was happening.
2 Darkness covered the scene.

3 The firemen were thinking of nothing.
4 The firemen could not relax.
5 Nothing could be heard.
A 1 and 3 only
B 1 and 5 only
C 2 and 3 only
D 2 and 4 only
E 4 and 5 only

25. The hours are described as 'indefinite' (line 14) because the firemen
A might be called to another incident at any minute
B did not know how long the fire would last
C found time passed slowly when they were at work
D were not interested in what they were doing
E thought that the fire would go on burning for ever

26. Which one of the following statements is implied by the expression 'a timeless second' (lines 17–18)?
A Time ceased to have any significance for the men.
B It seemed for a moment that time stood still.
C The wall did not pause but seemed to.
D There was no time to take evasive action.
E The poising was too brief to be measurable.

27. Which one of the following is closest in meaning to *panorama* as used in line 22?
A A detailed and colourful prospect
B A confused and bewildering sight
C An unbroken and extensive view
D A brilliant and theatrical scene
E A remarkable and changing spectacle

28. Which *two* of the following are implied by the sentence beginning 'New eyes opened . . .' (lines 20–21)? He
1 turned his head quickly, first to one side and then the other
2 had, till then, been aware only of what was before him
3 grasped the situation as a whole and in a moment
4 focused his attention on the objects which were nearest at hand
A 1 and 2 only
B 1 and 3 only
C 2 and 3 only
D 2 and 4 only
E 3 and 4 only

29. All the following information about fire-fighting is indicated in the first five paragraphs (lines 1–37) EXCEPT that
A a hose, if not restrained, will push the fireman towards the fire
B a mechanical pump keeps the water under steady and constant pressure
C hoses are made up of lengths, and swell when filled with water
D a nozzle enables the water to be directed at the fire
E a live hose will twist and turn alarmingly unless firmly held

30. The windows of the building are compared to 'the lighted carriages of a night express' (line 43) for all the following reasons EXCEPT that they were
A shaped as upright oblongs
B bright against surrounding darkness
C set in a moving surface
D spaced at regular intervals
E arranged in straight lines

31. In the sentence beginning 'In rigid rows of ten   ' (line 47) the lighted win-

dows of the building seem to be compared to
- A rows of flowers
- B a train at night
- C seats in a theatre
- D a framework of girders
- E soldiers on parade

32. All the following are suggested by the comparison of the fire to 'boiling jelly' (line 50) EXCEPT that it
- A seemed to protrude like a semi-liquid mass
- B was obviously at a very high temperature
- C seemed to be cooking on a metal grill
- D resembled some jellies in its colour
- E seemed to be moving constantly as though boiling

33. *Pivoted* (line 52) suggests that the top three storeys moved as if
- A turning on a hinge
- B rocking like a see-saw
- C forming a huge arch
- D hovering like a hawk
- E dropping into a pit

34. The wall is compared to an 'inverted' awning (line 56) because awnings normally
- A consist of canvas, not red-hot brick
- B slope downwards from the supporting upright
- C do not completely exclude the light
- D are meant to offer some protection
- E give shade from sunlight, not moonlight

35. Which one of the following best explains the sentence beginning 'But it was declining hope' (line 58)?
- A The writer's hope was lessening, because he felt that the wall was about to fall.
- B There was still some hope, but the extreme stillness suggested something dreadful would happen.
- C Although hope was growing dim, the writer believed that the wall would remain stationary.
- D As he began to lose hope, the writer realised he had to move at once.
- E It was useless to hope, because throughout the entire scene he could see slight movements.

36. 'An imminence of movement' (lines 59–60) is best explained as a movement which is
- A imperceptible
- B impending
- C impetuous
- D impressive
- E immediate

37. All the following are true of the sound of the falling wall, as described in lines 66–71, EXCEPT that it
- A shook the men out of their trance
- B made the men bend down low
- C climaxed in ear-splitting noise
- D filled the men with sudden terror
- E began with a series of rapid cracks

38. In the passage as a whole, all the following information is given about the collapse of the wall EXCEPT that it
- A began to fall when its bricks and mortar burst

B pivoted over from the top of the second storey
C swayed backwards and forwards at first before finally falling
D remained in one piece until parallel with the ground
E fell freely at the end with increased speed and noise

39. According to the passage, which *two* of the following statements about the writer are true?

    1 He noticed all the details of the scene.
    2 He did not realise the danger until too late.
    3 He abandoned hope when he saw the wall falling.
    4 He foresaw they might be framed by the window-space.
    5 He seemed unable to take action to save himself.

A 1 and 3 only
B 1 and 5 only
C 2 and 3 only
D 2 and 4 only
E 4 and 5 only

	A	B	C	D	E		A	B	C	D	E
1	(· ·)	(· ·)	(· ·)	(· ·(	(· ·)	21	(· ·)	(· ·)	(· ·)	(· ·)	(· ·)
2	(· ·)	(· ·)	(· ·)	(· ·)	(· ·)	22	(· ·)	(· ·)	(· ·)	(· ·)	(· ·)
3	(· ·)	(· ·)	(· ·)	(· ·)	(· ·)	23	(· ·)	(· ·)	(· ·)	(· ·)	(· ·)
4	(· ·)	(· ·)	(· ·)	(· ·)	(· ·)	24	(· ·)	(· ·)	(· ·)	(· ·)	(· ·)
5	(· ·)	(· ·)	(· ·)	(· ·)	(· ·)	25	(· ·)	(· ·)	(· ·)	(· ·)	(· ·)
6	(· ·)	(· ·)	(· ·)	(· ·)	(· ·)	26	(· ·)	(· ·)	(· ·)	(· ·)	(· ·)
7	(· ·)	(· ·)	(· ·)	(· ·)	(· ·)	27	(· ·)	(· ·)	(· ·)	(· ·)	(· ·)
8	(· ·)	(· ·)	(· ·)	(· ·)	(· ·)	28	(· ·)	(· ·)	(· ·)	(· ·)	(· ·)
9	(· ·)	(· ·)	(· ·)	(· ·)	(· ·)	29	(· ·)	(· ·)	(· ·)	(· ·)	(· ·)
10	(· ·)	(· ·)	(· ·)	(· ·)	(· ·)	30	(· ·)	(· ·)	(· ·)	(· ·)	(· ·)
11	(· ·)	(· ·)	(· ·)	(· ·)	(· ·)	31	(· ·)	(· ·)	(· ·)	(· ·)	(· ·)
12	(· ·)	(· ·)	(· ·)	(· ·)	(· ·)	32	(· ·)	(· ·)	(· ·)	(· ·)	(· ·)
13	(· ·)	(· ·)	(· ·)	(· ·)	(· ·)	33	(· ·)	(· ·)	(· ·)	(· ·)	(· ·)
14	(· ·)	(· ·)	(· ·)	(· ·)	(· ·)	34	(· ·)	(· ·)	(· ·)	(· ·)	(· ·)
15	(· ·)	(· ·)	(· ·)	(· ·)	(· ·)	35	(· ·)	(· ·)	(· ·)	(· ·)	(· ·)
16	(· ·)	(· ·)	(· ·)	(· ·)	(· ·)	36	(· ·)	(· ·)	(· ·)	(· ·)	(· ·)
17	(· ·)	(· ·)	(· ·)	(· ·)	(· ·)	37	(· ·)	(· ·)	(· ·)	(· ·)	(· ·)
18	(· ·)	(· ·)	(· ·)	(· ·)	(· ·)	38	(· ·)	(· ·)	(· ·)	(· ·)	(· ·)
19	(· ·)	(· ·)	(· ·)	(· ·)	(· ·)	39	(· ·)	(· ·)	(· ·)	(· ·)	(· ·)
20	(· ·)	(· ·)	(· ·)	(· ·(	(· ·)						

4 Summary

4.1 Definition and Description

A summary is

- a short, pithy restatement of the *chief points* made by a writer (or speaker); a *concise summing-up* of the contents of a passage of writing set by the examiners for that purpose.

A summary must be

- written in *continuous* prose (*not* in note form). As far as possible, it must be written in the summariser's *own words* (*not* in the words of the original passage).

A good summary is

- *accurate*. It includes *all* the chief points of the original passage and, although they must be expressed in the summariser's own words, they must *not* be altered. However much the summariser may dispute or dislike the facts set out or disagree with the ideas or opinions expressed in the passage, they must not be tampered with. The 'slant' and the 'feel' of the original passage must not be changed.

A good summary is

- *brief*. The summariser must *condense* the original passage by *selecting* the essential points and expressing them in *economical* language. Minor points must be omitted. All decorative writing, figures of speech, verbal flourishes, illustrations and examples must be omitted. In a summary there is room only for the essential meaning — the bare bones — of the original passage.

A good summary is

- *clear*. It must be *clearly planned* so that its successive items follow each other in a logical sequence. It must also be *clearly expressed* in plain, easily understood English.

4.2 The Importance of Summary

A summarising exercise is a compulsory question in every English Language examination, for two reasons. First, summarising is a frequently needed skill. For example, it is often necessary to make a summary of papers, correspondence, articles, books or sections of books in order to abstract important material needed for working purposes. Second, the mental activities and linguistic capabilities called into play when summarising are those that the examiners are rightly intent on measuring in an English Language paper.

4.3　The Skills Required

Summarising employs all the skills required for general competence in the use of language, for it is a test of reading comprehension and writing aptitude. To make a good summary you must be able to:

- understand what you read;
- and then express your understanding in words of your own.

The first step in summarising is to arrive at a thorough comprehension of the passage. Then, and only then, you are ready to plan and to write your summary. Those two operations demand:

- the *judgement* to distinguish between *essential points* (which must be included) and *minor points* (which must be omitted);
- the *organising ability* to work out a *coherent* and *logical* plan;
- the *writing skill* to frame *clear* sentences, *correct* in grammar, punctuation and spelling;
- the *word power* to *condense* the passage while restating its essential contents, and to select *appropriate* expressions to reflect the 'slant' and the 'feel' of the passage.

Each of those points is discussed and demonstrated in later sections of this chapter.

4.4　Different Kinds of Summary Questions

(a) Whole-passage Summary ('Précis')

The word *précis* (French) is still in common use as a synonym for *summary*, although it appears much less frequently in examination instructions than it did. Should you be instructed to 'Make a précis of this passage', just remember that it is simply another way of saying, 'Summarise this passage'.

Variations of wording occur in the instructions given by different boards, but the essentials are common to all.

(i)　*Typical Instructions: Whole-passage Summary (Précis)*

Summarise (make a précis of) this passage in clear and correct English. Some words and phrases in the original writing cannot be accurately or economically replaced, but you must not copy out long expressions or whole sentences. Use *your own words* as far as possible. Your summary *must not exceed 150 words*. State at the end the exact number of words you have used.

The word limit may be expressed in other ways. For example, '. . . in about 150 words'. In that case, you should aim at being not more than 5 words above or below the stipulated number. Detailed guidance on word limits is provided later.

A whole-passage summary question requires you to include in your summary *all* the chief points expressed in the passage set.

(b) Selective Summary

Selective-summary questions direct candidates to summarise a particular *part* (or *parts*) of the contents of the set passage. The examiners select one (or more than one) aspect of the subject matter and require a summary of that and *only* of that.

For example, the set passage might recount the history of a legal reform (the abolition of child labour, say) from the early days of the struggle to enlist public support to its passage into law and its effects on society. You might then be instructed to summarise *either* the early stages *or* the parliamentary battle *and/or* the subsequent effects.

Another exercise in selective summary might involve the selection and summarising of material occurring in various places throughout the passage. For example, in an account of the career of some famous person there might be material drawn from various stages of his/her life in which particular qualities led to success or failure. You might then be instructed to summarise the part that one quality (rashness, say) or another (ruthlessness, perhaps) played in his/her career.

A selective summary is often a shorter exercise than a whole-passage summary, but by no means easier to write, for the instructions demand particularly close attention and constant alertness. The examiners are testing your ability to reach the heart of the matter *in accordance with their precise instructions*. Much that is important in the passage must be disregarded in your summary because *it is irrelevant to the task you have been set*. You will lose marks if you include any point that does not bear on the answer asked for, however essential it may be to the passage as a whole.

(i) *Typical Instructions: Selective Summary*

1. This passage gives an account of the various courses of action open to the leaders of the new party. Summarise in not more than 100 of your own words their reasons for rejecting the policies that were pressed upon them by an influential group of their supporters.

You must summarise only that part of the passage that is concerned with the specified subject. Much that is important in the passage as a whole (for example: other courses of action open to the party leaders; the policies that they adopted) is irrelevant to the task you have been given.

2. Study these letters exchanged between Mr J. K. Smith and the Northtown planning authority. Summarise in one paragraph of about 100 words their points of disagreement about the roofing materials to be used on the house that Mr Smith seeks planning permission to build.

Other matters may be covered in the correspondence (design of roof and windows, colour of paintwork, access road to the house, and so on), but the subject matter of your summary must be restricted to the topic specified in the instructions.

(c) Short Summary

Short-summary questions are often set as part of the comprehension test, a fact that underlines how closely comprehension and summary are connected. Such questions are a condensed form of selective summary, requiring the same concentrated attention, the same mental processes and the same writing skills. However, the instructions do not always include the word *summarise* and its absence misleads some candidates.

You must learn to recognise the signals that indicate that a short summary is required. These are:

1. More words are allowed for the answer to a short-summary question than for a 'straight' comprehension question.
2. More marks are given.
3. The instructions usually stipulate an answer *in your own words*.

(i) *Typical Instructions: Short Summary*

(Look for the signals that indicate the short-summary exercise included among the comprehension questions in this paper.)

[PASSAGE]

1. Give *one* word meaning the same as *each* of the following as they are used in the passage: (i) tedious (1.3), (ii) parsimonious (1.6); (iii) dilatory (1.10); (iv) erring (1.12); (v) taunting (1.25). [5 *marks*]
2. From the first sentence quote the two words that indicate how risky the plan was. [4 *marks*]
3. Set out clearly in not more than 30 *of your own words* the excuses that Brown made for declining the invitation to take part. [10 *marks*]
4. Write down two of the facts that the investigation revealed. [4 *marks*]
5. What is implied in the final sentence about Brown's conduct during the investigation? [4 *marks*]

Question 3 is a short-summary question. It is to be answered 'in not more than 30 of your own words' and it carries 10 marks.

4.5 Summarising Method: Step by Step

Practice in whole-passage summarising ('précis writing') is the best way of learning the art of summary. While you are learning how to make a good summary of a whole passage, you are at the same time mastering the kind of thinking and the language techniques needed for selective-summary and short-summary questions.

Step 1 Get the *gist* of the passage. State it briefly and in your own words.
Step 2 Get to grips with the writer's *purpose* by 'tuning in' to the 'slant' and 'feel' of the passage.
Step 3 Make a *skeleton outline* of the writer's presentation of the *main theme* by noting each *key point* as it occurs in the passage.
Step 4 Use your list of key points as the framework of a *detailed plan* for your summary.
Step 5 Write a *draft* of your summary.
Step 6 *Prune* and *polish* the draft.
Step 7 Write the *final version* of your summary.

That list of the necessary steps may look daunting, but each step is explained and demonstrated later in this chapter.

Summary writing is an essential skill and you must take pains to learn it. Method is vital: nobody can make a good summary 'off the cuff'. With practice, you will speed up and become so versed in these well-tried procedures that you will find it second nature to apply them efficiently in your examination.

4.6 Applying the Method

(a) Step 1: Get the Gist of the Passage

Follow the reading method set out in Section 3.1(c) to arrive at a thorough comprehension of the passage. Then write (*in your own words*, as far as possible) a brief statement of the main theme(s) expressed in the passage. (The *theme* is the basic, bedrock subject.) Your statement should sum up in as few words as possible ('encapsulate') what the passage is essentially about: the very heart of the matter. You will find it helpful to begin your statement of the theme with some such formula as 'The writer argues that . . .' *or* 'This passage gives an account of . . .'. Such an opening helps you to make an objective and accurate statement of the writer's main subject matter.

(b) Step 2: Get to Grips with the Writer's Purpose

The need to be objective and accurate was emphasised in Section 4.1: 'However much the summariser may dislike or dispute the facts set out . . . they must not be tampered with.' You may not like the factual contents of the passage. You may even know or think you know that they are wrong, but *it is not your job to alter or correct them in any way*. If the passage states that the moon is made of green cheese, you must not query it or comment on it in your summary. When you make a summary you must reproduce *faithfully* the gist of the original. Your concern is with what the writer says, *not* with what you think he/she ought to have said.

The subject matter is not always factual. It may be an expression of ideas, opinions, arguments for or against a point of view or a course of action. Again, you must reproduce the writer's 'slant' accurately, however much you may disagree with it. It may arouse strong feelings in you – either for or against – but *you must not allow those feelings to appear in your summary*.

Again, without actually stating a point of view, the writer may indicate his/her standpoint indirectly. The passage may be satirical (mildly or savagely; in whole or in part). It may be objective or subjective, part factual, part persuasive. It may be warmly enthusiastic or 'tongue in cheek' writing. There are many possibilities, but whatever the 'feel' of the passage, you *must reflect it accurately and without comment* in your summary.

So, keeping in mind your brief statement of its theme, read through the passage again, looking for the writer's point of view and purpose in writing. As you read, note key words, phrases, sentences that indicate the 'feel' of the piece. Ask yourself these questions: '*What* is the writer trying to do?' '*Why* is the writer trying to do this?' '*How* is the writer trying to do this?'

(c) Step 3: Skeleton Outline—Key Points of Main Theme

Keep in mind your statement of the main theme as you look for the key points. Include every one that bears on that statement. If in doubt about a point, include it; you will prune later. You can list the key points either by underlining them in the passage or by jotting them down on rough paper.

(d) Step 4: Make a Detailed Plan for Your Summary

Base the plan on your list of key points. When writing the plan:

- Use *your own words* as far as possible.
- Include sufficient *detail* to enable you to write your draft summary from your notes *without referring to the passage*.

There are two good reasons for that advice. First, if you use the writer's words in your notes, you will be in danger of incorporating them in your summary. Second, if you have to refer to the passage as you write your draft, you will be in danger of departing from the scheme of key points worked out in Step 3 and will probably mix minor points and other irrelevant matter in with the key points.

A good summary plan is:

- *coherent* — all the items that sensibly go together are grouped together — they 'stick together' (*cohere*) — they are *not* 'dotted about' in various parts of the summary;
- *logical* — each part follows on sensibly from the preceding part — the summary is presented in an ordered sequence, *from* its beginning, *through* its middle, *to* its end.

(e) Step 5: Write a Draft of Your Summary

Stick to your plan. Do not be tempted to alter it as you go along. Revisions come later (Step 6). Choose your words carefully and think out well-framed sentences. The language of summary is:

- clear and easily understood;
- condensed — no wasted words or long-winded expressions;
- correct — in grammar, punctuation and spelling.

(f) Step 6: Prune and Polish the Draft

1. Count the number of words in the draft. You will probably be over the limit, but the excess can be pruned out. Word limits are expressed by the examiners in different ways. Here are some typical examples, with notes on how to proceed:

    . . . in not more than 150 words
    . . . must not exceed 120 words
    Those are to be treated as *absolute* limits. Words beyond the specified number will be ignored by the examiners, making nonsense of the end of your summary. On the other hand, you should not be more than 5–10 words

below the limit. If you are, you have probably omitted something important.

> *. . . between 180 and 220 words*

This is a wide 'band'. Try to be halfway or lower. You must *not* be above the upper limit or below the lower.

> *. . . in about 120 words*
> *. . . in 120 words*

In both cases you have a plus or minus 'allowance' of 5 words and your summary must be between 115 and 125 words in length.

However expressed, the word limit is extremely important. Failure to observe it (in accordance with the instructions just given) will cost you marks.

2. Prune by removing unnecessary words. Look especially for overworked, verbose expressions and tautologies (see Section 4.7 and Chapter 6).

EXAMPLES

check up on	= check
period of time	= period
in this day and age	= now *or* nowadays
advance forward	= advance
reverse backwards	= reverse

Apart from such misuse of language, some perfectly good expressions must be pruned because brevity is so important: figurative language, illustrative examples, rhetorical questions and repetitions, decorations — all of which have a part to play in writing *of a different kind*.

3. Condense wherever possible. Search your vocabulary for *compendious* words (see Section 4.7). Make every word tell.

EXAMPLE

Those who argued in favour of a nuclear generation plant raised powerful objections to their opponents' plan, which offered them some but not all of the resources for which they were contending.	The nuclear lobby objected strongly to their opponents' suggested compromise.

4. Check for errors of grammar, punctuation and spelling.
ing words and expressions such as *however, therefore, first, second, next, on the other hand, despite, considering* are needed.

5. Check for errors of grammar, punctuation and spelling.

6. Look out for and remove *all*: colloquialisms; slang; quotations; direct speech. See Section 6.7.

7. *Finally* ask yourself these questions:

   ● Would this summary be readily understood by a reader *who had not seen the original passage*?
   ● Would it convey to that reader *the essential meaning* of the passage?

If the answer to both questions is 'Yes', you have written a good draft which you can fair copy and confidently hand in.

(g) Step 7: Write out the Final Version

1. Head your summary with a suitable title and underline it. Keep it *short*. Do *not* try to write a 'clever', 'punchy', newspaper-type headline. A plain, accurate, brief title is what is wanted. It does *not* count towards the number of words used.
2. Write the final version in your best and clearest handwriting. Be sure to incorporate all the corrections and improvements made as you pruned and polished the draft.
3. State at the end the *exact* number of words in your summary, *excluding* the title. Do *not* be tempted to falsify the number. If it looks wrong (and the examiners have a shrewd idea of how many words occupy how many lines of the answer sheet), it will be checked.

4.7 The Language of Summary

(a) Plain, Clear, Brief

1. *Plain*, because a summary is a restatement of the bare bones – the *essential* meaning – of a given passage. So, no 'frills' of any kind: no figures of speech; no illustrative examples; no rhetorical questions or repetitions; no 'decorative' writing.
2. *Clear*, because a reader *who has not seen the original passage* must be able to grasp its essential meaning quickly, easily and accurately *from the summary alone*.
3. *Brief*, because the word limit imposes a strict discipline and not a word must be wasted.

That description sums up points made in earlier sections, but certain other features of the language of summary must now be singled out for special attention.

(b) Condensed

See Section 4.6(f). The use of *condensed* language (language that boils down a lot of meaning into very few words) is necessary. You must take every opportunity of contracting clauses into phrases and phrases into single words. *Compendious* words (*compendious* = 'space-saving') are needed to encapsulate the essential meaning of longer expressions.

You must also *remove* all *redundant* (superfluous) words. *Verbose* language (language that uses more words than are necessary) is always a fault: in summary, it is fatal.

EXAMPLES

1. The popular press is full of crime stories, violence in the streets, scandals, thefts and horrifying incidents of every kind.

   The popular press is full of sensational items.

2. She made a list of things she needed such as butter, cheese, raisins, salt, sugar, flour and frozen foods.

   She made a list of groceries she needed.

3. The auctioneer moved on to the old barn where harrows, ploughs, seed-drills, rakes and mowers were stored.

The auctioneer moved on to the old barn where agricultural implements were stored.

4. The ship was crowded with people who were leaving their native land for a new home.

The ship was crowded with emigrants.

5. Jean decided to train as a teacher of spinning, weaving, basket-making, china-painting and similar skills.

Jean decided to train as a handicrafts teacher.

6. He was handicapped in examinations by his inability to recall accurately facts and theories that he had learnt.

He was handicapped in examinations by his bad memory.

7. The book tells how Ben Gunn was put ashore and abandoned on an uninhabited island as a punishment.

The book tells how Ben Gunn was marooned.

8. Her small, unexpected good fortune was quickly and wastefully spent on tastelessly showy ornaments.

Her windfall was soon squandered on garish ornaments.

9. Brown says his new job involves a great deal of very hard work.

Brown says his new job is laborious.

10. We tried in vain to persuade the conflicting parties to agree to submit their respective cases to the decision of an independent umpire.

We failed to persuade the adversaries to go to arbitration.

11. The treasurer reported that there were serious financial difficulties in respect of the prospect of completing the new housing estate by the target date that had been set.

The treasurer reported that lack of funds was endangering the completion of the new housing estate on time.

12. In the majority of instances, householders informed the council through the investigating officers enquiring on the council's behalf that they were satisfied and had no complaints in the matter of the scheme regulating the system of differential rating.

Most householders told the council that they were satisfied with the differential rating scheme.

(c) Correct and Appropriate

Errors in *grammar, punctuation* and *spelling* will cost you marks in summary (as in all the other questions), but correct language alone is not enough: it must also be *appropriate*. The language of summary is *formal* (without being stiff or pompous). Therefore, you must *not* use:

colloquialisms ('free and easy' expressions suited to conversation and informal writing),

contractions ('didn't' = 'did not', and so on);
abbreviations;
slang.

(d) Reported Speech

The language of summary is *impersonal*. Therefore, you must *not* use direct speech. Any direct speech in the passage that contributes to the essential meaning must be turned into *reported* ('indirect') speech in the summary.

Direct speech is a *direct representation* in writing of the words *actually spoken*. Reported speech is a *report* in writing of what was said.

Direct speech	*Reported (indirect) speech*
Jones said, 'I shall be forced to resign.'	Jones said that he would be forced to resign.
(Quotation marks round the words actually spoken.)	*(No quotation marks, because no words are actually spoken.)*

(i) *The Rules*

1. A 'saying' verb followed by 'that' introduces reported speech. The use of an *expressive* 'saying' verb helps to convey the tone and 'flavour' of the speech being reported.

   EXAMPLE

   The customer *maintained* that the goods were faulty when delivered.

2. The tense of the 'saying' verb governs the tenses of the verbs that follow. When the 'saying' verb is in the past tense, the other verbs must also be in the past tense. When the 'saying' verb is in the present tense, the other verbs must be adjusted to fit the sense.

   EXAMPLES

   (i) The witness *declared* that he *had* often heard the accused threaten to set fire to the factory and that he *had* not been in any doubt that the threats *were* serious.

   (ii) Our agent in Brussels *reports* that the new regulations *will* favour our products and that he *foresees* a steadily growing market.

3. All pronouns and possessive adjectives must be in the third person: *I* becomes *he/she; we* becomes *they; my* becomes *his/her*; and so on.

   EXAMPLE

   (*Direct speech*)   The retiring president said, 'I am grateful for the support that I have always received from you, the officers of the association. Your help and friendship will remain a precious memory.'
   (*Reported speech*)   The retiring president expressed *his* gratitude for the support that *he* had received from the officers of the association, adding that *their* help and friendship would remain a precious memory.

4. All expressions indicating nearness in place and time in direct speech are 'distanced' in reported speech: *here* becomes *there; this* becomes *that; today* becomes *that day*; and so on.

(*Direct speech*)   Councillor Brown said, 'My supporters have not sent me here to prolong these conditions. They expect decisive action before this year is out.'

(*Reported speech*)   Councillor Brown said that his supporters had not sent him *there* to prolong *those* conditions. They expected decisive action before *that* year was out.

5. Colloquialisms, contractions and slang expressions used in direct speech must be removed in reported speech. If they contribute to the essential meaning, a formal equivalent must be substituted.

EXAMPLE

(*Direct speech*)   At this point, the sergeant blew his top. 'Don't dodge the question!' he yelled at the suspect.

(*Reported speech*)   The sergeant now angrily accused the suspect of being evasive.

6. As the examples have made clear, quotation marks must never be used in reported speech.

The following demonstration gathers together all the rules. Note that a rearrangement of the order of the original passage helps to condense the material. Note, too, the use of compendious words and the way in which the 'flavour' of the direct speech is reflected in the shortened version.

Direct speech

'May all the plagues of Hades fall upon you!' the furious Hassan shouted at the trembling courier. 'You arrive with a message from my brother, asking for instant help, and I find that you have been over a week on the way. This letter should have been in my possession last Tuesday at the latest. I've half a mind to string you up with my own hands!'

'Pardon your wretched slave, pardon!' howled the distraught courier. 'The river at the frontier was in high flood and I could by no means cross until the waters subsided. You know how swift and faithful I have been in your service for many a long year.'

Shortened version in reported speech

Hassan cursed the terrified messenger and threatened him with execution, saying that his brother's request for immediate help, which should have arrived no later than the previous Tuesday, had taken over a week to deliver. Begging for mercy and reminding Hassan of his past services, the messenger protested that he had been delayed by a flooded river.

4.8 Work out 1: Step by Step

Write a summary of the following passage in good continuous prose, using not more than 120 words. State at the end of your summary the number of words you have used. The passage contains 348 words.

When social historians look back, they will be astonished at our almost obsessive concern with sufficient supplies of energy. Our planet is, after all, one vast system of energy. The sun's rays that fall on the roads of North America contain more energy than all the fossil fuel used each year in the whole world. The winds that rage and whisper round the planet are a vast energy reserve caused by unequal solar heating of blazing tropics and arctic poles.

Nor should we forget the energy locked up in plants. Indeed, in some developing lands, ninety per cent of the energy is derived from wood. Experimentally, a U.S. Naval Undersea Centre has an ocean-farm project cultivating seaweed. The hope is that the solar energy captured by the plant on an ocean-farm of, say, 470 square miles could theoretically be converted into as much natural gas as is consumed in America at present. All in all, the fear of running out of energy must be said to have a social, not a rational base. Modern citizens simply do not see that their whole life is surrounded by a variety of energy reserves which not only exceed present sources but have a further advantage that they are not exhausted by use. A ton of oil burnt is a ton lost. A ton of seaweed will be growing again next year. Even more reliably, the sun will rise and release an annual 1.5 quadrillion megawatt hours of energy. There can be no running out of such resources.

But can they be harnessed? A tornado is a fine exhibit of energy unleashed but it is hardly a useful one. The fundamental question with all renewable sources of energy is how to develop the technologies for using and storing them at reasonable cost. Perhaps the first need is for citizens to open the eyes of their imagination and conceive of energy in new shapes, forms and sizes. If they do, they will find that the technologies *are* available, *will* become cheaper, and *could* even lead to a more civilised mode of existence.

Barbara Ward

(a) **Step 1**

Discover the theme. Make a brief statement of the gist of the passage.

> Writer argues that our worries about supplies of energy are unnecessary, since nature provides abundant renewable supplies if we learn how to tap them.

(*Notes:* (i) Objective statement, beginning with formula ('Writer argues that . . .'). (ii) Own words used.)

(b) **Step 2**

Read passage again, slowly and carefully. Jot down (or underline in passage) expressions that highlight writer's ideas/views/aims. Get to heart of subject matter.

> they will be astonished/our almost obsessive concern/Our planet . . . vast system of energy/fear of running out of energy . . . social . . . not rational/ simply do not see . . . whole life surrounded . . . energy reserves/exceed present sources . . . not exhausted by use/no running out of such resources/ can they be harnessed?/fundamental question . . . to develop the technologies/open the eyes of their imagination/conceive of energy in new shapes/ technologies *are* available/*will* become cheaper/*could* lead to a more civilised mode of existence

(*Notes:* (i) Writer believes people misunderstand true position. (ii) Uses facts to back this up. (iii) Wants to persuade people to look at position differently. (iv) All those points made clear by scrupulous examination of *what* writer says and *how* it is said.)

(c) Step 3

Keeping statement of theme in mind, make skeleton outline of key points.

1. . . . social historians . . . will be astonished at our almost obsessive concern with sufficient supplies of energy.
2. Our planet is . . . one vast system of energy.
3. All in all, fear of running out of energy must be said to have a social, not a rational base.
4. Modern citizens simply do not see . . . not exhausted by use.
5. There can be no running out of such resources.
6. But can they be harnessed?
7. The fundamental question . . . reasonable cost.
8. Perhaps the first need is for citizens to open the eyes of their imagination . . . energy in new shapes, forms and sizes.
9. If they do . . . more civilised mode of existence.

(*Notes:* (i) *Only* key points included. All supporting points and illustrative examples omitted (e.g. 'The sun's rays . . . the whole world'/'The winds . . . arctic poles'/'A ton of seaweed . . . next year'). (ii) This effects a considerable reduction of the original material; but there are nine major points, so condensed writing will be required. (iii) *Question*: How vital is 'social historians' point? Not sure, so include *at this stage*.)

(d) Step 4

Make plan for summary. Base plan on list of key points. Use own words in plan as far as possible and include sufficient detail to be able to write a draft of the summary without referring to the passage.

1. Future social historians will be very surprised by our constant worries about not having enough energy resources.
2. Since the planet is a huge reservoir of energy, it is not reasonable to be afraid of running out of energy. There must be a social reason for our fears.
3. People today do not see that there are many different sources of energy all around them. These sources are not only greater than those now used, but they cannot be used up because they constantly grow again or they are permanent forces.
4. There are technical problems of how to make use of these sources economically, but the chief problem is getting people to use their imagination and think about energy in new ways.
5. If they can manage to do that, they will see that we have the techniques to exploit the natural resources and that they will get cheaper and could make life more civilised.

(*Notes:* (i) The plan is based on the key points, but it 'telescopes' some of them: nine key points become a five-point plan. (ii) There is a lot of repetition of words in the plan (e.g. *energy/sources*) and this must be removed in the draft. The detail of the plan is important; polishing comes later. (iii) A good deal of rephrasing will be needed − compendious words must be found to boil down the meaning of some straggling expressions which waste words. (iv) Connecting phrases and linking words will be needed to turn the separate points of the plan into a piece of good, continuous prose.*)*

(e) Step 5

Write a draft of the summary, working from the plan. Refer to the passage *only* if stuck; but it should not be necessary to do so.

> Future social historians will be very surprised by our constant worries about not having enough energy resources. Since the planet is a huge reservoir of energy, it is not reasonable to be afraid of running out. There must be a social reason for our fears. People today do not see that there are many different sources of energy all around them and that these are not only greater than those now used, but they cannot be exhausted because they grow again or they are permanent forces. There are technical problems of how to use them economically, but the first necessity is for people to use their imagination and think about these new forms of energy. If they do that, they will realise that we have the essential technologies and that they will become cheaper and could make life more civilised.

(f) Step 6

Prune and polish the draft.

(i) *Word count* The word limit is 'not more than 120 words' and there are 139 words in the draft. Hard pruning is required: 19 surplus words make the draft 15% too long!

(ii) *Look for unnecessary material* First, check the 'social historians' point listed as 'doubtful' at Step 3. Further thought shows that it ties in with 'a *social* reason', so it makes an important point and must stay. All the other material seems essential, so words cannot be saved by pruning the subject matter.

(iii) *Look for wasted words* The language of the draft needs to be much tighter in construction and more condensed in expression. For example: '. . . it is not reasonable to be afraid of running out'/'. . . because they grow again or they are permanent forces'. The first is loose; the second is both loose and ambiguous. Disciplined rewriting will save words and put the meaning across much more crisply.

(iv) *Look for badly chosen words* One leaps out at once: *reservoir*. There is nothing wrong with the word itself, of course, but *in this context* it seems to suggest that the natural energy sources are all to do with water-power; and that is *not* what the writer says. Again, is there confusion in the use of *techniques/technologies*? Does 'very surprised' give the right 'feel'? Is it strong enough?

(v) *Is the draft a connected and readable piece of prose?* The last two sentences are not linked firmly enough to bring out their logical connection. Apart from that, the 'flow' of the draft seems satisfactory. The ideas and the argument move steadily forwards.

(vi) *Check grammar, punctuation and spelling*

(vii) *Final tests to be applied* Would this summary be readily understood by a reader who had not seen the original passage? Yes. Would it convey to that reader the essential meaning of the passage? Yes.

(g) Step 7

Write final version.

(i) *Head* the summary with a *suitable* (brief, plain, accurate) *title*.

(ii) *Write out* the final version in your best and *clearest* handwriting, remembering to incorporate all the improvements of Step 6.

(iii) *State* at the end the *exact* number of words used, *excluding* the title.

THE EARTH'S UNTAPPED AND RENEWABLE ENERGY RESOURCES

Our besetting anxiety about energy supplies will astonish future social historians. Since Earth is itself a huge energy system, our fear that our supplies may fail is not reasonable. Its cause is social. People today are blind to the fact that all around them are different kinds of energy, far greater than those now used. These natural sources of energy can never fail, for they are renewable and, therefore, inexhaustible. There is the problem of how to exploit them economically, but the first necessity is for people to think imaginatively about these new possibilities. Then, they will realise that we have the essential technologies, which will get cheaper and which could make human life more civilised.

(116 words)

4.9 Work out 2 (with Notes)

Summarise this passage in clear, concise English, *using your own words as far as possible*. You may retain words and brief expressions which cannot be accurately or economically replaced. Do *not* take whole sentences from the passage and simply replace key words. Write your summary in about 110 words and state at the end the exact number of words you have used. Spend about 45 minutes on this question.

A man can stand being told that he must submit to a severe surgical operation, or that he has some disease which will shortly kill him, or that he will be a cripple or blind for the rest of his life; dreadful as such tidings must be, we do not find that they unnerve the greater number of mankind; most men, indeed, go coolly enough even to be hanged, but the strongest quail before financial ruin, and the better men they are, the more complete, as a general rule, is their prostration. Suicide is a common consequence of money losses; it is rarely sought as a means of escape from bodily suffering. If we feel that we have a competence at our backs, so that we can die warm and quietly in our beds, with no need to worry about expense, we live our lives out to the dregs, no matter how excruciating our torments. Job probably felt the loss of his flocks and herds more than that of his wife and family, for he could enjoy his flocks and herds without his family, but not his family — not for long — if he had lost all his money. Loss of money indeed is not only the worst pain in itself, but it is the parent of all the others. Let a man have been brought up to a moderate competence, and have no specialty; then let his money be suddenly taken from him, and how long is his health likely to survive the change in all his little ways which loss of money will entail? How long again is the esteem and sympathy of friends likely to survive ruin? People may be very sorry for us, but their attitude towards us hitherto has been based upon the supposition that we were situated thus and thus in money matters; when this breaks down there must be a restatement of the social problem so far as we are concerned; we have been obtaining esteem under false pretences. Granted, then, that the three most serious losses which a man can suffer are those affecting money, health and reputation. Loss of money is far the worst, then comes ill-health, and then loss of reputation; loss of reputation is a bad third, for, if a man keeps health and money unimpaired, it will generally be found that his loss of reputation is due to breaches of parvenu conventions only, and not to violations of those older, better established canons whose authority is unquestionable. In this case a man may grow a new reputation as easily as a lobster grows a new claw, or, if he have health and money, may thrive in great peace of mind without any reputation at all. The only chance for a man who has lost his money is that he shall still be young enough to stand uprooting and transplanting without more than temporary derangement.

Samuel Butler, *The Way of All Flesh*

LOSS OF MONEY IS THE WORST OF MISFORTUNES

The prospect of a major operation, fatal illness or crippling disability is more courageously borne than financial disaster. Indeed, that worst of sufferings, loss of money, is followed by all other miseries. Health is lost because habitual comforts are removed. Friendships and social regard are destroyed because sympathy alone cannot sustain former relationships once they are seen to have been based on false financial assumptions. Loss of money is worse than loss of either health or social standing. With money, illness is endurable. Lost social standing is easily recovered or readily dispensed with if money and health are preserved, but financial ruin can be survived only by those young enough to start again elsewhere.

(113 *words*)

NOTES

1. The opinions expressed in the passage are contentious, deliberately challenging the usual points of view on these matters. The summariser must not be jolted out of an objective approach to the task. The writer's opinions must be restated accurately, without alteration or comment.
2. Because the writing is itself condensed, the word limit is hard to observe. In fact, the summary is just below the upper limit ('about 110 words' allows a plus or minus of 5 words). The material omitted consisted mainly of supporting points and illustrative examples (e.g. 'Suicide is . . .'/'Job probably felt the loss . . .'/'as easily as a lobster. . .').
3. Compendious words (e.g. 'crippling disability'/'habitual comforts'/'financial assumptions') were used to encapsulate longer but essential statements. Useful tips can be learnt by comparing the vocabulary of the summary closely with that of the original passage.
4. An attempt was made to convey the ironical tone of the writing (e.g. 'Lost social status . . . *easily recovered . . . readily dispensed with* . . .'), though the need to condense inevitably diluted the full flavour.
5. Some rearrangement of the order in which the key points are presented in the passage helped to establish coherence in the summary. For example, 'With money, illness is endurable' encapsulates the meaning of 43 words in the passage ('If we feel . . . torments.') *and* moves the point to a later stage in the summary than in the passage. Such shifts in the order are often necessary, for the coherence established in a longer piece of writing may be destroyed unless adjustments are made to preserve it in a small-scale version of the essential meaning.

4.10 Summary and Directed Writing

Questions combining summary with directed writing are often set. They are primarily tests of summarising skills, but they also require candidates to write 'to order' in accordance with very detailed instructions. First, *the specified aspects* of the subject matter must be *abstracted* from the passage and *restated* (selective summary). Second, the summarised material must be written up *in a form and style appropriate to a given writing assignment* (directed writing). Revise Chapter 2 before proceeding.

(a) Typical Instructions: Summary and Directed Writing

1. The following passage is an account of Napoleon's campaigns in Italy, Austria and Russia. In **two** paragraphs, restate *in your own words*: (i) the explanations given of his success in his earlier campaigns; and (ii) the evidence given to prove that when campaigning in Russia, he neglected to apply his own previous experience. You are to write in good clear English and in a style *appropriate* to a history essay. Use *only* the material supplied in paragraphs 2, 3 and 4. Your answer as a whole – i.e. both paragraphs together – *must not exceed 150 words*. State at the end the exact number of words you have used. Do not spend more than 40 minutes on this question.

    (20 marks)

2. *(Read the instructions very carefully before beginning your work.)*

    The following passage describes some of the effects of the Blitz on London in 1940.

    Write an article for a school or college magazine which sets out to describe clearly the difficulties Londoners faced during the Blitz.

    Your article should reflect your admiration of Londoners' behaviour. *Use only the information contained in the passage*; do not attempt to summarise everything in it but select only the material you need for your account. *Use your own words as far as possible*, although you may retain words and expressions which cannot be accurately or economically replaced. *The complete article should not exceed 160 words altogether and at the end you must state the exact number of words you have used.*

    Write in an appropriate style and use clear, accurate English.

    Spend not more than 1 hour on this question.

    (30 marks)

The length of those instructions is typical of questions of this kind. You must study them closely and then do *exactly what you have been told to do*. Their complexity is not so frightening when they are broken down into the component parts, as follows.

(b) Selective Summary

Question 1: 'Use only the material supplied in paragraphs 2, 3 and 4.'

Question 2: '. . . do not attempt to summarise everything . . . but select only the material you need for your account.'

The other summary instructions are such as you are familiar with.

Question 1: 'in your own words'/'must not exceed 150 words'/'state at the end the exact number of words you have used'
Question 2: 'Use your own words as far as possible'/'should not exceed 160 words altogether'/'state the exact number of words you have used'

(c) Directed Writing

The instructions governing the performance of this part of the question introduce features *not* found in 'straight' summary, and it is here that candidates are most likely to depart from their 'brief'. If you analyse the instructions, you will see that they break down into these two parts.

(i) *The Form of the Directed Writing*

Question 1: 'In two paragraphs . . .'

The total word limit is 150 and that must be apportioned between the two paragraphs. Generally speaking, they will be of roughly equal length, *but that depends on how the essential material is apportioned in the passage.* Each paragraph must deal with *one* and with *only* one aspect of the specified subject matter. Therefore, in the example given, the first will be longer than the second *if* the passage gives more space and more *weight* to Napoleon's earlier successes than to his failure in Russia. (Or, of course, the other way round.)

(ii) *The Style of the Directed Writing*

The basic requirement, of course, is to write clear, correct sentences, cogently linked to form a continuous and connected piece of prose; but direct writing makes a particular demand: the *style* in which you write must be *appropriate* to the particular task set.

Question 1: '. . . in a style appropriate to a history essay . . .'
Question 2: '. . . an article for a school or college magazine . . . Your article should reflect your admiration of Londoners' behaviour . . . Write in an appropriate style . . .'
(Notice that the *impersonal* style appropriate to many directed writing assignments would be a *fault* here. You must read every detail of the instructions very carefully to be sure that you are obeying them to the letter.)

Those are just two examples of the requirements of 'directed style'. You may be instructed to write up the summarised material 'in a style appropriate to a letter to the editor of your local paper'/'in a style appropriate to a letter to the principal of your college'/'in a style appropriate to a diary entry recording those events', and so on.

When the style required is not explicitly described, you must think out and write in the style that is appropriate to the given task: 'an article for your local paper'/'a report to the committee', and so on.

- Even though your summary is accurate, you will lose marks if its style is not appropriate.

4.11 Work out 3 (with Notes)

The passage below deals with certain aspects of vandalism. Using only the material contained in this passage write an article, in *two* paragraphs, for your local newspaper, setting out:

(*a*) the serious effects of vandalism; *and*
(*b*) the possible causes of vandalism.

Your two paragraphs should correspond to (*a*) and (*b*) above. *Do not add ideas of your own* but select and arrange material from the passage. *Write in good, clear, accurate English and use an appropriate style.* Your article should be in your own words as far as possible; do not copy out whole sentences or expressions.

Your final article should not exceed 175 words altogether; at the end you must state the exact number of words you have used.

You should spend about **1 hour** on this question.

(30 marks)

A feature of the last twenty years has been the rapid increase in vandalism in Britain. Vandalism itself, however, is not a new phenomenon, since through the ages there have always been those who preferred to destroy rather than to create; even the word 'vandalism' owes its origin to a race of barbarians
5   who devastated parts of Europe as long ago as the fifth century.
    The mis-spelt graffiti, uprooted newly planted trees, abused train carriages, smashed phone boxes, and bus-stop shelters recklessly destroyed spoil the environment and deprive the public of their amenities for which they have paid. Those who perpetrate such outrages seem to be without any self-
10   discipline and show scant respect for the rights of their fellow-citizens. Moreover, they increase the taxes and the rates that they themselves have to pay.
    Some argue that the vandals feel rejected by society with its predominant middle-class standards and have far too much time on their hands. It is conceivable that poor housing and squalid living conditions may lead to this
15   anti-social behaviour, but, if these are the principal causes, it needs to be explained why most of the socially deprived are not vandals. One thing is certain: in order to repair the damage done, local rates have to be increased and national levels of income tax have to take account of the increased expenditure needed to maintain services. Scarce material resources and human
20   skills are unnecessarily wasted in the attempts to reduce the danger to life and property caused by vandalism.
    Those who practise vandalism are often of poor education and without parental control. They would defend their behaviour, perhaps, by arguing that society provides them with few youth clubs and recreational activities
25   and that they have nothing better to do with their time. The truth is that they are insecure and feel they must put on a show of bravado in order to impress their peers and members of the gang. Perhaps the growth of gangs and movements such as the punks, mods and greasers has played a major rôle in the increase in vandalism.
30   It is a pity that the development of new schools and improved health

services has been jeopardised because of a lack of financial resources when these very resources are being squandered in repairing the damage and making good the destruction caused by vandalism. The situation poses a real challenge to those responsible for educating the young or maintaining law

35 and order. The evidence everywhere of vandalism demeans the standing of the country in the eyes of foreign visitors who are amazed to read the obscene remarks scrawled illiterately across walls or step through the broken glass of street lamps smashed 'just for a joke'. The pride, too, of local people in their environment is being eroded.

40 Some of the socially minded politicians give up their efforts to improve the quality of life in the face of such mindless destruction; imaginative designers and developers are reduced to designing amenities which are vandal-proof rather than beautiful and attractive. The older generation, with some justification, blames the younger one and age-groups become even more

45 sharply divided. Some local authorities have become reluctant to improve recreational and social facilities because of vandalism, which is aided and abetted, it is sometimes suggested, by the reduction in police surveillance and an apparently uninterested public which looks the other way when it sees vandals at work. Too many are content to blame the invention of the

50 aerosol can and the felt-tip pen, which make it easy to vandalise buildings and other people's property. Ostrich-like, many ignore what they see and hope that the trail of devastation will cease with the coming of a new generation.

(L., January 1983)

NOTES

1. Start work by abstracting the material asked for, listing each key point under one or the other of the headings provided in the instructions: (a) the serious effects of vandalism; *and* (b) the possible causes of vandalism. Use of the given headings ensures that all the material selected is *relevant* to the set task. Restate each key point *in your own words* as you note it down. Have an eye to the style required by the assignment (an article for your local newspaper) as you reword the points.

2. In the passage the relevant key points may be divided from each other. For example, the physical damage detailed in lines 6 and 7 is a serious effect of vandalism. So are the reactions of politicians, designers, developers, older people and local authorities described in lines 40–46. Having found one key point bearing on one of the set topics, do not conclude that you have finished with that topic. Keep looking.

3. When you are sure that you have abstracted *all* the relevant material and listed each key point under its correct heading, read through the passage again. Have you included any non-essential material? (For example, nothing in the first paragraph is relevant to the task you have been given; nor is the second sentence of the second paragraph.)

4. You are now ready to plan the article you must write. You know its shape: two paragraphs. As you plan, think out a sensible way of linking the two. Your paragraphs must be connected. Each is part of the *same* article, although each deals with a distinct aspect of the shared subject matter.

5. You must also look for a way of making each paragraph *coherent*. (All the items must 'stick together'.) Perhaps you see that the separate items fall into

groups? (For example, *paragraph (a)*: group 1, physical effects; group 2, financial burdens; group 3, less tangible effects — reactions of foreign visitors — erosion of local pride — widening of generation gap; and so on.) If you can hit on coherent groupings, you will be able to present the material in a logical sequence.

6. Now think hard about the style. An article for a local newspaper must be interesting and informative. If you have made an accurate selection of material from the passage, your article will be informative, but unless you present it in an interesting way, the information will not make an impact on your readers. Try to write *plain* but *lively* English. Your language must be *condensed* (or you will exceed the permitted number of words) and it must be easily understood. The *style* in which you write must not get in the way of *what* you write. It must be a smooth-running vehicle to carry information to your readers.

7. Finally, an article must have a *title*. Make it eye-catching (but *not* 'gimmicky'), brief, crisp, accurate. The title does *not count* towards the word limit.

LIFE IN VANDALISED BRITAIN

The visible effects of vandalism are sickeningly evident in our damaged surroundings. To repair the havoc, rates and taxes are increased and scarce funds diverted from pinched education and health services. Less tangible effects also diminish the quality of life. Foreign visitors think poorly of us. Local pride is worn down and local authorities hesitate to embark on amenities. Caring politicians lose heart. Innovative design and development must concentrate on security to the improverishment of aesthetics.

Conflicting theories explore the causes of this pernicious disease. Superficially, some blame the vandals' much-used tools, the aerosol can and the felt-tip pen. Public apathy and the removal of the bobby from the beat play their part. The alienation of vandals from a society whose values and advantages they cannot share undoubtedly contributes. Yet does not explain why most who are poor, badly housed and ill-educated do not turn to vandalism in protest. Certainly, insecurity and the consequent bravado — intended to impress fellow-members of proliferating anti-social gangs — underlies conduct that corrodes our national life.

(174 words)

COMMENTS AND QUESTIONS

1. The *title* was chosen to attract a newspaper reader's attention without being sensational or inaccurate. Can you improve on it?
2. In draft, the article overran the word limit. It was *pruned* in the following places:

Draft
The visible effects of vandalism are apparent in our damaged surroundings, from illiterate scrawls on buildings to wrecked bus-stop shelters.

Some simply blame the aerosol can and the felt-tip pen because they are often used by vandals, but this is surely to confuse means with reasons.

Final version
The visible effects of vandalism are sickeningly evident in our damaged surroundings.

Superficially, some blame the vandals' much-used tools, the aerosol can and the felt-tip pen.

It is often said, with some justice, that vandals feel shut out from the prevailing standards and occupations of a dominantly middle-class society.	The alienation of vandals from a society whose values and advantages they cannot share undoubtedly contributes.
Yet that does not explain . . .	Yet does not explain . . .
Certain it is that insecurity and its resulting bravado . . .	Certainly, insecurity and the consequent bravado . . .

3. The *order* in which the key points are presented in the passage was *extensively rearranged* in the article, partly because the imposed two-paragraph structure dictated this and partly because the passage itself is not remarkable for its coherence. Compare the two closely, trying to appreciate the reasons for the changes and weighing their effectiveness.

4. Consider the *style* in which the article is written. Remember that the given task was to write in a style *appropriate to a local newspaper*. Therefore, the relevant subject matter had to be presented in a lively, readable way without altering or distorting the information supplied in the passage. Note (and comment on) the use of emotive expressions — for example: 'sickeningly'/ 'pernicious disease'/'anti-social'/'corrodes our national life'. Remember that a style that is appropriate to *this* directed writing assignment would not be appropriate to another. (Nor, of course, to 'straight' summary.) If, for example, the required writing had to take the form of a report to a committee, then 'the removal of the bobby from the beat' would *not* be an appropriate rewording of 'the reduction in police surveillance'. When considering the effectiveness of the style, look closely at these points: (i) use of compendious words; (ii) compression of sentences to save words and tighten up the writing; (iii) the linking of the two paragraphs; (iv) the vocabulary. Finally, ask yourself whether the article would be easily understood by the readers of your local newspaper. If you think that you can improve its readability, do so; but do *not* exceed the word limit and do *not* omit or tamper with any of the essential information.

4.12 Test Papers in Summary

(*You will find suggested answers on pages 167–168, but do not look at them until you have completed your own summaries. Then study them closely, making detailed comparisons with your own work.*)

1. Make a summary of the following passage in not more than 100 words. Write good continuous prose. Provide a suitable title and state at the end the exact number of words you have used, *excluding* the title. You should spend about 40 minutes on this question. **(20 marks)**

Prospective students hoping to start this autumn should already be involved in making inquiries about getting grants from the local education authorities. The best advice is to start the process in January; there is certainly no need to wait until you have received an unconditional offer of a place at college or university. The rules are quite complicated and the forms which have to be filled in by the student (and, probably, his or her parents or spouse) will help to determine the nature and amount of the grant which can be expected.

These will depend on (a) the nature of the course to be followed, (b) the student's personal history (he or she must have been treated as an ordinary UK resident for three years and must not have received any previous grant for higher education) and (c) the financial status of the people involved.

Government regulations require LEAs to pay **mandatory grants** ('awards') to young people who are about to take first degrees at universities, polytechnics or colleges, as well as Diplomas of Higher education, B.TEC (Business and Technical Education Council), Higher or Higher National Diplomas, initial teacher training courses leading to PGCE or Art Teachers' Certificates or Diplomas, and a range of other eligible courses about which information can be obtained from the local education authority or direct from the Department of Education and Science.

Discretionary Awards are for those who take a variety of other courses and are made by LEAs in accordance with policies which are reconsidered at the beginning of each financial year.

They vary and some are competitive in terms of exam results. Wherever finite and diminishing public funds are concerned, it's best to get in early. It is worth noting, however, that if an LEA decides to offer a discretionary grant to someone who doesn't fill all the requirements of the Education Act (about residence, etc.) but has been accepted for a degree-equivalent course the award must be the same amount as a mandatory one.

Mandatory awards are expected to cover course fees, examination fees and compulsory contributions to students' unions; these sums are usually paid directly to the educational institution. At present, the undergraduate actually receives reasonable travel costs over £50 (this system is under review) and a maintenance grant, the amount of which is determined by the 'residual income' of the student, his or her parents, or possibly spouse. Deductions are made on a sliding scale when the undergraduate's own residual income is over £345 per annum, or that of the parents exceeds £7100. A minimum grant of about £410 is always payable. Special allowances will be paid to mature students and those with dependents and a grant of up to £520 may be paid at the discretion of the local authorities to students with disabilities.

The only people who can draw social security benefits during term time are single parents and handicapped people.

Education Guardian (April 1984)

---

2. Summarise the passage below in clear continuous English, using your own words as far as possible. Your summary should be about 150 words in length and you must state at the end the exact number of words you have used. Remember to provide a suitable title. Spend not more than 1 hour on this question. **(30 marks)**

In politics, again, it is almost a commonplace that a party of order and stability and a party of progress or reform are both necessary elements of a healthy state of political life; until one or the other shall so have enlarged its mental grasp as to be a party equally of order and of progress, knowing and distinguishing what is fit to be preserved from what ought to be swept away. Each of these modes of thinking derives its utility from the deficiencies of the other; but it is in a great measure the opposition of the other that keeps each within the limits of reason and sanity. Unless opinions favourable to democracy and to aristocracy, to property and to equality, to co-operation and to competition, to luxury and to abstinence, to sociality and to individuality, to liberty and to discipline, and all the other standing antagonisms of practical life are expressed with equal freedom and enforced and defended with equal talent and energy, there is no chance of both elements obtaining their due; one scale is sure to go up, and the other down. Truth, in the great practical concerns of life, is so much a question of the reconciling and combining of opposites that very few have minds sufficiently capacious and impartial to make the adjustment with an approach to correctness and it has to be made by the rough process of a struggle between combatants fighting under hostile banners. On any of the great open questions just enumerated, if either of the two opinions has a better claim than the other, not merely to be tolerated, but to be encouraged and countenanced, it is the one which happens at the particular time and place to be in a minority. That is the opinion which, for the time being, represents the neglected interests, the side of human well-being which is in danger of obtaining less than its share. I am aware that there is not, in this country, any intolerance of differences of opinion on most of these topics. They are adduced to show, by admitted and multiplied examples, the universality of the fact that only through diversity of opinion is there, in the existing state of the human intellect, a chance of fair play to all sides of the truth. When there are persons to be found who form an exception to the apparent unanimity of the world on any subject, even if the world is in the right, it is always probable that dissentients have something worth hearing to say for themselves and that truth would lose something by their silence.

John Stuart Mill, *On Liberty*

---

3. *Read the following instructions carefully before beginning your work.*
Write an article for inclusion in a local newspaper deliberately setting out to persuade the readers that noise is a real threat to everyone in today's society. It should consist of *three* paragraphs, as follows:
   (a) deploring the potential dangers of noise in modern life;
   (b) suggesting how the dangers can be reduced or eliminated;
   (c) admitting that it is neither possible nor desirable to eliminate all noise in life.

Your article should be between 170 and 200 words in length; at the end you must state accurately the number of words you have used.

Use only the information given in the passage and the table below; do not attempt to use all the details and examples given but select and arrange the material best able to make your article really persuasive. Use your own words as far as possible, although you may retain words and expressions which cannot be accurately or economically replaced.

As you write, bear in mind the kind of readers who take a local newspaper and your own attitude as a writer seeking to persuade others. You should use an appropriate style but you must write in clear and accurate English.

Remember that your work will be assessed on the number of facts you use and their accuracy, as well as on the way you direct your writing towards your readers.

Spend about 1 hour on this question. **(30 marks)**

NOISE

The unit in which noise is measured is known as the *decibel* (db). The threshold of hearing, that is the point at which man has the capacity to hear, is at zero decibels; somewhere around 180 decibels is the lethal level. Rats exposed to levels approaching this turn cannibalistic and eventually die from heart failure; short exposure to 150 db can permanently damage the human ear and cause excruciating pain; slightly lower levels can cause temporary deafness and if there is a long-term exposure to noise above that found near a motorway where traffic is continually passing there is a grave risk of permanent hearing-loss and nervous exhaustion.

Table: Common noise levels

Jet aircraft at 200 feet near a large airport	150 db
Pneumatic drill	130 db
A 'hard-rock' band	115 db
Power mower; accelerating motor-cycle	110 db
Food mixer (2 to 4 feet away)	100 db
Underground train (inside)	100 db
Heavy city traffic	90 db
Passenger cars on nearby motorway	65–86 db
Normal conversation	60–70 db
Telephone conversation	60 db
Quiet residential street noises	50 db
Tick of watch (2 feet away)	30 db
Leaves rustling in the wind	10 db

It is best, of course, to minimise the potential danger from noise at its source; much of it is within our control in the kitchen, living-room, and the play or work-room. Dishwashers, food-mixers, tumble-driers, electric drills and washing-machines can raise the noise level to dangerous levels but if they are placed or operated in rooms separate from the living accommodation the noise level is reduced or even eliminated; if the machines are stood on sound-absorbing pads the nuisance and risk are diminished. The acoustic power of a full orchestra is rarely more than ten watts and yet music systems used in some living-rooms can produce sounds at more than a hundred watts of audio power. Young people, too, often feel it necessary to amplify the sound of their musical instruments and they also plug their transistor outputs into their ears with the volume turned up at full blast. Perhaps they want to follow Beethoven into deafness.

Most television sets are turned up to dangerous levels while the viewers' attention is distracted from the threat by the picture flashing in front of their eyes. Noisy dustbins, squeaky gates or machines strangers to the oil-can, loud lawn-mowers shattering the peace of suburban afternoons, honking car-horns, and children reliving the latest TV Western in the street, all contribute to the noise pollution of our own time. Curtains, carpets, large furniture and wall-fittings help to reduce noise levels within the home by their deadening effect; outdoors, trees and shrubs, high walls and fences act as noise-breaks; even lawns and flower-borders make the environment quieter just as carpets reduce sound levels indoors.

However, there are those who think that noise is preferable to washing clothes by hand, cutting grass with scythes and walking long distances. Noise, they argue, is a necessary part of man's advance. One man's noise is another's sweet melody. Some think that a crying baby, the explosive roar from a motor-bike's exhaust, the throbbing beat of a pop-group or the rattling of bells as cows slither down idyllic mountain slopes are all beautiful sounds. The living world is full of sounds; only the world of the dead is uniformly silent.

(L., June 1983)

5 Using Words

Some examining boards set questions specifically designed as tests of correct English, basing them on particular points of vocabulary, usage (or grammar), style, punctuation and spelling. All these points are covered in Chapters 5–9 before being thoroughly tested in Chapter 10 by a wide-ranging series of typical examination questions. (Answers are provided at the end of the book.)

The particular points on which the examiners concentrate are carefully chosen as indicators of *the standards of written English which all candidates are expected to reach*. As earlier chapters have demonstrated, all the 'big' questions in all the papers (composition, practical writing, comprehension and summary) are tests of your competence in written English. So — even if your examining board does not set additional language questions — you must not neglect the topics dealt with in Chapters 5–9, nor must you dodge the labour of working through all the questions in Chapter 10. You need the guidance and practice provided there to bring your written English up to the level required by all the boards and made very clear in this representative instruction to candidates:

- Remember that this is an examination in English Language. It is important not only to answer the questions correctly but also to write *all* your answers in clear, careful English with proper attention to appropriate style and vocabulary, correct grammar, punctuation and spelling.

5.1 Enlarging Your Vocabulary

Your vocabulary is the range of words that you can use. The larger that range, the better your work in all the English Language questions — and the better your performance in all your other subjects.

To enlarge your vocabulary you must be interested in words: their meaning, derivation, pronunciation and spelling. While preparing for your examination (and afterwards, I hope) pay attention to every new word you meet: words that you have not heard or seen before; *and* familiar words used in ways that are new to you.

Get the dictionary habit. First, you must learn the 'signalling' system of abbreviations, different typefaces, brackets, and so on, that your dictionary uses to convey a lot of information in a small space. Different dictionaries use different 'codes', so, to get full help from the entries, you must study the 'preliminary matter' in your own dictionary. As this example shows, 'knowing' a word involves more than simple definition, although that is the essential starting point.

> **summary**, a. & n. Compendious, brief, dispensing with needless details, done with dispatch, (a *s. account*; *s. methods*, *jurisdiction*, etc.); hence **summarily**, adv. (N.) brief account, abridgement, epitome. [n. f. L. *summarium*.]

To build up a vocabulary that will be adequate for your examination, you must make frequent and proper use of your dictionary.

5.2 Meaning and Context

Examination questions, especially in comprehension tests, often draw your attention to the fact that the meaning of a word depends very largely on the context in which it is used. A typical instruction reads like this: 'Explain the meaning of the following words and expressions *as they are used in the passage*'.

- Remember that a word can have several meanings and can act as different parts of speech, *according to the context in which it is used*.

For example, my dictionary tells me that the word *pat* can be used as a noun, as a verb, as an adjective or as an adverb. It can mean (among other things): a stroke or tap; a small mass formed by patting; to strike gently; opportune(ly); apposite(ly). In all the following sentences, *pat* is correctly used but it means something different in each.

1. Get me a pat of butter.
2. Don't pat yourself on the back.
3. The startling news came pat to their purpose.
4. Question him again if you like, but he has his story pat.

Context must always be considered before meaning can be established. Your dictionary gives you as many meanings as it has space for and indicates the common ways of using a word, but it cannot tell you which particular meaning and which particular usage you need. Your study of the context provides the solution.

5.3 Prefixes and Suffixes

- A **prefix** is a letter or a group of letters joined on at the *beginning* of a word to change its meaning and to make a new word (*un* + 'happy' = unhappy).
- A **suffix** is a letter or a group of letters joined on at the *end* of a word to change its meaning and to make a new word ('friend' + *ship* = friendship).

You must learn to recognise the meaning and the function of the prefixes and suffixes most frequently found in English. Ignorance will cost you marks in the 'big' questions as well as in the language tests. For example, you must know the difference between *ante*date and *anti*dote; between *ab*ject, *in*ject, *ob*ject, *pro*ject and *re*ject; between occu*pancy* and occu*pant*; between wood*ed* and wood*en*.

The language tests in Chapter 10 provide useful practice, but you must reinforce them with work along the lines suggested in Section 5.1.

5.4 Synonyms, Antonyms, Homophones

- **Synonyms** are words having the same (or very nearly the same) meaning. For example: *blend/mixture*; *change/alteration*; *start/begin*.

But when you need to substitute one word for another, as so often in comprehension and summary, you must remember that words are *not* lifeless counters, instantly interchangeable. You have to consider whether the proposed substitute carries the required *shade* of meaning. The following points must be borne in mind.

1. Words often convey feelings as well as ideas; and the feelings associated with

a word are an important part of its meaning. For example, *evil* 'means' *bad* (and *bad* 'means' *evil*) but *evil* carries with it different (and much stronger) feelings than *bad*. The two words cannot simply be interchanged. You could not sensibly write (or say), 'Travelling overnight was an evil decision, for we were tired out when we arrived.' (See Section 5.7.)

2. Very rarely do two words mean exactly the same thing, although they may be close enough in meaning to be interchangeable. You have to be satisfied that the word you choose is precisely right for the particular meaning you want to express. For example, *end* and *finish* are very close in meaning and they may be interchangeable in some contexts, but they may convey quite different senses in other contexts. Compare: 'There was a dead heat at the finish of the Tadcaster Hurdle' with 'The loss of sponsorship funds means the end of the Tadcaster Hurdle'.

3. Words must be appropriate to their context. You have to consider not only the sentence in which a word is to be used, but also the paragraph in which that sentence occurs and — often — the passage as a whole. You have already seen that a particular use of language demands a fitting (appropriate) choice of words (see especially Sections 4.7, 4.10 and 4.11) and you must bear this in mind when selecting synonyms. For example, *respire* 'means' *breathe*, but the two words cannot be freely switched around. There are many contexts in which *breathe* is appropriate but in which *respire* would be inappropriate. Similar considerations apply to *buy/purchase*; *live/reside*; *house/residence*; and to many other synonyms.

- **Antonyms** are words of opposite meaning: *difficult/easy*; *happy/unhappy*; *strong/weak*.

The considerations that apply to the selection of synonyms apply equally to the selection of antonyms. In respect of length, a long journey is the opposite of a short journey. Opposite moral judgements are expressed in the two sentences: 'He is a good man'/'He is a bad man'. *But* is the meaning of 'Those sausages were bad' the opposite of 'Those sausages were good'?

- **Homophones** are words that sound the same or nearly the same, but are spelt differently and have different meanings: *complement/compliment*; *fair/fare*; *gait/gate*; *sail/sale*.

There are a great many of these 'confusables' — a name that epitomises the danger they present to a careless writer.

5.5 Compendious Words

The need to know (and to know how to use) these 'space-savers' was demonstrated in Chapter 4. Essential when summarising, they are invaluable in all uses of written (and spoken) language. They pack a tremendous punch. With a wide range of compendious words in your vocabulary, you can write and speak plain, forceful English, and steer clear of verbosity and the pretentious fluffiness that is death to the language. Many of the tests in Chapter 10 provide practice in substituting compendious words for long-winded expressions. (See also Section 6.5.)

5.6 Literal and Figurative Uses of Language

Figurative use of language is a frequent, useful, colourful element of everyday speech and writing. We are not usually confused by it. When we hear that somebody has been 'spurred on', we do not suppose that a sharp instrument has been applied to his/her sides. We understand that he/she has been impelled to make additional efforts. If 'the books were cooked', we do not suppose that they were boiled in a saucepan or baked in an oven. We understand that the accounts have been falsified.

A common mistake is to employ language figuratively and to make nonsense of it by inserting the word *literally*. ('How did you feel when you heard that you had been selected?' 'Astonished! You could literally have knocked me down with a feather.')

Of course, you would not make that silly mistake, but many people do — and it's catching! The example illustrates too the danger of *cliché* inherent in many popular figurative expressions. (See Section 6.8.)

Comprehension questions frequently require you to distinguish between these two uses of language, for the passages set often include vivid and emotive figurative expressions. (See Section 5.7.) When summarising, any figurative expressions that are essential to the key points must be reworded as literal statements.

Language questions explicitly test your understanding of literal and figurative uses by asking for a demonstration of your ability to handle both. For example:

> *Question*   Select two of the following words and use each in two sentences, literally in the first and figuratively in the second.
> *Answer*
> *fruit*   (i) We were warned of the danger of eating unripe fruit.
> (ii) A handsome cheque was the fruit of six months' work.
> *wooden* (i) In an age of plastics, a wooden dashboard has become a status symbol.
> (ii) His fine voice did not compensate for his wooden movements on stage.

You are not as a rule questioned directly about *figures of speech* but you should learn to recognise the following: alliteration; metaphor; paradox; onomatopoeia; personification; simile. They are in common use, and failure to recognise them causes misunderstanding of content and purpose. Figures of speech often play a major part in conveying the *nuances* of meaning which you must be able to detect in passages set for comprehension and summary.

Again, a question may be worded in a way that presumes your knowledge of these terms. For example: 'Use the following words metaphorically'/'What is the effect of the alliteration in line 23?'/'Bring out in your own words the full force of the simile in the last sentence'.

5.7   The Language of Fact and the Language of Feeling

Words may be used primarily to convey facts and ideas. They may be used primarily to communicate feelings or emotions. The former is described as a *referential* use of words. The latter is described as an *emotive* use of words.

- **Referential** use of language. Words are used as 'labels'. They name and describe things and their attributes. They are used factually and *objectively*. The writer (or speaker) says, in effect, 'I am using language to deal with things as they are.'
- **Emotive** use of language. Words are used to communicate feelings and emotional attitudes. They are used *subjectively*. The writer (or speaker) says, in effect, 'I am using language to communicate my feelings about these matters and I want to persuade you to share those feelings.'

Many words have both a denotation and a connotation. The *denotation* is the 'labelling function' of the word — what the word 'actually means' (to put it very crudely). The *connotation* is the feelings and emotions associated with the word — the 'emotional tones' that it carries with it. For example:

(i) They chose a *blue* car last time. (*denotation* of 'blue' uppermost)
(ii) We felt very *blue* when they left. (*connotation* of 'blue' uppermost)

Denotation is uppermost when words are used literally. Connotation is uppermost when words are used figuratively.

Referential language (stressing *denotation*) is the appropriate language for scientific, factual, practical and discursive writing.

Emotive language (stressing *connotation*) plays a large part in creative, persuasive, impressionistic writing.

Your understanding of these two ways of using words may be directly tested in language questions, particularly by exercises involving literal and figurative expressions. Directed writing and composition are, of course, sustained tests of the ability to use words in ways that are suitable to a particular kind of writing. The explicit instruction 'Write in an appropriate style' is the key to successful directed writing. A composition the style of which is not appropriate to the kind of subject chosen falls at the first hurdle.

5.8 Idiomatic and Proverbial Expressions

An **idiom** is a form of expression (or of grammatical usage) peculiar to a particular language. For example, English idioms using the word *heart* include: 'a person/ cause after one's own heart'; 'with all one's heart'; 'from the bottom of one's heart'; 'break one's heart'; 'by heart'; 'go to one's heart'; 'in good heart'; 'with a heavy heart'; 'know by heart'; 'learn by heart'; 'lose heart'; 'lose one's heart'; 'not find it in one's heart to' . . . . And that is only a selection of 'heart idioms'.

Mastery of its idioms is a sure mark of proficiency in the use of a language. That is why it is so difficult to speak or write a foreign language 'like a native'. We may have the vocabulary we need and know the grammar, but the idioms often defeat us.

Mishandled idioms cost marks in an English Language examination and, although nobody can sit down to learn all the idioms of English just like that, you can prepare yourself for the examination by checking the accuracy of the idioms you hear and read *and* of those you habitually use. Careful listening and reading and the use of reference books (such as Roget's *Thesaurus* and Brewer's *Dictionary of Phrase and Fable*) will increase your range and fluency and help you to guard against blunders such as confusing 'lose heart' with 'lose one's heart' — an increasingly common mistake.

Proverbial expressions, like idioms, are part and parcel (idiom!) of everyday speech and frequently used in written English. Many are centuries old and some, with constant use, have degenerated into clichés (see Section 6.8). Many retain their freshness and vigour and the stock is continually renewed. Again, you have to rely on your sense of style to guide you when writing. Is the expression that you are about to use stale and overworked? (No self-respecting writer could use 'over the moon' or 'sick as a parrot'!) Can you find words *of your own* to say what *you* want to say? If so, use them.

However, you must acquaint yourself with the meaning of the commonest proverbs, any of which may be encountered in a passage set for comprehension or summary. In the language questions, you may be asked to rewrite sentences containing idiomatic and proverbial expressions so that their sense is unchanged when those expressions have been reworded.

5.9 Good Writing

Chapter 6 discusses and illustrates the faults most commonly committed when using words. You will find that each offends against one or more of these basic rules of good writing:

- be plain;
- be direct;
- use no more words than are necessary;
- think hard to find the right word;
- use active verbs rather than passive verbs where you have a choice.

Your written English will reach the standard that the examiners expect if you make a consistent effort to apply those rules every time you write.

6 Misusing Words

The mistakes listed in this chapter are those most frequently made in written English and, therefore, the chief reasons for failure in the extended writing questions. Many of the additional language questions are designed to test your ability to recognise and correct these common misuses of words.

Each mistake is defined and discussed in a separate section, but it is helpful to think about their causes before looking at each of them in turn. They all arise from one or more of these bad habits:

- carelessly or ignorantly using the wrong word;
- using more words than are needed;
- using pompous expressions to sound important;
- using stale, tired words and expressions;
- using language that does not fit the occasion.

Because they have common origins, the faults overlap. For example, writers who use more words than are needed will probably be guilty of tautology or circumlocution, or both at once. *Verbosity* (see Section 6.7) manifests itself in different ways, all of which break the rules of good writing.

6.1 Malapropisms

DEFINITION

A malapropism is a word used in mistake for one that resembles it, often resulting in an unintended comic effect; *always* resulting in nonsense.

EXAMPLES

(i) All newly elected members of the society must attend the *propitiation* ceremony to be held at 6 p.m. next Friday.
(ii) The interviewer lost his temper and accused the shifty politician of *invading* his questions.
(iii) As the excise duty has increased, so have deaths caused by drinking *implicitly* distilled spirits.

COMMENTS

The mistake is as old as language itself, but it takes its name from Mrs Malaprop, a character in R. B. Sheridan's play *The Rivals* (1775). One of her most famous 'malapropisms' neatly demonstrates the mistake: 'a nice derangement (*arrangement*) of epitaphs (*epithets*)'. Shakespeare's character Dogberry (*Much Ado About Nothing*) was a specialist in malapropisms nearly two hundred years earlier than Mrs Malaprop herself: 'You are thought to be the most *senseless* and fit man for the constable of the watch.'

6.2 Tautology

Needlessly saying the same thing more than once in different words (*tauto-* = 'the same').

(i) The guests arrived *in succession one after the other*.
(ii) I have arranged to be called at 6 *a.m. in the morning*.
(iii) Brown then bought out his partner and so became the *sole and only* proprietor of a *thriving* business *that was doing well*.

Think hard about the sense and you will avoid tautologies. We all seem to have an itch to write (and say) more words than are needed, as if a plain statement is somehow not sufficient on its own. As a result, we use superfluous words which add nothing to the meaning but clog up the sense of what we want to say.

6.3 Circumlocution

A roundabout way of speaking and writing.

(i) Candidates who scored low marks in summary *in many cases* exceeded the word limit.
(ii) Your application is *under active consideration* by the Board.
(iii) Pensioners *received a disappointment in the shape of the fact that* their pensions were not increased.

Spotlighted, the fault is so obvious that we wonder how we can ever commit it; but we all do. Each of those examples needs just a little thought to turn it into good English.

(i) Candidates who scored low marks in summary often exceeded the word limit. (*Or* and *better*: Many candidates who scored low marks in summary exceeded the word limit.)
(ii) Your application is being considered by the Board. (*Or* and *better*: The Board is considering your application.)
(iii) Pensioners were disappointed because their pensions were not increased.

6.4 Pomposity

Self-important and inflated language. Using out-of-the-way words and expressions to impress, and avoiding the shorter, simpler and more familiar terms that would express the same meaning. Pompous language conceals the sense — and it is often meant to. Jargon (see Section 6.5) is usually present.

EXAMPLES

> (i) The *counterproductive trends* in the industrial *production situation* are *escalating* to a *serious degree*.
> (ii) Candidates must *operate* within the *time parameters obtaining*.
> (iii) The *prolonged state of belligerency occasioned severe financial stresses. Governmental fiscal imposts* were increased *prior to its termination*.

COMMENTS

Circumlocution usually goes with a pompous choice of words (*to a serious degree* = 'seriously'). In themselves, there is nothing wrong with long words or words outside an everyday vocabulary; but there is no justification for far-fetched language when there are simple and familiar terms to do the job. The examples just given can be rewritten in plain, direct English, without changing the intended sense and with greatly increased clarity and force.

> (i) Industrial production is falling seriously.
> (ii) Candidates must keep to the time limit.
> (iii) The long war cost a lot of money. Taxes had to be raised before it ended.

Plain English is crisp and it means what it says. Pomposity is woolly and it often does not mean what it appears to say. The 'vogue words' of pompous people are loosely used. Examples are: *parameters*; *syndrome*; *ambivalent*; *liquidate*; *interface*; *approximate*; *optimum*; *orientate*; *viable*. All those words (and dozens more) are fashionable today. They *can* be used accurately and precisely, but only in appropriate contexts.

6.5 Jargon

DEFINITION

The use of technical terms in an inappropriate context. Technical terms are words and expressions that are used in particular arts, sciences, professions and occupations: there are technical terms in acting, for example, in physics, in psychology, in law, in medicine, in politics. In their appropriate contexts, they are accurate, intelligible, indispensable tools of communication. They become jargon *only* when they are transplanted. Each of the vogue words listed above has an important job to do on its home ground. For example, *syndrome* is a technical term in medicine; *parameter* in mathematics; *viable* in biology.

Some technical terms have passed into general use without losing their accuracy and plain, honest dealing: *altering tack* (from sailing) is one such expression, used figuratively, as many of them are. The label 'jargon' (it means 'twittering'!) cannot be stuck on them.

Examples of and comments on jargon are included in the next section, which deals with a fault that is closely related to it.

6.6 Gobbledegook

DEFINITION

Pompous official writing, stuffed with the jargon of government departments: 'officialese'. Unfortunately, it has found its way out of the offices in which it first flourished and is now one of the commonest faults in written English. The word *gobbledegook* is onomatopoeic, imitating the sound made by a turkey-cock.

EXAMPLES

(i) The district surveyor has arrived at the conclusion that the physical properties and configuration of the terrain of the site make the proposal to erect habitations thereon a proposition of dubious viability.

(ii) Throughout a long period of time extending over several years there have been considerable and recurring variations in personnel in the establishments of this manufacturing agglomeration.

(iii) It has been decided by the minister that the incidence of the levying of prescription charges under the new regulations shall remain under active consideration and that, pending a decision being formulated, the current practice shall apply to such classifications of exemptees as would have remained exempt had the new regulations not been promulgated.

COMMENTS

Many of the faults already discussed come together in those examples. Jargon and gobbledegook (the jargon of officialdom) are usually accompanied by tautology, circumlocutions and pomposity.

The meaning of (i) and (ii) can be expressed plainly and directly:

(i) The district surveyor has decided that the shape and surface of the site make it unsuitable for house building.

(ii) For several years, the number of workers in this group of factories has varied considerably.

It is not so easy to turn the third example into plain, sensible English. Either the writer did not know what he wanted to say or he did not want his readers to know. The meaning seems to be:

(iii) The minister is still considering how the new prescription charges will be levied. Until he makes a decision, people who were exempt under the old regulations will remain exempt.

6.7 Verbosity

Using more words than are needed. The symptoms of the disease include tautology, circumlocution and pomposity. Writers who use jargon and gobbledegook always suffer from verbosity and – be warned – they are highly infectious. We are all in danger of catching the sickness.

6.8 Cliché

A cliché is an expression that has been used so often that it has lost its freshness and vigour. Some clichés have become so worn-out that they no longer add meaning. They have degenerated into verbal lumber, not worth the space that they take up.

EXAMPLES

    (i) *To all intents and purposes* the government appears to have changed its policies without telling the electors.

   (ii) As was only *right and proper*, the insurance company settled the claim *then and there*.

  (iii) After so many disappointments, we cannot rationally hope that he will *turn over a new leaf* at his *time of life*.

COMMENTS

In (i) the cliché adds nothing to the meaning of the sentence. Rewrite: 'The government appears to have changed its policies without telling the electors'. What does *to all intents and purposes* say that *appears* does not?

In (ii) the cliché *right and proper* is not a tautology, though it sounds like one (*right* = 'correct' and *proper* = 'seemly'). But are the two senses needed? In this context the only relevant point is the legal correctness with which the insurance company behaved. The second cliché, *then and there*, means 'at once', 'promptly'. The clichés take up space without doing enough work to justify their presence.

Rewrite (iii): 'After so many disappointments, we cannot rationally hope that he will reform at his age.'

Clichés are usually verbose and they are *always* a sign of a stale mind. Whenever you are about to use a well-worn expression, stop. Then ask yourself, 'Do I need this formula? Can I find another — a more direct — way of putting my meaning in my own words?' Remember George Orwell's advice:

- '. . . cut out all prefabricated phrases'.

6.9 Colloquialisms

DEFINITION

Expressions and grammatical forms used in familiar speech, but not appropriate in formal writing.

EXAMPLES

    (i) 'Come on, Bill! We're going to be late.'
       'Can't hurry. Breathless this morning.'
       'You smoke too much.'
       'I know. Shouldn't smoke at all, the doctor says.'
       'Give it up, then.'

   (ii) 'As I see it, there's a simple answer.'
       'Show me.'

'Cut this para — this one. Begins, "Everyone has an active vocabulary and a passive vocabulary." Save six lines if we lost the last two sentences.'
'Yes, I see — but — hold on. Let's see — better — take it back. Whole para, I mean. Back to — yes that's it. Not happy about cutting it. There's a short page on proof 67 — see? Slot it in there — no damage done if we re-word connectives.'

COMMENTS

The following characteristics of colloquial English, illustrated in those two ex-amples, are inappropriate in formal written English.

1. Free and easy expressions (*hold on*).
2. Contractions (*we're; there's; that's*).
3. Abbreviations (*para*).
4. Verbless sentences (*Breathless this morning*).
5. Omission of subjects, especially pronouns (*Save six lines . . .*).
6. Rapid leaping about from one topic to another (the second speaker's last utterances in (ii)).
7. Reliance on tones and gestures to fill out the meaning of the spoken words ('act out' the dialogue in (ii)).

Naturally, when you are writing dialogue (in a story composition, for example), colloquialisms are appropriate. Nobody will believe in your characters if they talk like a book.

6.10 Slang

DEFINITION

The *Concise Oxford Dictionary* defines slang as: 'words and phrases in common colloquial use, but generally considered in all or some of their senses to be outside of standard English'.

EXAMPLES

(i) There's this *geezer* standing at the corner.
(ii) I gave him *the old one two*.
(iii) They *hopped it pretty smartish.*

COMMENTS

In Example (i) the slang word *geezer* is preceded by a characteristic construction of present-day slang: *There's this* . . . . In Example (iii), *pretty smartish* is also a slang construction. Such non-standard uses of grammar are often associated with slang vocabulary.

It is not always possible to make a clear distinction between colloquial English and slang. Slang is often, but by no means always, a feature of familiar speech. You would certainly use colloquial English in conversation with your grandmother or an old family friend, but you would probably not use slang; at least, not as frequently as you would use it in conversation with people of your own age.

It is helpful to think of language as being in 'levels of appropriateness'. Taking that view, *man* is the word for formal written English; *chap* for colloquial English; *bloke*, *guy*, *geezer* (or whatever word happens to be 'in') for slang.

Slang is a matter of fashion. Slang expressions originate in the specialised vocabularies of particular occupations, hobbies, social groups. (In this, slang resembles jargon.) These expressions are taken up by other users of English and are the 'in thing' for a time. Then they fall out of use and are forgotten. Today's slang is old-fashioned and unintelligible tomorrow.

It is wrong to use slang expressions in formal written English because: (a) their meaning may not be understood outside the comparatively small circle in which they happen to be used; (b) they go out of date very quickly; and (c) like jargon, they are 'prefabricated phrases', used by writers who are too lazy to find their own ways of expressing their own thoughts.

7 Correct Grammar

Faulty grammar in your written English will cost you marks in composition, practical writing, comprehension and summary. The additional language questions that you may have to answer test your ability to recognise and correct the errors most commonly made.

This chapter will help you to reach the grammatical standard required by the examiners. (You must also work through the follow-up exercises in Chapter 10.) It sets out the basic grammar that all candidates are expected both to know and to be able to make use of when writing. Then it lists and gives examples of all the common mistakes, supplying the corrections needed to turn them into good English. It is not a complete account of English grammar. Much information that would appear in a full study of the subject is deliberately omitted. It concentrates on the grammatical points usually tested — both implicitly and explicitly — in the examination for which you are preparing.

Candidates are not sufficiently aware that poor grammar is a frequent cause of failure in English Language examinations. A large vocabulary is important, but a knowledge of words alone is not enough. We may know all the words that we need to express a particular meaning, but unless we use those words grammatically, we cannot get their meaning across. If our handling of grammar is very poor indeed, we can hardly make ourselves understood at all; but *any* misuse of grammar is enough to slow communication down and cause misunderstanding. That is why your examiners require you to show them that you can write grammatical English.

Your ability to handle grammar correctly depends on your understanding of:

- the work that words do in sentences: words as *parts of speech*;
- the changes that must be made to word-forms according to the work that they are doing: *inflexions*;
- the grouping together and positioning of words in sentences: *syntax*.

7.1 Words as Parts of Speech

First, you must remember that:

- a word is a particular part of speech *by reason of the particular work that it does in a sentence*.

It is not useful to look at a word in isolation and say, 'This word is a noun'; but it helps our understanding of grammar to look at a word in a sentence and say, 'This word is doing the work of a noun in this sentence'.

The same word may do different work — and, therefore, function as a different part of speech — in different sentences. For example:

1. A child's *top* lay on the floor. (noun)
2. We shall easily *top* last year's results. (verb)
3. He seems to be their *top* man. (adjective)

There are *eight* parts of speech: nouns, pronouns, adjectives, verbs, adverbs, prepositions, conjunctions, interjections.

A **noun** is a word used in a sentence to name someone or something. For example: '*Jane* was sitting in that *chair*.' 'They all showed great *loyalty* to their *team*'.

A *common* noun names a member of or an item in a whole class of people or things. For example: 'It was a huge *book* of six hundred *pages*.' A common noun is the name *common to* all the members of or all the items in the class.

A *proper* noun names a particular person, place or thing. For example: '*Jean* is the best swimmer in *London*.' The name 'Jean' is *proper to* (belongs to) Jean. It distinguishes her from the others. The name 'London' is proper to one particular place. It distinguishes it from the others. Proper nouns begin with a capital letter.

An *abstract* noun names a quality or a state of mind or feeling. For example: 'Marks will be awarded for *accuracy* and *neatness*.' Abstract nouns name non-physical things: concepts that exist only in the mind: loyalty, honour, jealousy, anger, welfare.

A *collective* noun names a group or collection of people or things: *crew*, *team*, *library*, *flock* are words that are often used as collective nouns.

A **pronoun** is a word used in a sentence to stand for (or in place of) a noun. For example: 'The plate was so hot that *it* burnt the table.'

A *personal* pronoun stands for (or in place of) a person or thing. For example: 'Pass the ticket on to Robert if *you* don't want *it*.'

A *demonstrative* pronoun points to or at a person or a thing. For example: 'I like *these* but they would not be as useful as *those*.'

A *relative* pronoun relates to (refers to) a noun or pronoun used earlier in the sentence. That noun or pronoun is called its 'antecedent'. For example: 'My purse was in the bag *that* I left on the counter.' (The antecedent of *that* is 'bag'.)

An *interrogative* pronoun is used in some questions. For example: '*What* were you going to say?'

A pronoun of *number* or *quantity* indicates how many or how much. For example: 'Customers are restricted to *three* because we have *few* left.'

An **adjective** is a word used in a sentence to describe ('qualify') the person or thing named by a noun or a pronoun. For example: 'The *little* boy was used to crossing *busy* streets.'

A *descriptive* adjective qualifies a noun or a pronoun by describing its qualities. For example: 'Shall I wear my *green* dress?' A descriptive adjective may be separated from the noun or pronoun that it qualifies. For example: 'I think her dress was *green*.'

A *possessive* adjective indicates possession or ownership. For example: 'Was *her* dress green?'

A *demonstrative* adjective points to or at the noun or pronoun that it qualifies. For example: '*That* dress was hardly suitable for *this* occasion.'

A *relative* adjective introduces a subordinate (or dependent) clause (see Section 7.4) and links it to another clause. For example: 'We let them have *what* money we could spare.'

An *interrogative* adjective is used in some questions. For example: '*What* train did you catch?'

An adjective of *number* or *quantity* indicates how many or how much. For example: '*Few* customers showed *any* interest and we sold only *ten* books that day.'

(*Note:* Do not confuse adjectives with pronouns. An adjective is always used to qualify a noun or a pronoun. A pronoun always stands in place of a noun. For example: '*My* car [possessive adjective] is for sale and I want to put in a bid for *yours* [possessive pronoun].' 'Is *this* hat [demonstrative adjective] the right size?'

'No, but I think *that* [demonstrative pronoun] is.')

A **verb** is a word used in a sentence to indicate action or being. For example: 'We *ran* for the train but we *were* too late.'

Person and *number*. There are three persons and two numbers. For example:

	Singular	Plural
1st person	I laugh	we laugh
2nd person	you laugh	you laugh
3rd person	he/she/it laughs	they laugh

Tense. The time in which the action takes place or the state of being exists: present, past or future. For example: 'I ride' (present); 'I rode' (past); 'I shall ride' (future).

Voice. There are two voices: active and passive. For example:

Active	Passive
The mechanic repaired the car.	The car was repaired by the mechanic.
The expert is studying the evidence.	The evidence is being studied by the expert.

Transitive and *intransitive*. A verb is used transitively when it has an object. It is used intransitively when it does not have an object. For example:

Transitive	Intransitive
She sang an aria.	She sang.
The government is negotiating a new treaty.	The government is negotiating.
They fought a good fight.	They fought hard.

When a verb is used transitively, the action is carried across (*trans-*) from the subject of the verb to the object of the verb. Many verbs can be used both transitively and intransitively.

Finite and *non-finite* verbs. A finite verb has a subject. Because it has a subject, it is 'limited' (made *finite*) by having person, number and tense. A non-finite verb does not have a subject; therefore, it does not have person, number or tense. The non-finite forms of the verb are: the infinitive, the present participle, the past participle and the gerund.

The infinitive. The verb-form containing the word 'to'. For example: to walk; to read; to sing.

The present participle. The verb-form ending with *-ing* and functioning as an adjective. For example: 'This is a *teasing* problem.' The present participle is also used with the verb 'to be' to form the continuous ('imperfect') tenses of verbs. For example: 'We *were waiting* for the bus.'

The past participle. Like the present participle, it functions as an adjective, but it does not end with *-ing*. It takes many different forms. For example: 'A *beaten* and unhappy team flew home.' '*Bought* bread does not taste like home-*baked* loaves.' 'The election resulted in a *hung* parliament.' The past participle is also used to combine with auxiliary (helping) verbs to form the perfect (completed) tenses and the passive voice of verbs. For example: 'Those greedy children *have finished* the cake.' 'Their offices *were raided* last week.'

The gerund. Like the present participle, it is a verb-form ending with *-ing* but, whereas the present participle functions as an adjective, the gerund functions as a noun. For example.

The *dripping* tap kept us awake. (*dripping* is a present participle, functioning as an adjective qualifying the noun 'tap')

The steady *dripping* kept us awake. (*dripping* is a gerund, functioning as the noun subject of the verb 'kept')

Mood. The infinitive has already been noted. For example: '*To be asked* for my ticket again annoyed me.' The indicative is the 'mood' in which statements are made or questions are asked. For example: 'He *was* quite angry, *wasn't* he?' The imperative is the 'mood' in which orders are given or requests are made. For example: '*Go* away!' The subjunctive has few uses in modern English and, in any case, since most verbs have the same form for both the subjunctive and the indicative, the question of its use hardly arises. However, it is still correct to use the subjunctive mood of the verb 'to be' when expressing a wish or stating a condition that is very unlikely to be fulfilled. For example: 'If I *were* a millionaire, I would endow a research centre for peace studies.' 'She would still be champion if she *were* a few years younger.'

An **adverb** is a word used in a sentence to add to the meaning of ('modify') a verb, an adverb, or an adjective. For example: 'We did the journey *quickly*.' 'We travelled *quite* comfortably.' 'It was not a *very* crowded train.'

(*Note:* Adverbs often, but by no means always, end with *-ly*. You cannot safely identify a part of speech by its form. Its *function in the sentence* is the decisive factor.)

Simple adverbs may be classified as follows:

(a) Adverb of *time*. For example: 'They always arrive *late*.' (arrive *when*? – late)

(b) Adverb of *place*. For example: 'Stop *there*.' (stop *where*? – there)

(c) Adverb of *manner*. For example: 'He works *well*.' (works *how*? – well)

(d) Adverb of *quantity*, *extent or degree*. For example: 'I have eaten *enough*.' (eaten *how much*? – enough)

(e) Adverb of *number*. For example: 'We wrote *twice*.' (wrote *how often*? – twice)

Interrogative adverbs are used to ask questions. For example: '*When* are you going?' '*Why* are you leaving?'

Relative adverbs connect two clauses (see section 7.4). They *relate* the clause that they introduce to a word in another clause which they modify. For example: 'May is the month *when* Paris looks its best.' (The relative adverb *when* joins the two clauses and it relates its own clause to and modifies the verb 'is'.)

A **preposition** is a 'relating' word. It introduces a phrase (see Section 7.3) that contains a noun or a pronoun. It relates that noun or pronoun to a word elsewhere in the sentence. For example: 'I backed the car *into* the garage.' (The preposition *into* relates the noun 'garage' to the verb 'backed'.) 'We chose the house *at* the end.' (The preposition *at* relates the noun 'end' to the noun 'house'.) Note that the preposition introduces a phrase: 'into the garage' functions as an adverb; 'at the end' functions as an adjective. The word *preposition* means 'placed before'. A preposition is always placed before a noun or a pronoun in the phrase that it introduces and it relates that noun or pronoun to another word. For example: 'There was a present *for* me.'

(*Note:* Many words can be used either as prepositions or as adverbs. For example: 'Leave the parcel *inside* the porch.' (The preposition *inside* relates the noun 'porch' to the verb 'leave'.) 'Leave the parcel *inside*.' (The adverb *inside* modifies the verb 'leave'.))

A **conjunction** is a joining word. It joins two separate items in a sentence. It may be used to join one word to another. For example: 'Toast *and* marmalade, please.' It may be used to join one phrase to another. For example: 'It is a bad journey by rail *or* by road.' It may be used to join one clause to another. For example: 'The old man left a lot of money *but* his son soon spent it.'

Co-ordinating conjunctions connect items that do the same work in the sentence. They are 'of equal standing'. In the three examples just given, the items are linked by a co-ordinating conjunction.

Subordinating conjunctions connect subordinate clauses to main clauses (see Section 7.4). For example: 'He went on working *although* he was tired.' 'The government lost support *because* it ran out of energy.'

An **interjection** is a word or a group of words 'thrown in' to a sentence to express a feeling (of surprise, boredom, tiredness, etc.). It has no grammatical connection with or function in the rest of the sentence. For example: '*Oh dear*, he is going to be late again.' '*Hello*! who's that?'

7.2 Inflexions

The grammar of some languages requires many changes of word-forms. For example, in German – a 'highly inflected' language – adjectives change their word-forms according to the person, gender, number and case of the nouns that they qualify. In this respect, English is an uncomplicated language. Adjectives do not change their forms. ('A *red* dress was hanging in the cupboard.' 'She always wore *red* dresses.')

Nevertheless, correct grammar demands some changes in word-forms, the chief of which occur in the use of:

1. *Personal pronouns*. For example: Kate and *I* were invited. They invited Kate and *me*.
2. *Verb-forms*. For example: The cause of many grammatical errors *is* [*not* 'are'] carelessly used inflexions.
3. Plural noun-forms. For example: *baby/babies*, but *donkey/donkeys*.
4. *Comparative and superlative word-forms*. For example: *sad/sadder/saddest*; *little/less/least*; *favourable/more favourable/most favourable*.

As you will see in Section 7.5, the inflectional errors crop up time and time again.

7.3 Phrases and Sentences

Written English makes clear sense only when words are grouped together and positioned in sentences in grammatically correct ways. The rules that govern the arrangement of words in sentences are the rules of syntax. (*Syntax* = 'marshalling'; 'setting out in order'.)

(a) Phrases

- A phrase is a group of words that does not make *complete* sense.

EXAMPLES

1. in that photograph
2. sitting at the back
3. scorched by the sun

Each of those word groups makes some sense, but not complete sense. They are unfinished utterances.

(b) Sentences

- A **sentence** is a group of words that makes complete sense. It can stand on its own without the addition of other words. It is an *independent*, self-contained, finished utterance.

EXAMPLES

1. She smiled.
2. People could not hear.
3. The plants wilted.

Each of those word-groups makes an independent self-contained, *finished* utterance. It does not need additional words to make sense, although its meaning can be *expanded* by the addition of a phrase.

1. She smiled in that photograph.
2. People sitting at the back could not hear.
3. Scorched by the sun, the plants wilted.

(c) Subject and Predicate

A sentence makes complete sense because it contains two parts: a subject and a predicate.

- The **subject** of a sentence is the part that names (identifies or announces) the person, idea or thing about which the sentence is saying something.
- The **predicate** of a sentence is the part that says something about the subject.

EXAMPLES

Subject	Predicate
1. She	smiled.
2. People	could not hear.
3. The plants	wilted.

Every sentence must contain both of those parts. Take either away and it ceases to be a sentence, because it is no longer able to make an independent, self-contained, *finished* utterance.

(d) How Phrases Work

A phrase does the work of: an adjective *or* an adverb *or* a noun (see Section 7.1).

1. That chair *by the fireplace* is his. (The adjective-phrase qualifies the noun 'chair'.)
2. They have gone *on holiday*. (The adverb-phrase modifies the verb 'have gone'.)
3. He hoped *to win*. (The noun-phrase is the object of the verb 'hoped'. It answers the question *what*? They hoped *what*? — to win.)

Many of the common errors in written English are caused by incorrect positioning of phrases. If you are clear about the work that a particular phase is doing, you will position it correctly.

(e) Phrase Structures

Phrases are classified according to the work they do (adjective-phrase; adverb-phrase; noun-phrase) *and* according to their structures.

1. A *prepositional* phrase begins with a preposition.

EXAMPLES

(a) The crowd pressed *against the barriers*. (The prepositional phrase functions as an adverb modifying the verb 'pressed'.)
(b) A man *with a gun* was arrested. (The prepositional phrase functions as an adjective qualifying the noun 'man'.)

2. A *participial* phrase begins with a present participle or with a past participle.

EXAMPLES

(a) *Living in the country*, we were not used to crowds. (The participial phrase functions as an adjective qualifying the pronoun 'we'.)
(b) *Bought at a sale*, the car was a bargain. (The participial phrase functions as an adjective qualifying the noun 'car'.)

3. A *gerundive* phrase begins with a gerund.

EXAMPLES

(a) *Practising daily* perfected his skill. (The gerundive phrase functions as a noun. It is the subject of the verb 'perfected'.)
(b) She started *having nightmares*. (The gerundive phrase functions as a noun. It is the object of the verb 'started'.)

(*Note:* The gerund and the present participle both end with *-ing*, but they have different grammatical functions — and so do the phrases that they introduce. In the sentence 'Practising daily perfected his skill' the gerundive phrase functions as a noun. In the sentence 'Practising daily, he perfected his skill' *practising daily* functions as an adjective qualifying the pronoun 'he'. A gerundive phrase always functions as a noun. A participial phrase always functions as an adjective. This is far from being a mere quibble. Failure to recognise those two different functions is the cause of a great many errors in sentence construction.)

4. An *infinitive* phrase begins with an infinitive.

(a) *To sit and mope* is no answer to the problem. (The infinitive phrase functions as a noun. It is the subject of the verb 'is'.)

(b) They were ready *to go out*. (The infinitive phrase functions as an adverb modifying the adjective 'ready'.)

Accurate and fluent written English depends on correct structuring of phrases and their correct positioning in sentences.

7.4 Kinds of Sentences

(a) The Simple Sentence

In the subject of a sentence the most important word is the subject-word. In the predicate of a sentence the most important word is the verb. Provided that those two words are present, you have a sentence.

EXAMPLES

1. Stunned by explosions, fish rise to the surface of a river.
2. Having spent too long on comprehension, candidates often hurry their summaries, with disastrous consequences.

Subject	Predicate
1 Stunned by explosions, fish	rise to the surface of a river.
2 Having spent too long on comprehension, candidates	often hurry their summaries, with disastrous consequences.

Subject-word	Verb
1 fish	rise
2 candidates	hurry

Each of the original sentences can be stripped down to its two essential components (the verb and its subject-word) and *remain a sentence*: 'Fish swim.'/ 'Candidates hurry.'

The term *simple* does not refer to the length of the sentence or to its intellectual content. It is a grammatical term, referring solely to the structure of the sentence: a structure that is built on *one* finite verb.

The simple sentence is the bedrock construction on which the writing of good English rests. All the other kinds of sentences are based on the simple sentence. They extend its framework, but they do not alter its fundamental structure.

The simple sentence provides the backbone of written English and, as you will see in Section 7.5, many of the common errors arise because that backbone is broken; as happens when, for example, a writer splits a participial adjective-phrase away from the noun to which it refers, or separates a subject-word so far from its verb that he forgets to make them 'agree'.

(b) Clauses and Sentences

Many sentences contain *more than one* finite verb.

1. He *started* the car and *drove* down the street.
2. She *opened* her bag and *looked* in her purse, but it *was* empty.

There are two finite verbs in Example 1 and three finite verbs in Example 2. Put the same fact in different words: there are two *clauses* in Example 1 and three *clauses* in Example 2.

- **A clause** is a group of words containing a finite verb and forming *part of* a sentence.

(c) Main (or Independent) Clauses

Each of the clauses in Examples 1 and 2, above, can stand on its own and make complete sense without the help of the others.

1. He started the car./He drove down the street.
2. She opened her bag./She looked in her purse./It was empty.

Clauses of that kind are called *main* (or *independent*) clauses.

- **A main clause** makes a self-contained, *finished* utterance. It can stand alone without needing help from another clause.

(d) Subordinate (or Dependent) Clauses

Some clauses need help from other clauses to make complete sense. They cannot stand alone.

1. They rewarded the boy *who found the wallet*.
2. *When I feel tired*, I relax in the garden.
3. They were certain *that he would be elected*.

On their own, the italicised clauses cannot make complete sense. Clauses of that kind are subordinate (or dependent) clauses.

- **A subordinate clause** does not make a self-contained, finished utterance. It cannot stand alone. It needs help from the main clause.

Such a clause is *subordinate* because it is 'lower in rank' than a main clause. It is *dependent* because its meaning depends on a main clause.

Subordinate clauses function as: adjective-equivalents (Example 1, above); adverb equivalents (Example 2, above); noun-equivalents (Example 3, above).

(e) Sentences: Simple; Complex; Double; Multiple

Classified by grammatical structure, there are four kinds of sentences. Here is a check-list.

Sentence class	Grammatical structure
1. Simple	*one* finite verb
2. Complex	*one* main clause
	AND
	one or *more* subordinate clauses
3. Double	*two* main clauses
	WITH or WITHOUT
	subordinate clauses
4. Multiple	more than two main clauses
	WITH or WITHOUT
	subordinate clauses

EXAMPLES

1. *Simple sentence (one finite verb)*   Finding their hotel comfortable and welcoming, the travellers decided to rest in Melbourne for a few more days before continuing their long journey.
2. *Complex sentence (one main clause with, in this example, two subordinate clauses)*   Because their hotel was comfortable and welcoming, the travellers decided that they would rest in Melbourne for a few more days before continuing their long journey.
3. *Double sentence (two main clauses without, in this example, subordinate clauses)*   Their hotel was comfortable and welcoming and the travellers decided to rest in Melbourne for a few more days before continuing their long journey.
4. *Double sentence (two main clauses with, in this example, one subordinate clause)*   Their hotel was comfortable and welcoming and the travellers, who had a long journey ahead, decided to rest in Melbourne for a few more days.
5. *Multiple sentence (in this example, three main clauses and no subordinate clauses)*   Their hotel was comfortable and welcoming and the travellers decided to rest in Melbourne for a few more days, but their long journey lay ahead.
6. *Multiple sentence (in this example, three main clauses with two subordinate clauses)*   Their hotel was comfortable and welcoming and the travellers decided to rest in Melbourne for a few more days but they knew that their journey, which was a long one, lay ahead.

The content of all six sentences is the same, but the simple sentence expresses it more directly and plainly than any of the others. Its greater effectiveness does not come solely from its verbal economy. It is, in fact, only one word shorter than the next most economical sentence (3), though nine words shorter than the wordiest (6). It is the best sentence because it is the most *sinewy*, all its parts held firmly together and in place. Even its nearest 'rival' (3) is looser ('. . . and . . . and . . .'). The rest are sprawling in comparison.

This is not to argue that a simple sentence is always the best. For some purposes and on some occasions, one of the other structures will be more suitable. What the comparison does prove is that good written English depends very greatly on the care and skill with which sentence structures are selected and handled.

7.5 Common Errors

(a) Errors in 'Agreement'

The verb must 'agree with' its subject in number and in person. This is the rule of *subject/verb concord*.

(i) *Faults Caused by 'Attraction'*

When the subject-word (noun or pronoun) is separated from its verb by nouns or pronouns of a different number, the verb may be 'attracted' to agree with a noun or a pronoun that is not its subject-word.

EXAMPLES

Wrong	*Right*
1. A crate of empty bottles were left at the back door.	A crate of empty bottles *was* left at the back door.
2. Recent technological developments of that long-known material, glass, has influenced industrial design.	Recent technological developments of that long-known material, glass, *have* influenced industrial design.
3. A new computerised system controlling the stock and despatch of thousands of spare parts were installed at the factory.	A new computerised system controlling the stock and despatch of thousands of spare parts *was* installed at the factory.

(ii) *Collective Noun Subjects and Their Verbs*

Treat a collective noun as a singular subject when the group or collection is thought of as a *whole* — as *one*. Treat it as a plural when the sense stresses that it comprises *separate members or items* and that they are being thought of as *individuals*.

Wrong	*Right*
1. The government have lost support.	The government *has* lost support.
2. My family have lived in this house for a hundred years.	My family *has* lived in this house for a hundred years.
3. The crew was inoculated against various tropical diseases.	The crew *were* inoculated against various tropical diseases.

This particular subject/verb problem spills over to pronouns and possessive adjectives referring to the collective noun subject. They must be made to agree with it. Be consistent and stick to the number you first settled on. A haphazard mixture of singulars and plurals is confusing.

Wrong	*Right*
1. The government is being harried by their opponents.	The government is being harried by *its* opponents.
2. The BBC has announced that	The BBC has announced that *it* will

they will not increase the fees that it has offered for racing coverage.

3. After a poor season, the Midlands club informs our sports editor that their new manager has its full confidence.

not increase the fees that *it* has offered for racing coverage.

After a poor season, the Midlands club informs our sports editor that *its* new manager has *its* full confidence.

(iii) *Relative Pronoun Subjects*

A relative pronoun is the subject of the verb in the subordinate clause that it introduces. The relative pronoun must agree with its antecedent, and the verb in the subordinate clause must agree with the relative pronoun.

Wrong

1. This is one of the best books that has been published by this enterprising firm.
2. She is among those talented minor stars who has received consistently poor publicity.

3. Scholarship is still indebted to research into the derivations and meanings of English placenames that were pioneered by Sir Frank Stenton.

Right

This is one of the best books [*plural antecedent of 'that'*] that *have* been published by this enterprising firm.
She is among those talented minor stars [*plural antecedent of 'who'*] who *have* received consistently poor publicity.
Scholarship is still indebted to research [*singular antecedent of 'that'*] into the derivations and meanings of English placenames that *was* pioneered by Sir Frank Stenton.

(iv) *Other Troublesome Pronoun Subjects*

Difficulties arise with these pronouns: *anybody, anyone, each, either, everybody, everyone, neither, none*. Generally, they are treated as singulars.

Wrong

1. Anybody hoping to win a fortune on the pools are almost certain to be disappointed.
2. Neither of those proposals seem practical.
3. We do not impose decisions on our members, each of whom have a personal contract.

Right

Anybody hoping to win a fortune on the pools *is* almost certain to be disappointed.
Neither of those proposals *seems* practical.
We do not impose decisions on our members, each of whom *has* a personal contract.

However, there are times when *none* is used in a plural sense to mean 'not any' rather than the clearly singular sense of 'not one'. The verb should then be plural. Most writers would prefer the latter of these versions: 'Although the box of eggs hit the floor from a considerable height, none was broken.'/'Although the box of eggs hit the floor from a considerable height, none were broken.'

The problem of the 'follow-up' pronouns and possessive adjectives is more acute. According to the rule, this sentence is correct; but is it sensible? 'When the victorious team arrived at the station, everybody rushed forward, shouting his head off in the excitement of the moment.' Surely 'shouting *their heads* off' would make better sense?

Again, the absence of 'common gender' personal pronouns and possessive adjectives makes for clumsiness and/or inaccuracy. The sentence 'Each UK citizen must show *his* passport at the barrier' is grammatically correct, but carries the nonsensical implication that all UK citizens are males! The 'official explanation' that, in such uses, 'he' means 'he or she' is pretty thin. Often *he and/or she* (*his and/or her*) will get us out of the difficulty, but repetition of the formula is clumsy. Often, plurals can perfectly well be substituted for singulars. Instead of 'Everyone wanting to pay by cheque must provide evidence of his identity', we can write 'People wanting . . . of their identity.' Here, as always, hard and clear thinking is needed.

(v)   *'Either . . . or'/'neither . . . nor' Subjects*

The construction involves two separate subjects and one verb. When both subjects are of the same person and number there is no difficulty. 'Either Joan or Freda *is* certain to call.' 'Neither the children nor their grandparents *want* to go out.' When the two subjects are of different persons and/or number, the verb must agree with the *nearer* subject. 'Neither the pupils nor their teacher *welcomes* Monday morning.' 'Either one of my assistants or, in an emergency, I *am* available after closing hours.'

(vi)   *Parenthesis in Subjects*

The punctuation of what appears to be a double (and, therefore, a plural) subject may throw all the stress onto the first part of the subject. The verb then agrees with it. 'Truth-telling, and all its attendant inconveniences, seldom *attracts* a politician.' 'The new weapon, with its technicians, *was* flown out in great secrecy.' The punctuation is all-important. Remove the parenthetical commas and the subject is clearly plural.

(vii) *Appositional Words in Subjects*

Words in apposition to the subject-word must not be allowed to break subject/verb concord.

Wrong	*Right*
1. The treasure-trove, coins, medals, precious stones, were sold.	The treasure-trove, coins, medals, precious stones, *was* sold.
2. Two wretched companies, the ill-fed and despairing residue of the rebel army, was captured.	Two wretched companies, the ill-fed and despairing residue of the rebel army, *were* captured.

(viii) *'It' as a 'Provisional' Subject*

Always singular, however 'attractive' the plurals that it may introduce. 'There seems little doubt that it *was* those blocked culverts that caused the flooding.'

(ix)   *'Here' and 'there'*

Used as introductory adverbs, they are often mistaken for the subject of the verb.

Wrong	*Right*
1. Here, in remarkably good condition, is the chancel, the altar and the east window of this great ruin.	Here, in remarkably good condition, *are* the chancel, the altar and the east window of this great ruin.
2. After the quiet introduction, there follows energetic and near-dissonant passages of great power.	After the quiet introduction there *follow* energetic and near-dissonant passages of great power.

(b) Wrong Case

(i) *Nominative, Accusative, Genitive Cases*

1. *Nominative* case: the case of the subject-word.
2. *Accusative* (or *objective* case): the case of the object-word *and* of the noun or pronoun following ('governed by') a preposition.
3. *Genitive* case: the case of a 'possessing' word.

(ii) *Case in Nouns*

The genitive case is signalled by an apostrophe. (The rules are given in Chapter 8.) English nouns do not have special word-forms for the other cases. The commonest trouble spots in the use of genitive nouns are pinpointed and corrected in these examples.

Wrong	*Right*
1. The tomatoe's on that stall are too dear.	The *tomatoes* on that stall are too dear.
2. That boys' handwriting is illegible.	That *boy's* handwriting is illegible.
3. Victorian girl's clothes look very odd to us.	Victorian *girls'* clothes look very odd to us.
4. He was knocked out in the third round of the mens' competition.	He was knocked out in the third round of the *men's* competition.
5. Several of Dicken's novels have been filmed.	Several of *Dickens'* (or *Dickens's*) novels have been filmed.

(iii) *Personal Pronouns*

Nominative and accusative case forms are often misused.

Wrong	*Right*
1. They are making an exception of you and I.	They are making an exception of you and *me*.
2. It is a good crop in warm areas, but not practicable for we who garden in the north.	It is a good crop in warm areas, but not practicable for *us* who garden in the north.
3. This group — it includes Jane, Rosie and I — moves off after they.	This group — it includes Jane, Rosie and *me* — moves off after *them*.

(iv) *Relative Pronouns: 'Who' (Nominative) and 'Whom' (Accusative)*

Wrong	*Right*
1. We have appointed a principal whom we think will give leadership.	We have appointed a principal *who* we think will give leadership.
2. We have appointed a principal who we think the staff will support.	We have appointed a principal *whom* we think the staff will support.
3. We have appointed a principal to who we think the staff will respond.	We have appointed a principal to *whom* we think the staff will respond.

(v) *Personal Pronouns in Comparisons*

Note the difference between: (a) 'That firm is offering you a bigger salary than I.'/ (b) 'That firm is offering you a bigger salary than me.' The meaning of (a) is: 'That firm is offering you a bigger salary than I am offering you.' The meaning of (b) is: 'That firm is offering you a bigger salary than it is offering me.'

(vi) *The Genitive Case of Personal Pronouns*

Never use an apostrophe to mark the genitive of personal pronouns. The correct word-forms are: *mine, yours, his, hers, its, ours, yours, theirs.*
(*Note: it's* is the contracted form of 'it is'.)

(c) Wrong verb-forms

(i) *The Verbs 'to lay' and 'to lie'*

The verb 'to lay' must be used transitively. The verb 'to lie' must be used intransitively.

Wrong	*Right*
1. I was laying down when the door bell rang.	I was *lying* down when the door bell rang.
2. Lie the material on a flat surface.	*Lay* the material on a flat surface.
3. They have lain six courses of bricks.	They have *laid* six courses of bricks.

(ii) *The Verbs 'to raise' and 'to rise'*

The verb 'to raise' must be used transitively. The verb 'to rise' must be used intransitively.

Wrong	*Right*
1. Rise the girder another foot.	*Raise* the girder another foot.
2. As the sun was raising, we rose the flag.	As the sun was *rising*, we *raised* the flag.

If you want an increase of pay, ask for a *rise* not a *raise*, or you may find yourself being hoisted off the floor!

They are 'defective verbs', so called because they lack the full range of tenses and forms. (For example, there is not an infinitive 'to may', nor is there a future simple tense, 'I shall can'!) The other defective verbs are: *must, ought, shall, will.*

May and *can* have different meanings. Correct usage is illustrated by these examples:

1. *May* I go out?
2. You *may*, if you *can* afford the time.
3. He *can* play a good game but his form is erratic.
4. He *may* play a good game but he must be calm.
5. The Act says that we *may* not import livestock without a licence.

(d) Phrases in the Wrong Places

This is a very common fault and one of the most serious that a writer can commit. Remember that a phrase does the work of an adjective *or* an adverb *or* a noun. (See Sections 7.3(d) and 7.3(e).) A phrase cannot do its proper work unless it is put in its right place in a sentence.

Wrong	*Right*
1. Old books are always in demand by collectors with coloured plates.	Old books with coloured plates are always in demand by collectors.
2. Rabbit wanted for a little boy with floppy ears.	Rabbit with floppy ears wanted for a little boy.
3. I remembered that I had not switched off the electric fire while running for the bus.	While running for the bus, I remembered that I had not switched off the electric fire.
4. Arriving at the ground late, the seats we wanted had been sold we found.	Arriving at the ground late, we found that the seats we wanted had been sold.
5. Alarmed by falling sales, millions were spent on advertising by the brewers.	Alarmed by falling sales, the brewers spent millions on advertising.

(e) Pronouns Used with Vague or Wrong Reference

A pronoun must always be seen to refer clearly and accurately to the noun (or noun-phrase) that is its antecedent. Woolly use of pronouns — particularly *this, that, these, those* and *it* — is a frequent cause of poor communication in writing.

For example: The team's record had not been inspiring despite a splendid month in mid-season. *This* was a cause for concern, but *it* should be remedied shortly, our reporter was told. *This* accounted for falling gates, but the setback was temporary and *it* was improving. Supporters, the club said, should bear *this* in mind when reading the results and forming an opinion. *These* would improve drastically if *it* was given time.

(f) Sudden Shifts of Voice, Tense and Person

Wrong

1. Once the plumber had found the leak it was able to be repaired quickly by him.

2. The examiners referred to poor handwriting, reporting that you had difficulty in reading many scripts.

3. Unfortunately, many people were bored by the sermon and lose interest in the message.

Right

Once the plumber had found the leak *he was able to repair it* quickly.

The examiners referred to poor handwriting, reporting that *they* had difficulty in reading many scripts.

Unfortunately, many people were bored by the sermon and *lost* interest in the message.

8 Punctuation

Correct punctuation plays a crucial part in the writing of clear English. The various marks are used to indicate:

1. stop or pause (full stop, question mark, exclamation mark, comma, semi-colon, dash);
2. possession and omission (apostrophe, ellipsis marks);
3. direct speech or quotation (inverted commas or quotation marks);
4. apposition, bracketing, parenthesis (pairs of commas, pairs of dashes, round brackets, square brackets);
5. joining up (hyphen).

8.1 Full Stop .

The full stop is used:

(a) *To mark the end of a statement sentence*
This is its most important function. It is the sign that a self-contained utterance has been completed. It marks a finished, independent statement off from the one that follows. Every statement sentence must begin with a capital letter and end with a full stop. The full stop is also known as 'the period' because it 'puts a period to' a sentence (brings it to an end).

(b) *To mark an abbreviation*
Oct. = October. Note the difference between an abbreviation (*Nov.* = November) and a contraction (*Dr* = D(octo)r). Most writers use a full stop to mark an abbreviation but not to mark a contraction. Many well-known and commonly used abbreviations (such as BBC) are not punctuated. Acronyms (NATO, UNESCO) are never punctuated.

(c) *To mark an omission (three full stops)*
The three full stops marking an omission are called 'ellipsis marks'. When they occur at the end of a sentence, they are followed by a full stop. Study these examples:

Read the sentence 'Good written English . . . clearly punctuated' and express its full meaning in your own words.

Express the full meaning in your own words of the sentence beginning 'Good written English . . .'.

8.2 Question Mark ?

The question mark is used to *mark the end of a question sentence*. Do not use a full stop as well.

Have you heard the news?

Do not use a question mark at the end of an indirect question.

I asked whether you had heard the news.

8.3 Exclamation Mark !

The exclamation mark is used to *mark the end of an exclamation, interjection or sharp command*. Do not use a full stop as well.

He's dropped it!
Oh dear! I shall be late.
Hand it over!

Use an exclamation mark only when strictly necessary. Do not try to add emphasis or to draw attention to the point that you are making by using this overworked punctuation mark.

8.4 Comma ,

The comma is used:
   (a) *To separate words used in a series or list*
        She bought tea, jam, milk and flour.
   (b) *To separate phrases used in a series*
        She walked quickly down the street, round the corner and into the main road.
   (c) *To separate clauses used in a series*
        She found the bus stop, waited a few minutes, got on the first bus and took an upstairs seat.

As a rule, when the last item in a series is joined on by *and*, a comma is not used before the conjunction. (Conjunctions *join*, but commas *separate*.) However, the sense may sometimes require a final comma.

She bought tea, jam, milk, bread, and butter.

Do not put a comma after the last word in a list: always one comma fewer than the number of items.

Nuts, ginger, cloves are the ingredients. (3 items, 2 commas)
   (d) *In pairs, to mark off words in parenthesis*
        Some candidates, it was clear, had mis-read the question.
        He is upset, I know, but he will get over it.
   (e) *In pairs, to mark off words in apposition*
        Jones, the man responsible, is to be relied on.
        They sent their senior representative, the district inspector, the next day.
   (f) *To mark off the beginning of direct speech or quotation*
        The witness replied, 'I have no knowledge of that.'
        Look at the line beginning, 'Now the setting sun . . .'.

Remember that the presence or absence of a comma (or of a pair of commas) can change (or even destroy) the meaning of a sentence. For example, these two sentences are worded identically, but their meanings are different:

(i) The language questions, which are compulsory, must be answered on the special sheet provided. (*All* the language questions are compulsory.)
(ii) The language questions which are compulsory must be answered on the special sheet provided. (*Some* of the language questions are compulsory.)

Which of the two sentences is correctly punctuated depends on what the writer meant to say.

The use of a comma to separate main clauses is often a matter of choice. I chose to use a comma to separate the two main clauses in this sentence because I wanted to bring out a contrast:

These two sentences are worded identically, but their meanings are different.

It would not have been wrong to omit the comma after 'identically'.

Generally, a comma is not needed between two main clauses having the same subject.

They were nearly home when they ran out of fuel.

However, there will be occasions when a pause (marked by a comma) will add something to the sense or make it clearer.

They were nearly home and they were confident of winning, when they ran out of fuel.

Most writers would argue for the comma in that sentence.

8.5 Semi-colon ;

The semi-colon is used:
(a) *To separate items in a list when the items themselves contain commas*

Accessories for this model include: supplementary lenses, ranging from 28 mm to 400 mm; dedicated electronic flash; filters, both for colour and black-and-white film; an aluminium-framed hold-all.
(b) *To separate clauses the sense of which would be weakened if they were split off into a new sentence.*

When we started, we hoped to complete the cataloguing in six months; but, after a year, we had not made much progress.
Baffled by the absence of clues, the investigators were looking for a new lead; they suspected that one might have been overlooked in the initial confusion.

8.6 Colon :

The colon is used:
(a) *To introduce a list*

The following items will be sold on Tuesday: livestock, hay, implements, gates and fencing.

(b) *To introduce quotation or lengthy items of direct speech*

Keats wrote: 'A thing of beauty is a joy for ever'; and critics have been arguing about its meaning ever since.

The precise words in the agreement are: 'We shall waive our customary practice in your case and free you from the obligation to maintain the paths.'

(c) *To mark a dramatic break between two main clauses*

Man proposes: God disposes.

They cannot win: we cannot lose.

We do not know: we have faith.

(d) *To introduce a clause that explains or expands on a statement made in an earlier clause*

The seedlings are in a bad way: there has been no rain for a month.

I received a rebate from the Inland Revenue: a great surprise.

8.7 Apostrophe '

The apostrophe is used:

(a) *To mark the genitive case of a noun*

(i) Singular noun: add 's

book   The book's pages were defaced.

(ii) Plural noun ending with *s*: add '

books   The books' previous owner was at the sale.

fairies   The fairies' wings came off in the amateur pantomime.

Remember: It is the number of the genitive (possessing) noun that matters, not the number of the possessed noun. Compare: 'Those are my boy's books.'/'He played for the boys' under-11 team.'

(iii) Plural noun not ending with *s*: add 's

men   Use the men's entrance.

mice   There are mice's nests in the attic.

(iv) Proper noun ending with *s*: add ' *or* 's

Marks   Marks' (or Marks's) bowling has improved.

Dickens   Which of Dickens' (or Dickens's) novels have you read?

Generally, add 's; but you may think that 'Ulysses' bow' *sounds* better than 'Ulysses's bow'. Either word-form is correct.

(v) When two (or more) proper nouns share the ownership, mark the one nearer (or nearest) to the 'possessed' noun.

Pete and Dud's comic act delighted us.

(b) *To mark the omission of a letter or letters*

They can't (cannot) pay.

He'll (He will) write soon.

Ten o'clock (of the clock).

8.8 Inverted Commas ' ' " "

Inverted commas are also called 'quotation marks' or 'speech marks'. Either single marks ' ' or double marks " " may be used. Inverted commas are used:

(a) *In direct speech to indicate the words actually spoken*

'I can hear a noise in the basement', Bill said.

Bill said, 'I can hear a noise in the basement.'

'I can hear a noise', Bill said, 'in the basement.'

Note that *only* the words actually spoken are enclosed in the quotation marks.

(b) *In quotations within quotations*

The policeman asked Bill, 'Did you say, "I heard a noise in the basement"?'

Note: In that example double quotation marks were used inside single quotation marks. It is also correct to use single marks inside double.

The policeman asked Bill, "Did you say, 'I heard a noise in the basement'?"

Note: The question mark was included with the words actually spoken by the policeman, who was asking Bill a question. Bill's quoted words did not include a question mark, since they took the form of a statement not a question.

(c) *To indicate the title of a film, book, play, poem, newspaper*

Have you seen 'Star Wars'?

Do you read 'The Trumpet'?

I learnt Keats's poem 'Ode to Autumn' by heart.

(*Note:* Titles are sometimes underlined instead of being enclosed within quotation marks: There is an excellent account in *Racing Times*.)

Remember that quotation marks are never used in reported speech (nor are question marks).

Direct speech   Their lawyers asked, 'Are you ready to sign the contract?'

Reported speech   Their lawyers enquired whether we were ready to sign the contract.

8.9   Dash —

The dash is used:

(a) *As a pause mark before an explanation*

They sold their heirlooms — furniture, pictures, books.

(b) *To separate a 'summing up' from the items preceding it*

The gearbox, transmission, suspension — all constitute a revolutionary design concept.

(*Note:* Be on your guard. The dash is often overworked. *Never* use it as a substitute for a full stop or a comma.)

8.10   Round Brackets ( )

Round brackets are used:

(a) *To enclose additional information or explanations*

Hardy's long life (1840–1928) spanned the reigns of three monarchs.

(b) *To enclose apposition or parenthesis*

After his death, his impoverished widow sold his finest painting (the portrait of Sir Digby Wood) to a scoundrelly dealer for £25.

A pair of dashes may be used for this purpose instead of round brackets. Both dashes and brackets should be reserved for occasions when a pair of commas does not provide a strong enough effect.

8.11 Square Brackets [ ]

Square brackets are used to *indicate that a word or words included in quoted matter are not part of the original material.*

Johnson answered, 'I have no doubt that they [the poems of Ossian] are forgeries.'

8.12 Hyphen -

The hyphen is used:

(a) *To join up two (or more) words that are regarded as a compound word*
   mother-in-law; twenty-two; self-contained

Many expressions begin as hyphened words and lose the hyphen with continued use: *sea-plane/seaplane; look-out/lookout.*
Remember that the presence or absence of a hyphen can change the meaning of a word.

   (i) They hope to recover that valuable chair.
   (ii) They hope to re-cover that valuable chair.

(b) *To indicate that an unfinished word at the end of a line is completed at the beginning of the next line*
   The scientists are still look-
   ing for the answer.

Remember that the unfinished word must be split at the end of a syllable and that the hyphen must be placed at the end of the line, not at the beginning of the next.

9 Spelling

9.1 Self-help

English spelling does present some difficulties, but not nearly so many as people like to believe when they are excusing themselves for being bad spellers. The main causes of bad spelling are inattention and laziness — not the problems inherent in English orthography. Tackle your spelling difficulties on the lines suggested here and you will reach the required standard by the time you take your examination.

(a) Visualise and Syllabise

Pay attention to the look of words as you read and when you use your dictionary: *observe* their spelling. Look at and remember their *syllables*; not all of which may be sounded in their correct pronunciation, but all of which are present in their correct spelling (*vet/er/in/ary*). Look at and remember *silent letters*, too. Some are silent because they are not pronounced in sloppy speech (Feb*r*uary; arc*t*ic). Some are silent because they are not pronounced in correct speech (de*b*t; vi*ctu*aller).

(b) Prefixes and Suffixes

The commonest of all spelling errors occur at word joints, where a prefix is affixed at the beginning of a word or a suffix is affixed at the end (see Section 5.3). There is no excuse for misspelling (mi*s* + *s*pelling) 'disappoint' (di*s* + appoint), 'dissatisfy' (di*s* + *s*atisfy) or 'keenness' (kee*n* + *n*ess), to give just a few examples of the kind of words that are frequently the cause of lost marks.

(c) Pinpoint Your Mistakes

When you misspell a word, you do not get all of it wrong. You make the mistake at a particular point. Look it up. Write it out, underlining your trouble spot(s) (to*b*acco; a*cc*o*mm*odation; pa*r*a*ll*el). Learn it.

(d) Donkey Work

There is only one way to get better at spelling: work at it. The advice I am giving will help you to approach spelling intelligently, but it cannot remove the hard labour.

1. Resolve not to repeat your mistakes.
2. Make a list of the words you get wrong — and *learn* them.
3. Invent your own ways of avoiding your besetting errors. I used to have trouble with *mantelpiece*. I put it right by working out this *mnemonic*: 'You

don't put a man*tle* on a man*tel*piece'. It may sound silly to you, but it cured me of misspelling *mantelpiece*.

4. Face the fact that you will simply have to memorise the correct spelling of some words by repeating it over and over again. It is a long time now since I went wrong with 'ono-mato-p-o-e-i-a' (= *onomatopoeia*); but it took hard work to fix it in my memory. I did it partly by the syllables, partly by individual letters — and mostly by sheer determination to get it right.

9.2 Trouble Spots

Study these examples. Whenever you misspell a word in one of these categories, add it to the list and learn it.

- (a) *Silent-letter words*
  - *silent b:* bomb, climb, lamb
  - *silent g:* design, gnash, sign
  - *silent k:* knife, knob, knuckle
  - *silent p:* pneumonia, psychic, receipt
  - *silent w:* wrap, wrestle, wrist
- (b) *Words containing au*
  - auction, gauge, somersault
- (c) *Words containing ua*
  - equal, qualify, quay
- (d) *Words spelt with gh*
  - *silent gh:* bough, fought, thorough
  - *gh = f:* coughing, laughter, trough
  - *gh = g:* ghastly, ghetto, ghost
- (e) *Words spelt with ph*
  - *beginning ph:* pheasant, physical, physics
  - *ending ph:* autograph, paragraph, triumph
  - *containing ph:* emphatic, nephew, symphony
- (f) *Words spelt with ch*
  - *ch = k:* aching, chemist, scheme
  - *'soft' ch:* bachelor, machinery, which
- (g) *Words spelt with tch*
  - butcher, match, wretch
- (h) *Double-letter words*
  - *bb:* abbreviate, rabbit, rubbish
  - *cc:* accelerate, according, occur
  - *dd:* address, muddle, sudden
  - *ff:* afford, paraffin, toffee
  - *gg:* aggravate, luggage, suggest
  - *ll:* collision, excellent, pillar
  - *mm:* command, common, grammar
  - *nn:* beginning, channel, tyranny
  - *pp:* apparent, appoint, support
  - *rr:* barrel, carriage, quarrel
  - *ss:* dismiss, harassed, profession
  - *tt:* attitude, lettuce, mattress

9.3   Word Groups

Grouping words by their beginnings or endings is a useful way of remembering how to spell them. Bear these classifications in mind and add to the examples provided.

(a) *Beginning des-*
describe, deserve, destroy

(b) *Beginning dis-*
disastrous, discipline, dissolve

(c) *Ending -ance or -ant*
assistance, nuisance, tenant

(d) *Ending -ence or -ent*
absence, present, prominence

(e) *Ending -al*
educational, horizontal, municipal

(f) *Ending -el*
chapel, chisel, parcel

(g) *Ending -le*
axle, muscle, vehicle

(h) *Ending -sion*
collision, occasion, transmission

(i) *Ending -tion*
ambition, partition, volition

(j) *Ending -ar*
calendar, irregular, similar

(k) *Ending -er*
cylinder, traveller, surrender

(l) *Ending -or*
corridor, governor, interior

(m) *Ending -our*
colour, harbour, vigour

(*Note:* When a noun ending with *-our* adds *-ous* (to form an adjective), *u* is dropped from *-our*.

glamour *but* glamorous
humour *but* humorous
vigour *but* vigorous)

9.4   Common Confusables

Homophones and near-homophones (see Section 5.4) are often confused. Take care when using the words in this list.

accept/except; access/excess; affect/effect; allusion/illusion; altar/alter; ascent/ assent; capital/capitol; choose/chose; clothes/cloth; coarse/course; complement/ compliment; conscience/conscious; council/counsel; descent/decent; desert/ dessert; dairy/diary; dual/duel; dyeing/dying; formally/formerly; later/latter; lead/led; loose/lose; peace/piece; personal/personnel; principal/principle; quiet/ quite; respectfully/respectively; stationary/stationery; their/there; to/too/two; weather/whether

9.5　Some Spelling Rules

Some of the traditional spelling rules are complicated and riddled with exceptions. The donkey work recommended earlier in this chapter yields much better results. However, there are a few comparatively simple rules to which there are not many exceptions.

(a)　Rule 1

The prefix/suffix rule (see Section 9.1(b)). Never add or subtract a letter at the 'joint' in a word.

EXAMPLES

disservice, misunderstand, underrate

(b)　Rule 2

With *suc(c), ex* and *pro*, double e must go. By applying that rule, you can remember how to spell prec*ee*ding and proc*ee*ding and similar words.

EXAMPLES

exceed, succeed, proceed (N.B.: procedure)
concede, precede, recede

(c)　Rule 3

i before *e* when the sound is *e*, except after *c*.

EXAMPLES (The Sound is 'e')

ie achieve, grief, piece
ei conceit, deceive, receive

EXCEPTION

seize breaks the rule: *e* sound; no *c*; but *ei*

EXAMPLES (The Sound is not 'e')

ie cried, fierce, friend
ei eight, rein, their

(d)　Rule 4

When a word ends with *e* and you add to it, drop the *e* when the addition begins with a vowel or *y*.

acquire/acquiring; bone/bony; hate/hating

EXCEPTIONS

argue/argument; awe/awful; due/duly; true/truly
(*Note:* Words ending with *ce* or *ge* keep the *e* when the addition is *able* or *ous*: courage/courageous; notice/noticeable.)

(e) Rule 5

When a word ends with *e* and you add to it, keep the *e* when the addition begins with a consonant.

EXAMPLES

advance/advancement; hate/hateful; like/likewise

(f) Rule 6

Most words ending with a single consonant double that consonant when an addition beginning with a vowel is made.

EXAMPLES

blot/blotting/blotted; mat/matting/matted
begin/beginning; transmit/transmitted; propel/propelling
refer/referring; signal/signalled; travel/traveller

EXCEPTIONS

develop/developing/developed
limit/limiting/limited
profit/profiting/profited

(g) Rule 7

When *full* is joined to another word, it loses one *l*.

EXAMPLES

boast + full = boastful
fear + full = fearful

(h) Rule 8

When *full* is joined to another word ending with double *l*, both words lose one *l*.

full + fill = fulfil (*but* fulfilled)
skill + full = skilful (*but* skilfully)
will + full = wilful (*but* wilfully)

(i) Rule 9

When a word ends with double *l*, it loses one *l* when it is joined to another word.

EXAMPLES

all + so = also
well + fare = welfare

(j) Rule 10

Words ending with *our* drop the *u* when *ous* is added.

EXAMPLES

humour/humorous; valour/valorous; vigour/vigorous

(k) Rules for Plurals

1. Most words add *s*: lamp/lamps.
2. Most words ending with *o* add *es*: tomato/tomatoes.
   Exceptions: cuckoo/cuckoos; piano/pianos; solo/solos; studio/studios.
3. Words ending with *consonant* + *y* change the *y* into *i* and add *es*: memory/memories; lady/ladies.
4. Words ending with *vowel* + *y* keep the *y* and add *s*: donkey/donkeys; toy/toys.
5. Words ending with *f* or *fe* change the *f* or *fe* into *v* and add *es*: calf/calves; half/halves; loaf/loaves.
   Exception: roof/roofs.
6. A few words change their vowels: foot/feet; goose/geese; tooth/teeth; man/men; mouse/mice.
7. A very few make no change: deer/deer; salmon/salmon; sheep/sheep.

10 Work Out Problems: Language, Comprehension, Summary

The problems in this chapter are variously worded so as to reflect the kinds of questions set by different examining boards. They are tests of: vocabulary, style, usage (including grammar), comprehension, summary, punctuation and spelling. Answers are provided on pages 168–171, but do not look at the answer to a problem until you have written out your own solution. Use your dictionary and revise the relevant section (or sections) of this book while you are working out each problem and studying the answer.

PROBLEM 1 (answers on page 168)

Form the negative of each of the following words by adding a prefix: confirmed, defensible, honourable, logical, proper, rational.

PROBLEM 2 (answers on page 168)

For each of the following words write down a homophone. Then use each of the homophones that you have supplied in a sentence (six sentences in all) to show that you understand its meaning and use: beech, birth, maize, stake, taught, vale.

PROBLEM 3 (answers on page 168)

Part of each of the sentences in this question is underlined. The underlined part is repeated after the letter **A** (printed below the sentence). After the letters **B** and **C** two other versions of the underlined part are given. By writing down the appropriate letter (**A, B** or **C**), indicate which of the three versions would be the best English in the context of the sentence.

1 The north face of a wall generally suits shade-loving <u>plants, the plants may not like the cold however.</u>
  A plants, the plants may not like the cold however.

B plants, however the plants may not like the cold.

C plants; the plants, however, may not like the cold.

2 An unemployed person, the report shows, is <u>spending less than half on food than the weekly sum</u> spent by those in employment.

   A spending less than half on food than the weekly sum

   B spending on food less than half the weekly sum

   C spending less than half on food as compared with the weekly sum

3 Some diesel cars are as fast as petrol-engined cars of the same capacity and far more economical with fuel.

   A as fast as petrol-engined cars

   B equally as fast as petrol-engined cars

   C as equally fast as petrol-engined cars

4 We are hardly surprised <u>nowadays</u> when a popular newspaper, hungry for circulation, announces that there are fortunes to be won in its latest lucky dip.

   A nowadays

   B in this day and age

   C currently

5 The candidate assured the voters that he would spend <u>the majority</u> of his time on parliamentary business.

   A the majority

   B the maximum amount

   C most

6 Seeing my old friend again after so many years, <u>he seemed very fit.</u>

   A he seemed very fit.

   B I thought he seemed very fit.

   C he struck me as seeming very fit.

7 The promoters of this entertainment must be either lacking in all sense of artistry <u>or they are shamelessly exploiting</u> their simple-minded audiences.

   A or they are shamelessly exploiting

   B if not shamelessly exploiting

   C or shamelessly exploiting

8 Ten minutes before the final whistle, United's careful tactics literally came <u>unstuck</u>.

   A literally came unstuck.

   B came unstuck.

   C definitely came unstuck.

9 Both my son and my daughter did well in the examination but his career, unlike <u>hers</u>, lay in science.

   A hers

   B hers'

   C her's

10 If the new vaccine can be perfected, <u>hopefully this disease will be conquered</u>.

   A hopefully this disease will be conquered.

   B this disease will — hopefully — be conquered.

   C it may be hoped that this disease will be conquered.

PROBLEM 4 (answers on page 169)

Rewrite the following sentence in reported speech, using each of the given introductions in turn (three sentences in all):

Do you always go to the seaside for your holidays?

    A Jane will ask me . . .
    B I have asked Jane . . .
    C Jane asked her aunt . . .

PROBLEM 5 (answer on page 169)

Rewrite the following passage in reported speech:
    'I can't understand what's wrong with my new saw', said Mr Brown. 'It's so blunt, it wouldn't cut butter.'
    'There's nothing wrong with it, Dad', replied his seven-year-old son Tommy. 'I know, because I cut through a big nail with it only yesterday.'

PROBLEM 6 (answers on page 169)

Bodily labour is of two kinds: either that which a man submits to for his livelihood or that which he undergoes for his pleasure. The latter of them generally changes the name of labour for that of exercise, but differs only from ordinary labour as it rises from another motive.

A country life abounds in both these kinds of labour and, for that reason, gives a man a greater stock of health, and consequently a fuller enjoyment of himself than any other way of life.

---

1 Supply a suitable short title for the passage.
2 Make clear in your own words the distinction drawn between exercise and labour.
3 Make clear in your own words the three stages of the argument in the second paragraph by which the writer seeks to prove the superiority of a country life.

PROBLEM 7 (answers on page 169)

Fill each gap in the following sentences with a word that, in the context, is of opposite meaning to the italicised word.

1 Although most of the characters in this novel are *fictitious*, some . . . persons are introduced.
2 The . . . vegetation of the upper slopes was now replaced by the *prolific* growth of the plains.
3 The *natural* charm and simple dignity of the old king were in sharp contrast to the . . . manner and foppish airs of his son.
4 In less than six months, the financier sank from the *zenith* to the . . . of his fortunes.
5 The *clumsiness* of the clown, his partner in the double act, heightened our appreciation of the juggler's . . . .

Some of the following sentences are examples of good usage; others are faulty. Each of the faulty sentences contains an error of one of the kinds indicated by **B, C, D, E** below.

    A No error.

    B Wrong choice of word — i.e. mistaken use of a word for one that it resembles.
      Example: We could not except their invitation.

    C Lack of agreement (subject/verb or noun/pronoun).
      Examples: A packet of chocolates were given to each child.
                A person can only do their best.

    D Incorrect punctuation.
      Example: Fan belt, distributor, sparking-plugs, were carefully checked.

    E Unattached or wrongly attached phrases.
      Examples: They enjoyed their hot drinks, cold after a swim.
                Crossing the street, the church is a fine spectacle.

If a sentence contains no error of the kind **B, C, D** or **E**, mark it **A**; otherwise mark it with the letter corresponding to the kind of error it contains.

1. He designed a remarkable engine and being air-cooled he was able to cut production costs.
2. They promised the electors less interference and fewer taxes.
3. One of Europe's most imminent scientists then addressed the meeting.
4. Red Rum was one of the finest racehorses that has ever been seen.
5. People, who are over 65, qualify for age-relief under present tax regulations.
6. An editor's decision to publish or not to publish a scandalous story depends on what his criteria are.
7. After 1900, the merit of Hardy's poetry was widely recognised, but formally he was better known for his novels.
8. Labouring in heavy seas, the trawler put out distress signals at midnight.
9. Keeping up with fashion, the old furniture was sent to auction and replaced by modern pieces.
10. With those qualifications, you could try to become a journalist; alternately, you could train as a librarian.

Which of the two sentences in each of the following pairs more accurately conveys the sense intended?

    1(a) I had a letter from my father, who was staying in London.
    1(b) I had a letter from my father who was staying in London.
    2(a) Visitors are requested not to give the animals food, which will harm them.
    2(b) Visitors are requested not to give the animals food which will harm them.
    3(a) My experience has been that horses, which are mealy-muzzled, run well.
    3(b) My experience has been that horses which are mealy-muzzled run well.

Bring each of these sentences into line with good English usage. Make as few changes as possible and do not alter the intended sense.

1 All students do not learn German.
2 The reason why he was not elected to the committee was because he made such a bad speech.
3 Cowering under the bridge, an enemy patrol saw the bedraggled and frightened fugitives.
4 Walking is perhaps the best form of relaxation for, unlike golf, fishing or motoring, no elaborate equipment is required.
5 In recent years, sales have proved conclusively that customers prefer automatic than twin-tub washers.

PROBLEM 11 (answers on page 169)

Select the appropriate letter from the list below to indicate which of these sentences are grammatically correct.

1 His alibi was good.
2 The criteria was questionable.
3 The ensemble was playing at the Wigmore Hall.
4 The parenthesis was marked off with commas.
5 The phenomena was thoroughly investigated.
   A 1 and 2 only
   B 2 and 3 only
   C 3 and 5 only
   D 1, 3 and 4 only
   E 2, 4 and 5 only

PROBLEM 12 (answers on page 169)

Select the appropriate letter to indicate the correct meaning of each of these words.

1 mortuary is: A brickwork
               B a keen sense of disappointment
               C a building in which dead bodies are kept for a time
               D a deadening sensation in the limbs
2 plummet is: A a small plum
               B a sounding-line
               C graphite
               D a nestling's feather
2 ossification is: A being snubbed
               B becoming stupid
               C over-eating
               D turning (or being turned) into bone
4 proselytise is: A to demonstrate angrily
               B to turn verse into prose
               C to make converts
               D to take precedence

5 subjugate is: **A** to strangle
                       B to conquer
                       C to name the inflexions of a verb
                       D to delegate authority

PROBLEM 13 (answers on page 170)

Read this passage carefully and then answer the questions.

In our time it is broadly true that political writing is bad writing. Where it is not true, it will generally be found that the writer is some kind of rebel, expressing his private opinions, and not a 'party line'. Orthodoxy, of whatever colour, seems to demand a lifeless, imitative style. The political dialects
5 to be found in pamphlets, leading articles, manifestos, White Papers and the speeches of Under-Secretaries do, of course, vary from party to party, but they are all alike in that one almost never finds in them a fresh, vivid, home-made turn of speech. When one watches some tired hack on the platform mechanically repeating the familiar phrases — *bestial atrocities, iron heel,*
10 *blood-stained tyranny, free peoples of the world, stand shoulder to shoulder* — one often has the curious feeling that one is not watching a live human being but some kind of dummy: a feeling which suddenly becomes stronger at moments when the light catches the speaker's spectacles and turns them into blank discs which seem to have no eyes behind them. And this is not
15 altogether fanciful. A speaker who uses that kind of phraseology has gone some distance towards turning himself into a machine. The appropriate noises are coming out of his larynx, but his brain is not involved as it would be if he were choosing his words for himself. If the speech he is making is one that he is accustomed to make over and over again, he may be almost unconscious of
20 what he is saying, as one is when one utters the responses in church. And this reduced state of consciousness, if not indispensable, is at any rate favourable to political conformity.

---

1 As used in the passage, 'Orthodoxy, of whatever colour' (lines 3–4) means much the same as
   A any style of writing
   B religious belief of any kind
   C conformity with the accepted beliefs of any political party
   D emotive expressions of the right or the left
2 The writer asserts in lines 4–8 that
   A dialects hamper politicians
   B the political speeches of Under-Secretaries are more vivid than pamphlets, leading articles and manifestos
   C the various parties differ widely in their propaganda
   D the language of political speeches and writing is stale, ready-made stuff
3 The 'tired hack on the platform' (line 8) is
   A a weary rebel
   B a partly defaced slogan behind the speaker
   C part of the public address system
   D a politician mouthing platitudes
4 The suggestion in lines 12–14 is that
   A the speaker's eyesight is poor
   D the speaker is dehumanised

C the speaker lacks political insight

D the speaker is not the centre of attention

5 The phrase 'that kind of phraseology' (line 15) refers to

    A the 'private opinions' mentioned earlier

    B expressions such as those in italics

    C home-made turns of speech

    D the responses made in church services

6 The writer is highly critical of the political language 'of our time' for all but one of the following reasons; which one?

    A It is repetitive.

    B It is not the product of hard thought.

    C It increases party differences.

    D It reflects a lowered level of political awareness.

PROBLEM 14 (answers on page 170)

Study this passage carefully and then answer the questions.

There are many striking similarities between English and German. Some of the most commonly used words in the two languages look alike and sound similar: *Gras* = grass; *Korn* = corn; *Haus* = house; *bringen* = to bring; *hart* = hard; *gut* = good. These are but a very few of many possible examples. Philologists have proved that many English and German words which no longer look or sound similar, and which now have very different meanings, go back to a common origin. In grammar, too, the languages share certain characteristics, notably in the formation of comparatives and superlatives, the conjugation of verbs, and the genitive case. The evidence that the two tongues derive from the same source is overwhelming; but it is equally true that they have developed along very different lines, as anyone who is in a position to contrast the complications of German grammar with the simplicity of English grammar will readily agree.

---

1 In not more than 10 words, provide a suitable title for the passage.

2 Identify three points mentioned in the passage that are used to prove a common origin for the two languages.

3 Which of those points serves to bring out both their similarities and their differences?

4 Summarise the passage in not more than 40 of your own words.

PROBLEM 15 (answers on page 170)

Rewrite the following sentences in plain, direct English. Do not change the meaning.

1 It is regretted that your claim, which has been under active consideration, cannot be accepted by the District Assessor.

2 In the majority of cases, it was possible for students to be found placements operative within the period of time elapsing between the conclusion of the summer term and the commencement of the September session.

3 If it is decided that your application for admission to this course has been successful, you will receive notification on or before 1 November.

4 For a period of several years after the cessation of hostilities, the availability of new cars to the consumer was adversely conditioned by the supply situa-

162

tion then obtaining, and a severe shortage developed in relation to the considerable demand experienced.

5 In my mind it is much to be deplored that the Council has thought fit not to give an affirmative response to the proposal to refurbish the seating accommodation in the concert hall on the grounds of self-imposed financial constraints.

PROBLEM 16 (answers on page 170)

Write out the following, supplying the correct punctuation.

1 The students buses were unloading at 9 oclock.
2 Its necessary said the teacher to use punctuation youll confuse your readers if you dont.
3 The childrens enthusiasm increased as the conjuror performed trick after trick reaching a climax when a white rabbits head emerged from a top hat.
4 The builder said that he could paint the metalwork but stresses and strains were engineers problems he couldnt be expected to be responsible for the structures strength.
5 I very much doubt said Tom whether you fully understand the message I want you to deliver to Fred I certainly do replied Jack you want me to tell him that the practice will be on Thursday this week thats just the point exclaimed Tom Thursday next week not Thursday this week its on Wednesday as usual this week is it yes Ive said so twice already perhaps youd better give him the message yourself perhaps I had

PROBLEM 17 (answers on page 170)

Select the correct word to fill the gaps in these sentences.

1 He was the kind of leader . . . everybody admires. (who/whom)
2 I am sure he is the man . . . we saw at the bus stop yesterday. (who/whom)
3 If the experienced players cannot understand the new rules, what hope is there for . . . beginners? (we/us)
4 The cause underlying these recurrent disagreements, which are dangerous in present circumstances, . . . for international action. (call/calls)
5 Nobody . . . enter the keep . . . obtaining written permission. (can/may; unless/without)
6 He will, I know, be grateful if you . . . help him to raise money for this project. (could/can)
7 The plot of the play centres . . . intricate personal relationships. (round/on)
8 The inquest exonerated the nurse . . . blame; congratulated her, in fact, on a . . . decision (from/against; couragous/courageous)
9 Candidates must not enter the examination room more than 15 minutes before the paper is due to begin . . . leave before it is due to end. (or/nor)
10 If that . . . a knock at the door, it was probably the postman. (were/was)

PROBLEM 18 (answers on page 171)

At some of the numbered points in the passage below, the usual marks of punctuation have been omitted. The punctuation marks omitted are of the following kinds: comma, semi-colon, colon, full stop followed by capital letter. At some of the points numbered, on the other hand, none of those marks should be used, as it would be superfluous or even contrary to the sense of the passage. Indicate by one of the letters **A** to **E** which mark of punctuation, if any, you would use at each of the places numbered, as follows:

A no mark of punctuation
B comma
C semi-colon
D colon
E full stop followed by capital letter

Three possible explanations of the accident were put forward (1) a worn tyre, unnoticed at the time because of the many (2) radical changes in maintenance procedures at the garage (3) inadequate lubrication of the gearbox (4) and the fracture of a vacuum pipe (5) on which smoothly progressive braking depended (6) each of these theories was investigated (7) none provided a satisfactory explanation (8) in view of these findings (9) we may never know the cause of a most unusual accident (10) which cost lives and money (11) unless (12) that is (13) some quite remarkable (14) and unsuspected evidence is eventually uncovered.

PROBLEM 19 (answer on page 171)

With one exception, each of the following sentences uses two expressions where one would suffice. Which sentence does *not*?

1 When the lights changed to green, the learner-driver reversed at a brisk pace back into the front of the car behind.
2 The government made great use of its argument that most of the electors would find it more preferable to pay less in taxes rather than to have increased pay.
3 You could use inferior materials, but the job would not last and it would be only marginally cheaper.
4 As expected, Betty won in the final, being a very strong forehand player and relatively superior to Celia at the net.
5 We called at the hotel in Birmingham at which, so the local news led us to believe, the touring team intended to stay at when they left London.

PROBLEM 20 (answers on page 171)

Read the following passage and then answer the questions.

The letter, which was signed by several of the disaffected soldiers, painted in gloomy colours the miseries of their condition, accused the two commanders of being the authors of this, and called on the higher authorities to intervene by sending a vessel to take them from that desolate spot while some of them might still be found surviving the horrors of their confinement. The letter concluded with a paragraph in which the two commanders were stigmatised as partners in a slaughterhouse: one being employed to drive in the cattle for the other to butcher.

---

1 Give the meaning of the following expressions as they are used in the passage: (a) disaffected; (b) painted in gloomy colours; (c) the authors of this; (d) be found surviving the horrors of their confinement; (e) stigmatised.
2 Without using figurative language, reword the soldiers' description of their commanders.

Answers

TEST PAPER, pages 62–66

1

  (a) openness to visitors

  (b)

     (i) natural renewal

     (ii) wearing away

  (c) When the wardens talk to visitors, they draw on their experience as naturalists or foresters to explain countryside matters to them. In this way, *their knowledge contributes directly to the pleasure of visitors.*

  (d) without being paid for doing the job

  (e)

     (i) He means those National Trust estates that are teeming with visitors in the holidays (see line 37).

     (ii) He is referring to the imaginary airman (line 35) who – like the imaginary buzzard (line 36) – would see the busiest estates stirring 'like anthills'.

  (f)

The main problems caused by the popularity of National Trust properties are litter, hooliganism and the damage done to animal and plant life. On some estates, visitor pressure is wearing away the vegetation beyond the point at which natural renewal can take place. As far as it can, the Trust is alleviating the ill-effects by increasing the number of wardens and by persuading people to visit the 'open spaces', thus taking pressure off the overcrowded estates. The Trust's policy does not permit closure but, if the pressure continues to mount, it will be forced to restrict access either by charging for admission or by rationing the numbers admitted on certain days.

114 words

2

  (a)

     (i) The literal meaning of *prima donna* is 'first lady'. The term is used of the principal female singer in an opera company.

     (ii) The *title-role* is the 'name-part'. In the opera *Carmen*, Fiammetta was to sing the part of Carmen.

  (b)

     (i) old-fashioned, hackneyed, and, therefore, not very exciting.

     (ii) It creates an impression of bright, warm colour.

     (iii) His heart beat faster with excitement.

  (c)

     (i) It means that it is *customary* for Carmen to wear a scarlet costume.

     (ii) Because he would insist on redesigning all the other costumes and the scenery.

(d)
    (i) They were afraid of the fury with which she would react.
    (ii) I should have explained to her that her beauty and individuality would not shine out as they should unless the other costumes and the scenery were designed around her. Freeman hints at this in his indirect explanation.

(e)
    (i) In this context, *disdain* means 'scorn' or 'contempt'.
    (ii) In this context, *calculation* means 'shrewd and cunning thoughts'.

(f)
    (i) I make no claims to being honourable.
    (ii) I have risen from low origins.
    (iii) I do not burden myself with foolishly affected notions.

(g)

They quarrel because she insists on having a yellow dress and he refuses to design one for her without altering all the other costumes and the scenery. Finding that he will not budge, Fiammetta tries to seduce him into agreement, though Freeman warns her that he will take her kisses without yielding over the dress. She recognises her own ruthlessness in him and makes a passionate bid to win him. He believes that she is still trying to trick him, and they confront each other furiously. Then, they recognise their fundamental similarities and mutual attraction. Their anger dissolves in laughter. She says that she no longer cares about the yellow dress, which he still refuses to make, but as they embrace, he promises her a wonderful new scarlet dress, fit for a brilliant guttersnipe, as he laughingly and lovingly calls her.

140 words

TEST PAPER, pages 73–78. See Answer sheet, page 78

    1 = D
    2 = C
    3 = B
    4 = B
    5 = A
    6 = D
    7 = D
    8 = A
    9 = C
    10 = C
    11 = A
    12 = D
    13 = B
    14 = B
    15 = D
    16 = C
    17 = B
    18 = C
    19 = A
    20 = A
    21 = B
    22 = D

23 = B
24 = A
25 = B

TEST PAPER, pages 79–88. See Answer sheet, page 88

1 = B	21 = B
2 = C	22 = D
3 = D	23 = C
4 = E	24 = A
5 = C	25 = B
6 = A	26 = B
7 = D	27 = C
8 = E	28 = C
9 = A	29 = A
10 = C	30 = C
11 = E	31 = E
12 = B	32 = C
13 = C	33 = A
14 = D	34 = B
15 = D	35 = A
16 = D	36 = B
17 = A	37 = D
18 = A	38 = C
19 = D	39 = B
20 = B	

TEST PAPERS, pages 110–113

1

STUDENTS' GRANTS: AN INTRODUCTION

Approach the local education authority in good time. Eligibility is determined by: the nature of the course; a three-year UK residency; no previous grant. Mandatory grants must be paid to students accepted for degree courses. Discretionary grants may be paid for other courses. Grants for tuition, examination fees and union contributions are paid direct to the educational institution. Travel costs and maintenance are paid to the student. Above the minimum grant, maintenance depends on student and parental income. Mature or disabled students receive special grants. Social security in term is restricted to single parents and handicapped people.

98 words

2

WHY MINORITY OPINIONS MUST BE PROTECTED AND ENCOURAGED

Both a conservative and a radical party are essential to political health because the standpoint of each corrects the errors of its opposite and each exerts a restraining influence on the other. The complete triumph of one would suppress the truth represented by the other, for truth is not the monopoly of one point of view and the continuing struggle between embattled opposites is a necessary condition of betterment. It follows that minority opinions embody an aspect of truth and that minorities should be not merely tolerated but protected and encouraged. Political truth is so complex that the utmost freedom must be afforded to all opinions. Whenever a minority — however small — differs from the rest of mankind, its voice must be heard. Even if the received opinion is correct, it is likely that its opponents have something valuable to say and truth itself would suffer if they were silenced.

149 words

3

LIFE IS DANGEROUS IN A NOISY WORLD

Noise kills and injures — and we are at risk every day. At 0 db (db = *decibel*), it can just be heard. At about 180 db, it is fatal. Danger begins at 65–86 db, the noise level near a motorway. Above that, prolonged exposure deafens and enfeebles. A quick dose of 150 db (low-flying jets near an airport) inflicts agony and may wreck ears. Daily noises are in the damage band: motor mowers or revving bikes (110 db); 'hard rock' (115 db); pneumatic drills (130 db); even food mixers (100 db at 2–4 feet).

Defend your house against noise. Operate useful but noisy appliances away from the living area and stand them on padding. Keep radios and television down to safe levels. Repel outside noises with trees, shrubs, walls and fences. Quell those that penetrate with carpets, curtains, and big floor and wall furniture.

Agreed, we can't banish all noise, nor should we try. Liberation from domestic drudgery and Shanks's pony are worth a decibel or two. And noises *can* delight — a baby's crying, a roaring exhaust, throbbing 'pop', nature's music. Total silence means death. But so does unrestricted noise!

192 words

PROBLEM 1 (page 156)

unconfirmed, indefensible, dishonourable, illogical, improper, irrational

PROBLEM 2 (page 156)

beach, berth, maze, steak, taut, veil
1 A sandy beach is a great asset to a holiday resort.
2 The yacht was at its berth near the old quay.
3 No visitor had ever succeeded in finding the way out of the maze, which was formed of high yew hedges.
4 Traditionally, large, juicy steaks have been the principal diet of boxers and rowing-men.
5 They pulled hard on the slack mooring rope until it was taut.
6 Her features were hidden by a veil of black lace.

PROBLEM 3 (page 156)

1 C.   2 B.   3 A.   4 A.   5 C.   6 B.   7 C.   8 B.   9 A.   10 C.

PROBLEM 4 (page 158)

A Jane will ask me if I always go to the seaside for my holidays.
B I have asked Jane if she always goes to the seaside for her holidays.
C Jane asked her aunt if she always went to the seaside for her holidays.

PROBLEM 5 (page 158)

Mr Brown said that he could not understand what was wrong with his new saw, which was so blunt that it would not cut butter. His seven-year-old son Tommy replied that he knew that there was nothing wrong with the saw because, only the day before, he had cut through a big nail with it.

PROBLEM 6 (page 158)

1 A Country Life: Healthiest and Best.
2 Labour is the physical work undergone for a living; but exercise is the physical work undertaken for pleasure.
3 The first stage of the argument states that both kinds of labour are plentiful in a country life. The second stage claims that better health follows from that. The third stage concludes that, as a result, a country life provides greater pleasure derived from enhanced self-fulfilment.

PROBLEM 7 (page 158

1 historical.   2 sparse.   3 artificial.   4 nadir.   5 dexterity.

PROBLEM 8 (page 159)

1 E.   2 A.   3 B.   4 C.   5 D.   6 A.   7 B.   8 A.   9 E.   10 B.

PROBLEM 9 (page 159)

1(a).   2(b).   3(b).

PROBLEM 10 (page 160)

1 Not all students learn German.
2 The reason he was not elected to the committee was that he made a bad speech.
3 An enemy patrol saw the bedraggled and frightened fugitive cowering under the bridge.
4 Walking is perhaps the best form of relaxation for, unlike golf, fishing or motoring, it does not require elaborate and expensive equipment.
5 In recent years, sales have proved conclusively that customers prefer automatic to twin-tub washers.

PROBLEM 11 (page 160)

D

PROBLEM 12 (page 160)

1 C   2 B   3 D   4 C   5 B

PROBLEM 13 (page 161)

1 C.   2 D.   3 D.   4 B.   5 B.   6 C.

PROBLEM 14 (page 162)

1 The similarities and the differences between English and German. (*9 words*)
2 (i) Many of their most frequently used words look and sound alike. (ii) Many other words have a common origin. (iii) They have similarities of grammar.
3 The grammatical evidence.
4 The similarities between and shared origins of many English and German words, together with some grammatical affinities, prove the kinship of the two languages. Nevertheless, they have moved far apart, as their contrasting grammars show.

35 words

PROBLEM 15 (page 162)

1 Your claim has been considered carefully, but the District Assessor is sorry to say that he cannot accept it.
2 Placements for the summer vacation were found for most students.
3 You will be told by 1 November if you have been accepted for this course.
4 For several years after the war ended, fewer cars were made than there were customers for them.
5 I deplore the Council's decision not to spend money on new seats for the concert hall.

PROBLEM 16 (page 163)

1 The students' buses were unloading at 9 o'clock.
2 'It's necessary', said the teacher, 'to use punctuation. You'll confuse your readers if you don't.'
3 The children's enthusiasm increased as the conjuror performed trick after trick, reaching a climax when a white rabbit's head emerged from a top hat.
4 The builder said that he could paint the metalwork, but stresses and strains were engineers' problems; he couldn't be expected to be responsible for the structure's strength.
5 'I very much doubt', said Tom, 'whether you fully understand the message I want you to deliver to Fred.'
'I certainly do', replied Jack. 'You want me to tell him that the practice will be on Thursday this week.'
'That's just the point!' exclaimed Tom. 'Thursday next week, not Thursday this week. It's on Wednesday, as usual, this week.'
'Is it?'
'Yes. I've said so, twice, already.'
'Perhaps you'd better give him the message yourself.'
'Perhaps I had!'

PROBLEM 17 (page 163)

1 whom. 2 whom. 3 us. 4 calls. 5 may; without. 6 can. 7 on. 8 from; courageous. 9 or. 10 was.

PROBLEM 18 (page 163)

1 D. 2 A. 3 C. 4 C. 5 A. 6 E. 7 E. 8 E. 9 B. 10 A. 11 C. 12 B. 13 B. 14 A.

PROBLEM 19 (page 164)

Sentence 3.

PROBLEM 20 (page 164)

1 (a) disloyal; (b) described in depressing words; (c) responsible for their situation; (d) be still alive despite their suffering in prison; (e) described in abusive terms.

2 Their commanders inflicted casualties mercilessly upon them; one driving them into the killing ground where the other slew them.

Index *

*Page numbers in italic type refer to worked examples.